MOVING THE MOUNTAIN

MOVING THE MOUNTAIN

INSIDE THE PERESTROIKA REVOLUTION

ABEL AGANBEGYAN

TRANSLATED BY HELEN SZAMUELY

BANTAM PRESS

LONDON · NEW YORK · TORONTO · SYDNEY · AUCKLAND

TRANSWORLD PUBLISHERS LTD
61–63 Uxbridge Road, London W5 5SA

TRANSWORLD PUBLISHERS (AUSTRALIA) PTY LTD
15–23 Helles Avenue, Moorebank, NSW 2170

TRANSWORLD PUBLISHERS (NZ) LTD
Cnr Moselle and Waipareira Aves,
Henderson, Auckland

Published 1989 by Bantam Press
a division of Transworld Publishers Ltd
Copyright © Abel Aganbegyan 1989
Translation © Helen Szamuely

British Library Cataloguing in Publication Data

Aganbegyn, Abel, *1932–*
    Moving the mountain: inside the Perestroika
    revolution
    1. Eastern Europe & Soviet Union. Economic policies
    I. Title
    330.947'0854

ISBN 0-593-01818-4

Photoset in Linotron Baskerville by
Rowland Phototypesetting Ltd
Bury St Edmunds, Suffolk
Printed in Great Britain by
Mackays of Chatham Plc, Chatham, Kent

MOVING THE MOUNTAIN

CONTENTS

CONTENTS

Afterword. Statistical Review: Three Years of Economic Reconstruction

A NEW STAGE IN PERESTROIKA –
THE RESTRUCTURING OF
MANAGEMENT IN THE USSR

A critical period: this is sink or swim

We have reached a crucial, some might say critical, stage in perestroika, the restructuring of management in our country. The years 1985–7 were spent wholly in formulating a complete new system of administration, together with a programme of radical economic reforms. What we did was to study carefully our own past and that of other countries and conduct a series of economic experiments which helped us to define certain aspects of the new economic and administrative system.

The main aim is to change the economic management of our country from the administrative ('diktat' or command) system developed over the last fifty years to a radically new one, based on economic levers such as market forces, financial credits, and other stronger economic stimuli. The whole process must be carried out alongside a general democratization of our society and a transition to self-administration in our enterprises.

What lies at the root of the new system of administration is the offer of economic independence to the various enterprises and

9

conglomerates which make up our national economy. The state will no longer be responsible for their financial affairs, and they for their part will not be responsible for the state. Another new idea we have incorporated is that of pluralism in property. A large co-operative sector is to exist alongside the state enterprises. We have already seen a leap in personal productivity which in due course will spread to every aspect of the economy. The new economic mechanism is based on three laws enacted for the whole Union of Socialist Republics: the Law on State Enterprises and Conglomerates (in force since 1 January 1988); the Law on Co-operatives (in force since 1 July 1988); and the Law on Individual Labour Activity (in force since 1 May 1987).

On the basis of these laws the Central Committee of the CPSU* and the USSR Council of Ministers have taken a number of decisions that will radically transform the administration of the socialist economy and all facets of the economic mechanism. In July 1987 a series of decisions was taken that profoundly affected planning, finance, banking and price formation. The system of material and technical supplies and the practices of the various agencies dealing with labour and social problems, as well as those that deal with science and technology, are being transformed. As a result of these decisions there will be changes in the administration of industry and of the various regions, in the generation of state statistics, and so on. Earlier still, decisions were made about foreign economic affairs.

Together these form the basis for the radical reforms of our administration. This basis is not static – it is evolving, gradually affecting the whole of the economic and administrative system. This development is the result of a single new concept adopted at the June 1987 Plenum of the CPSU Central Committee, formulated in a document entitled *Basic Tenets for the Radical Restructuring of the Administration of the Economy.*

If required, one short phrase can express exactly the nature of this crucial stage in our work: from words to deeds. Since early 1989 all enterprises in the production sphere have been working on the basis of complete cost accounting, self-financing and self-administration. Around 75,000 new co-operatives have been formed. In 1988 they turned over more than 4 billion roubles in

* Communist Party of the Soviet Union.

10

production and services. Approximately 2 million people work in the new co-operatives or are self-employed.

Furthermore, we constantly review the new economic conditions and change our planning ideas as a result. The number of centrally planned tasks has decreased sharply as the new economic rules for enterprises have gained importance. The whole system of financing is being regularized. We have established new specialized banks whose purpose it is to gauge the needs of enterprises and organizations and to serve those needs. We have begun a reorganization of the administration in order to simplify the administrative structure, abolish unnecessary branches, and reduce the central and republican apparatus by 30–50 per cent.

In other words we are in transition between the old and the new systems of administration, a period in which the two methods co-exist. The old pricing structure has for the time being been retained, but a total reform of prices and price formation is scheduled for 1990. Once our financial and credit relations have been reformed and the new price structure is in place, we shall be able to move away from the present system of centralized distribution of the means of production* by direct funding. In the future we aim to work through a mutually profitable multi-channelled wholesale trade system with direct commercial links between producer and consumer, or indirect links through middlemen or intermediary bodies. Next year will see the reform of the banking system. Specialized banks will increase their commercial activity, and at the same time they too will become completely self-financing. As resolved by the 19th Party Conference, the economic mechanisms of the republics and regions, and, consequently, the economy of the country as a whole, will be radically transformed. The republics and regions will be offered economic independence and the opportunity to change to a system of self-administration, self-financing and self-provision.

As can be seen from all this, the year 1989–90 will be crucial in the transition from the old to the new economic mechanism. The resolutions of the 19th Party Conference make this clear: we intend to enter the nineties with a new economic and administrative system.

However, we must now look at the realities of moving to new

---

* The capital equipment which is used to produce goods.

economic conditions. It has to be said that the process has turned out to be slower, more difficult and more painful than anticipated. There are certain objective difficulties connected with the conditions of a transitional stage. Until we actually have new prices and a wholesale trade in the means of production, each enterprise's economic possibilities will necessarily be restricted. Further problems derive from the fact that this transitional period lies in the middle of the 12th Five-year Plan, whose tasks, not yet completed, were adopted while the old conditions were still in force. But these objective difficulties are not the real problem. The real problem lies in the fact that the central economic planners made serious mistakes right at the start of their attempts to implement the economic reforms.

Mistake number one was made when the concept of state purchase orders on enterprises and concerns was incorrectly developed in the plan for 1988. Under the guise of a new economic method, *goszakaz* (state purchase), created as part of the transition to economic methods of administration, was really a retention of the old idea of a directive plan from above. The central offices delegated decisions about state purchase orders to the various ministries, while the latter included in the *goszakaz* virtually the whole of their 'shopping list', leaving no room for independent economic activity.

Mistake number two was that the whole process of establishing economic regulations was farmed out to the ministries. These rules and regulations were to govern the charges on each enterprise's profits and how much was to be budgeted to them or to the various ministries' centralized funds. Further, rules were to be established for the use of amortized deductions and for the allocation of any remaining profit to various incentive funds within the enterprises and concerns. Many of the ministries approached this task without due care and consideration and simply reallocated the old five-year plan figures proportionately to each enterprise. As a result the economic rules and regulations generally turned out to be ad-hoc solutions involving the removal of means from efficient enterprises to subsidize inefficient ones.

Mistake number three, in my opinion, was the retention of the formulation of the wage fund in relation to the dynamics of production. This method was adopted in 1984–6, a period of large-scale experimentation. As a result, the ideas and conditions of the new economics did not affect the lower echelons, the working masses.

Worst of all, I think, is that in three years now of perestroika we have not managed to advance the process of financial renewal within the economy. Income in the country is still well ahead of the provision of goods and services, and the gap between paying ability and the ability to satisfy demand is not diminishing but increasing.

We must follow the spirit of the 19th Party Conference, which analysed critically the long and basically productive path of perestroika in the preceding three years, and understand the reasons for our mistakes and inadequacies. On the one hand we quite clearly underestimated the forces of inertia and of resistance to perestroika in sections of the administration, in the central economic offices, in the various ministries and among a large number of managers. We misjudged matters and compromised in the formulation of the state purchase orders regulations in the Law on Enterprises and other related laws. When we formulated the plan for 1988 we did not suggest reforms that were radical enough to create an economic system of management. Our measures were half-measures which made it possible for administrative 'diktat' to overrule the decisions of enterprises and concerns. Secondly we did not completely democratize the discussion and decision-making processes. These processes did not touch the large masses of working people. So the size of the state purchase orders and the establishment of economic rules and regulations were decided by committees. Representatives of working collectives were not invited to join the decision-making process. Such important problems as the price of spirits, the use of hard currency cheques and the amount of consumer goods to be imported were resolved by even smaller groups. During the countrywide discussion of the forthcoming Law on Co-operatives, the Ministry of Finance and higher bodies prepared, in secret, a statute for taxing the co-operatives. This statute virtually destroyed the new law. Only the open discussion of these problems by the Supreme Soviet in May 1988 enabled us to reject the statute as unsatisfactory. Now a new statute on the tax system is being discussed, this time with greater popular involvement. Undoubtedly the result will be much better.

These examples very clearly illustrate the importance of the various measures adopted by the 19th Party Conference to develop more realistically our first democratic ideas, to maintain glasnost and to intensify the fight against bureaucratism in all spheres, particularly in the administration.

Paradoxically, however, I think it was perhaps actually a good thing that our first efforts at establishing new economic conditions were quite clumsy. Our lack of success has given us a chance to understand how resilient those administrative methods are and that there really is no turning back. Most importantly, it has allowed us to take certain decisions for the future that will prevent backsliding of this kind in the administration. Let me draw a parallel with the notorious article by Nina Andreyeva in the newspaper *Sovietskaya Rossiya*. This proposed an anti-perestroika political platform and as a result was, I think, very beneficial for our further advance. The article sharpened our wits and allowed us to pinpoint the conservative ideas that would drag us back lurking behind the demagogic phrases about high socialist principles. The loud rejection of the article made us see more clearly that we must move ahead faster. Similarly, we are now rejecting all attempts to conserve the old administrative methods and to allow old thinking to enter new economic forms such as state purchase orders and economic regulations.

So what have we done in concrete terms? There was a rapidly prepared temporary directive about state orders, limiting these severely for the next two years. According to my calculations, if this directive is followed through, then state purchases will take up only 60 per cent of the volume of production in 1989 and less than 50 per cent in 1990. In 1988 they had taken up 90–100 per cent of production. Moreover, we have ensured that state purchases come under government authority, through Gosplan (the State Planning Agency) or Gossnab (the State Supply Agency), not under that of individual ministries or departments. Certain additional steps have been taken to encourage efficient enterprises even further by allowing them more of their profits than was left to them by the ministries when the economic rules and regulations were first established. It was decided that for the 13th Five-year Plan, unified rules would be established and developed. This would put efficient enterprises into a better position than inefficient ones and create strong incentives for the increase of efficiency and profitability.

We intend to change the principle upon which the wage fund is formed to one that is based on production. More enterprises will use a second model of cost accounting which goes even further. Here the wage fund will not be decided on by a formula but will be the residual fund after the enterprise has paid off its other expenses. Experience has shown that this second model provides extremely strong incentives for increased efficiency and accelerated production. For example, in those concerns of the Ministry of Geology where model two has been applied, labour productivity has risen by 25 per cent in a year. This growth was twice as rapid as that of average income in the rest of the country. Other qualitative work indices in geological organizations also leapt ahead. In the relevant concerns under the Ministry of Electrical Technology and Industry the rate of increase in production doubled in the first half of the year.

In order to make sure that the restructuring of the economic mechanism should stretch further than just the administration of enterprises and their R & D sections, and should affect the entire work force, we have decided to widen the scope of every possible collective contract that is based on cost accounting. In particular we want to widen the scope of the highest form of this contract, the lease contract, which is connected with a complicated system of incentives for increased efficiency in the use of every kind of resource and in the betterment of the quality of production. At the 19th Party Conference it was decided to speed up measures that would facilitate wholesale trade and would remove as fast as possible the limitations that are still being imposed on the control exercised by enterprises over their own income. Once again it was pointed out that we can no longer put off the development and accomplishment of a special programme aimed at the renovation of our country's economy.

All these measures will without doubt alter the time span needed for the transition to a complete new system of administration based on economic realities.

Our success in this respect will depend greatly on our ability to utilize the socialist market. Along with the consumer market, we aim to create in our country in the near future a market for capital goods. As the price reform progresses, the specific gravity of centrally established prices will be greatly reduced and will be retained only for the most important goods, including those that actually define the working people's standard of living, while the number of free and contract prices will increase. It is important at times like these to prevent inflationary tendencies, and for that purpose we must create market conditions under which competition can flourish, abolish monopolization, and create a financial credit mechanism that will work against inflation and ensure a proper correlation between the flow of money and the real flow of material goods. We shall have to ensure that the state's economic departments are flexible and dynamic. They will have to use their state budget allocations to balance supply and demand and to maintain stability in the market. In other words, we must learn to work in a socialist market place, particularly as this market will expand.

A number of enterprises have already begun to issue shares to their workers. I think this idea will spread enormously with time. We are preparing regulatory measures for the issue of shares in our socialist conditions. It is intended to start issuing certificates for the population and for various economic organizations. A new market in negotiable papers will grow up alongside the goods and services markets.

The June 1987 Plenum of the CPSU Central Committee on the problems of radical perestroika proposed that consideration be given to the creation of a convertible rouble. This means that in time there will be a currency market in the USSR. One of the most important steps along this road will be the price reform scheduled for the year 1990. This reform will bring prices within the Soviet Union closer to world prices, with allowances for duty tariffs but in accordance with recommendations made by GATT. Having done this we shall attempt to introduce a single exchange rate for the rouble instead of the number of different ones we have now, introducing what we call internal convertibility, which means that enterprises and organizations will be able to exchange roubles for hard currency according to an exchange rate established within the country. An alternative idea is to establish an exchange according to a floating rate that will take into account supply and demand. We shall aim to make currency convertible at first within the market formed by the socialist countries, then, with increased Soviet exports and closer links with western financial organizations, on the world market.

Making the rouble convertible will obviously be a difficult and complicated task and, naturally enough, will depend on other people, not just on us. But it is absolutely essential if we wish to develop external economic links between the Soviet Union and all other countries. Our view is that we must develop foreign trade more rapidly than home trade in order to increase the USSR's share of the world market. Clearly one reason for this is the need for the mutual economic benefit that accrues from such activities, a benefit that is to be measured not simply in terms of hard currency and goods but also in the exchange of personnel, in our understanding of the market, and in an ever-increasing ability to produce and sell competitive goods. But that is not all. Foreign trade is of immense importance from the point of view of greater co-operation and trust between countries and peoples. This in turn will lead to a better management of thorny political problems and, in particular, to disarmament.

Finally, let us look at what we mean by our perestroika of the administration, what we are aiming to reconstruct. Perestroika cannot be the aim in itself. It is simply a method of solving looming socio-economic development problems. Furthermore, while we are discussing this, we shall examine what we have achieved in the three years of perestroika and especially in 1988, when a sizeable number of enterprises and organizations at last went over to management by cost accounting, self-financing and self-administration.

The first and most important task of the new administrative system is to abolish the dictatorship of the producer and to overcome the deficits of our economy. It must achieve a position where production is aimed directly at the satisfaction of society's needs and is governed by the demands of the consumer.

People's social needs and their satisfaction are of especial importance. During perestroika we have abandoned the old principle of residual allocation of means to the social sphere and have redirected our economic development towards the satisfaction of people's needs. We have managed to overcome stagnation in the construction industry, in food production, in life expectancy and in the social services. But we have not yet achieved a radical transformation. The majority of Soviet families do not feel that perestroika has resulted in any real change. The point where results and real changes will be felt is a long way off, especially given ever-continuing shortages. However, this applies only to material goods. In the spiritual sphere, that is to say glasnost, we can feel a complete change, though even here there are certain unresolved problems.

The new economic conditions introduced at the beginning of 1988 have speeded up the production of consumer goods, the

17

dynamics of commodity circulation and of paid services by one and a half times compared with the same period in the previous year. At the same time wages have grown far more than before. For the first time since 1978 we have managed to increase the GNP of the country by 5 per cent and the use of consumer goods and services by 7.5 per cent.

The satisfaction of social, including individual, needs will depend on economic efficiency and the quality of production. The new administrative system aims to redirect our development, to substitute intensive for extensive growth, to emphasize quality and to economize on resources. Success will depend on how well we can mobilize all our organizational, economic and technological progress. At the moment this progress is often achieved at the expense of socio-economic conditions. At the same time we are working towards the creation of a new technical base in many branches of our economy. Under perestroika we have managed to increase labour productivity quite noticeably. For the first time in our history the growth of social production is due to greater labour productivity, which in industry increased by 4.7 per cent in 1988. Enterprises that have gone over to the new administrative methods have increased productivity by 6.4 per cent, while those which have not yet gone over achieved only 4.2 per cent. The rate of increase in labour productivity in building and transport is even higher. An even worse problem in the past was the economic mismanagement of resources. Here, too, a notable change could be seen in 1988. There has been a great improvement in the return on capital investment, though much needs to be done to stabilize and raise these particular qualitative indices.

The results we have achieved in improving the quality and competitiveness of goods have been more modest. We have overcome negative tendencies in Soviet export and for the first time in three years there was a 3-per-cent growth in exports in the first half of 1988.

The positive changes are apparent to all. But these changes are not basic enough, and perestroika in economics is not yet irreversible. I believe that if we achieve all we have planned, if we advance fearlessly towards a radical reform of the administration, our positive tendencies will become stronger with each passing year. The greatest leap will probably come in the early nineties, at the start of the new Five-year Plan.

18

The key problem – the financial overhaul of the economy

One of the main problems in the transition to an economics-based method of administration is that of restructuring the financial credit system. It is, after all, through finance and credit mechanisms that the state will influence the development of various enterprises and of the economy as a whole.

In this connection it is worth pointing out that under an administrative method of management the role of finance and credit was artificially diminished. These aspects of the economy developed not according to their own laws but according to dictates from above. This could not but lead to serious financial imbalances and to a loss of linkage between the circulation of money and of goods. A financial imbalance in the country has a detrimental effect on all aspects of economic and social life. It leads to shortages and to inflation. It undermines the idea of material incentives, since work is paid for in cash. It is the economic basis for various anti-social phenomena such as speculation, the abuse of official position for private gain and the existence of special shops restricted to senior officials and so on.

Financial reform of the economy is therefore of the utmost urgency. In my opinion it is the key to the whole of the economic reform. Unfortunately we have not devoted sufficient attention to solving this problem. Naturally, in the three years of perestroika various measures have been taken. For example we have tried to ensure that supply matches purchasing power. But this and other measures were uncoordinated and did not reach the root of the problem. What we tried to do was to solve the most urgent problems we had inherited from the period of stagnation by a little tinkering, a little improving, whereas it is clear that what was needed was a series of revolutionary changes. By the time of the June 1987 Plenum of the CPSU Central Committee the vital importance of this problem was fully understood and one of the Plenum's resolutions is concerned with the need to develop and implement a financial overhaul.

A year has passed since that decision was taken and the programme has not yet been developed. Individual local measures have been taken, but these will not solve the crucial problem. On the contrary, a number of decisions have also been taken that have actually aggravated matters. Some of these decisions were justified and have for one reason or another been forced on us. I am referring here to the redirection of resources towards the development of the social sphere. In particular, a large proportion of the wages fund was swallowed up when teachers' pay was increased on average by 40 per cent and doctors' and nurses' pay on average by 30 per cent. But unfortunately we have, in my opinion, made a number of mistakes, allowed a number of inefficiencies. I don't think it was right, for example, to limit the import of consumer goods, other than food. This was done because our income from exports of oil and other raw materials decreased in the last two years because of a general 10-per-cent lowering of world prices. We could instead have reduced our imports of ordinary metal products or of standard industrial equipment. This would have balanced out the hard currency shortages. Or we could instead have mothballed a number of our building projects, for which we were in any case ill prepared. (An obvious example, inter alia, would be the Astrakhan gas condensing and hydrogen producing complex.) We need not then have reduced imports of goods meant for mass consumption, or at least not by so much.

A far greater mistake, in my opinion, was made in the fight against drunkenness. There is no doubting that this is an important task. It is impossible to overestimate the favourable social, moral and economic results that success in this fight will bring. When we talk about drunkenness and our struggle against it, we are talking about the health of the nation and of the next generation, about the moral well-being of the whole population, about healthy family life and the proper upbringing of our children. And some positive results were achieved. On 17 May 1985 we introduced a number of measures to fight drunkenness, and the consumption of alcohol in the USSR went down considerably as a direct result. If the wine and vodka sold in 1984 amounted to 8.4 litres of pure alcohol per capita, then in 1985 this was down to 7.2 litres and in 1986 only 4.3 litres of pure alcohol. At the same time the consumption of sugar decreased in the first half of 1985 by about 2 kg per head of population, indicating that the manufacture of moonshine had also gone down.

We ought at the same time to have begun painstaking educational work and to have strengthened the Temperance Society to help it become a major lever in our fight against drunkenness. Instead of that, a new, tough, and in my opinion mistaken measure was introduced that raised prices of wine and spirits, while at the same time decreasing the number of places where alcoholic drinks could be purchased and in many areas severely restricting the amount that could be sold. This immediately created queues, excited discontent among the population and caused a number of people to take up the distillation of moonshine liquor. In 1987 the consumption of sugar went up from 42 kg per head of population to 46 kg, showing that the manufacture of moonshine had become even more widespread than it had been before the start of the campaign against drunkenness. At the same time sales of alcoholic drinks in state shops went down to 3.26 litres of pure alcohol per capita in 1987. Yearly losses to the state because of these measures amount to between 8 and 10 billion roubles. These losses are not compensated by any decrease in the amount of alcohol that is being consumed or by better health among the population at large. On the contrary, we have taken a step backwards. The state has lost its monopoly on wine and spirits; there is a greater gap between supply and demand in the retail trade; there is a shortage of sugar and an unprecedentedly high demand for and consumption of sugar all over the country. We have now had to resort to rationing, which has in turn made the sugar shortage worse and increased dissatisfaction.

Why do we make these and other mistakes? In my opinion the root of the problem lies in the absence of any democratic discussion of important economic problems and participation in the decisions about them. The decision to increase the price of wine and spirits was taken behind the scenes, without any research and without regard to its effect on popular opinion. And look at the result! This is just one of many examples showing how right the party line is in its insistence on the democratization of all aspects of social life and on a transfer of power to the people as part of the political reforms decided on by the 19th Party Conference.

However, let us return to the problem of achieving a financial balance. There can be no easy solution to it and none will be immediate. But the situation is not hopeless. What we need is three or four years of purposeful work within an overall programme, work that will involve the discussion and implementation of a whole range of interconnected radical measures. This will precipitate the change we want to see: the saturation of the market with goods, the reduction of queues, and the establishment of a certain balance between purchasing power and the supply of material goods.

Several socialist countries have achieved a great deal in this direction. I shall not discuss here the experience of the German Democratic Republic or Czechoslovakia – both highly developed socialist countries with advanced levels of labour productivity – but should like to look instead at Hungary's experience. Hungary launched its economic reform on 1 January 1968 and in the ensuing twenty years has managed to maintain, despite certain difficulties and shortcomings, a certain equilibrium in the consumer goods and services market. Those who are not familiar with the details of the Hungarian economy always respond to this with the following explanation: our Hungarian comrades manage to keep an equilibrium in the consumer goods market because of the large credits they have received from the West and therefore they can regulate the market with the aid of various loans. This is to miss the point. The best period for balancing low prices and consumer goods in Hungary was towards the end of the sixties and the first half of the seventies, at which time Hungary had no foreign debt. Therefore it was not by means of foreign credits that the consumer market was created and its balance maintained. If we examine the nature of Hungary's foreign debt we can see that it is connected not with the production of mass consumer goods or with the service industry but mainly with the production of the means of production (i.e. machine tools and so forth). The loans were taken out, in other words, not to develop those sections of the economy that serve the people directly but to develop heavy industry. Not only that, but the existence of a large and burdensome debt has a negative effect on the balance created in the consumer market, as money that could be used for improving people's lives goes instead to service the foreign debt. It is partly for this reason that we see annual price rises in Hungary. (Of course incomes rise at the same time, but they do not rise in every category proportionately to the rise in prices.)

Of course, Hungary is not the USSR. Our accumulated problems are immeasurably greater and more complex. Nevertheless the experience of this socialist country (as, indeed, that of other countries) shows that much can be achieved in a comparatively short period of time. I shall now adduce another, more tenuous example: China. As we all know, economic reforms have been carried out in China since 1978. The agrarian reforms were successful and as a result China has doubled its agricultural production. In the cities, too, economic reforms are being carried out. I am not going to discuss these reforms in detail and will restrict myself to one aspect of the whole process that is most interesting: the Chinese, while carrying out a series of economic changes, also managed to a great extent to fill the market with mass consumer goods and with services. Of course in many ways the process was a painful one. Many of the consumer goods became more expensive. But wages rose at the same time, and overall the standard of living rose considerably. This was not easy for China: but it was done; and it will not be easy for us.

Take the most important aspect of the projected renewal of the economy – the need to balance supply and demand in the field of consumer goods and services. What exactly can we achieve? We could enact a series of measures to control the amount of money paid out to the population, though this in itself would not amount to much. I am not talking about placing limits on individual earnings but about a general limitation on the amount of money in circulation. Within such a limitation those who work well will still earn well.

But we have a number of immediate tasks connected with increases in pay. For instance we need to introduce a new law about pensions, enabling them to be increased, especially for members of collective farms. I think we should find a formula whereby part of the pension fund, maybe even a considerable part of it, could be financed by other funds created in enterprises, and in collective and state farms, and partially covered by money set aside for the incentive fund and the wages fund.

We should look at ways of providing incentives to managers and other people involved in the administration of the wages fund and the contingency fund. In my opinion it would make sense to introduce some sort of sliding scale of deductions from that portion of an enterprise's profits which is directed into the fund for material incentives. This could be adjusted on a sliding scale if the wages and material incentives funds, that is the entire payment fund, were to grow too fast. Naturally this sliding scale must not be prohibitive. It must leave a considerable part of the increase in the wages fund with the workforce involved. Nevertheless it would be advisable to take the top off this increase if the fund showed extraordinary growth. If we adopted such an approach, we could allow the enterprises to decide for themselves how to allocate residual profits from the various incentive funds. This, incidentally, is how it is done in many countries. It is very important to link such payments to a realistic indicator. They ought not to be tied, as they are now, to the production of goods or to the fulfilment of production quotas, but to net production after costs have been met. This would on the one hand provide an enterprise with a considerable economic incentive and on the other enable it to adjust its payments to various funds far more efficiently.

We also need to think about taxation. At the moment we are devising a tax scale for members of co-operatives. Our intention is to tax those with an income of less than 700 roubles a month on the same scale as blue- and white-collar workers. For those with an income of over 700 roubles a month the tax would grow progressively. It would not be right to have several different scales of taxation in the country. Usually a country has a single scale, and it would be sensible for us to apply the new scale for members of co-operatives who earn more than 700 roubles a month to blue- and white-collar workers with similar incomes. At present only very few people earn more than 700 roubles a month. Any measure that would increase tax on higher-income groups would be popular. Obviously wages will continue to rise and the number of people with incomes of more than 700 roubles a month will grow rapidly. This measure will therefore prove useful in the long term in that it will help restrict excessive growth in the amount of money actually in circulation.

As I have said, these proposals would not on their own reshape the economy. That will come about from the steps taken to fill the market with goods and services.

Let me supply some figures here to illustrate the extent of the problem we are facing. The total turnover in retail trade by the state, co-operative and collective farm sections (including food and catering) in 1987 was 350 billion roubles. In the same year the turnover of the services industry was 54 billion roubles, making a total of 404 billion roubles. At the same time, the nation's disposable earnings in 1987 amounted to 586 billion roubles. Of this income, 441 billion roubles, or 75 per cent, was spent on food and consumer goods. To gain a correct impression of the nation's disposable income after taxes and other deductions, we must also take account of savings. In 1987 roughly 24 billion roubles were deposited in the Savings Bank of the USSR. This left an increased amount of money in people's pockets. In order to redress the imbalance between demand by people with money to spend and what is actually available, we must find goods and services worth tens of billions of roubles, a considerable amount of money. This we call 'frustrated demand', and its extent can be estimated partly by the amount of money in the mobile deposits in the savings bank and partly by the amount of money that people keep at home. I would say that in gross terms we shall have to find in the next few years consumer goods and services worth 70 billion roubles a year if we are to keep pace with income levels.

I also think that in the next three or four years we will be able to find supply to meet the demand. First of all we can encourage people to buy their homes, something they will do if their standard of living is thereby improved. Obviously we cannot make people pay for housing conditions that are deteriorating. In the next few years the Soviet Union is planning to build 2.5 million flats and houses, with an average area of 60 square metres. When families move to these new homes, others will move into the vacated ones, thus improving their living conditions. If we put first half, then two-thirds, of the newly built housing up for sale, this would generate a minimum turnover of 10–15 billion roubles a year. Naturally we have to assume that people will not be able to pay the full price of their new homes immediately and will deposit, say, 20–25 per cent of the price. An important role offers itself here to various enterprises and organizations which could assist purchasers from sources such as their incentive funds. Interesting possibilities deriving from combinations of state and privately supported housing provisions could arise. For example, a family living in a one-bedroom flat provided by the state might well want a two-bedroom one, but not be able to afford it. Since they would be moving out of a one-bedroom flat subsidized by the state, we could institute a system whereby they would have to pay only for the extra space they were getting, rather than for the whole flat. We could reach a situation on the housing market in two, or at most three, years where anyone wanting to improve his living conditions could do so simply by paying extra. In other words, we could balance supply and demand in this market. At the same time we ought to increase our efforts to stimulate private building, particularly of the dacha or 'country cottage' type. For this purpose, land should be made available and the proper infrastructures (i.e. utilities, building materials) supplied.

Equally the question of raising rents for people whose accommodation space is greater than what is considered to be the social norm needs to be put. Bearing in mind that living conditions are improving all the time, the sooner we introduce this idea of a social norm along with a higher rent for those with more living space, the less painful the process is likely to be. Average living space for one person at present is slightly more than 16 square metres. We could set the social norm at 20 or even 22 square metres. It would not, I think, be sensible to demand additional rent from a single person living in a one-room flat, but with families we could make the following arrangement: anyone who lives in less than the space allowed by the not ungenerous 'social norm' would pay rent according to the old valuation, while anything in excess of the set norm would be charged for in full, that is to say, the rent ought to correspond exactly to the amount the extra space is costing the state. The system would need to be arranged in such a way that only 10–15 per cent of the population would be subject to these extra living space surcharges. One solution would be to delegate the appropriate powers to the republics. The legislation for increased rent would be enabled by each republic and the money thus raised could then remain in the republic and be used for the upkeep of the available accommodation.

Looking at another field where supply could be made to match demand, we could take steps to increase sharply the production of cars and consumer durables in the USSR. At the moment the USSR produces 1,330,000 cars a year. Production has not increased since 1980. But even so the state earns around 8 billion roubles a year from the sale of new cars. If we include the sale of spare parts and fuel, the sum rises to around 10 billion roubles, which makes up 3 per cent of retail turnover in the country. Of all the middling to highly developed countries, the USSR has the lowest car-ownership figures – 16 for every 100 families. Western Europe's least developed country – Portugal – has 60 cars for every 100 families. The USSR not only produces fewer cars than the United States, Japan and West Germany. We produce fewer cars than Great Britain, France and Italy, countries with one fifth of our population. Moreover the cars we produce at the moment cannot be called cars for popular consumption. The most popular car is the Zhiguli (Lada in the West), which is sold for 8,000 roubles and requires an expenditure of 100 roubles a month to run. With a national average salary of 200 roubles a month, a standard Soviet family cannot think of owning such a car. It is meant for a family whose standard of living is twice, or more likely three times, as high as the average. The pathetic numbers of cheaper cars in production, cars like the Zaporozhets or the forthcoming Oka, do not alter this abnormal situation.

To make the USSR into a car-owning society will need some really big thinking: we must build a whole series of factories to produce annually about 2 million cars in the 700 to 1,100 cc range, costing 4–5 thousand roubles and with fuel consumption in the 60 mpg class. Such cars are what is popular now in the world. These are cars like the Seat from Spain, the Fiat Uno and Panda from Italy, the Renault from France, the Mini from Britain and others. At the same time we ought to start producing half as many Zhiguli again, lifting production to 1,200,000 a year. To do this we could set up automobile manufacturing enterprises jointly with western companies. The western firms could be paid in our more traditional goods for their share of the capital investment, which we would aim to set at 20–30 per cent of the value of the plant. At the same time the state could sponsor a nationwide programme to build and set up filling and service stations and garages to meet the demand generated by the increased number of car owners. And a further 20 billion roubles' worth of 'frustrated demand' would be satisfied.

These factories would in all likelihood take five to seven years to work up to full production, but the first cars could be rolling off the production lines after three or four years; and orders could be taken and deposits collected as soon as building work had begun. People would buy bonds for the cars with a guarantee that those who bought bonds worth more than half the price of a car would get priority delivery when the cars were produced.

But enough of cars. In the USSR there is a huge potential market for video cassette recorders. Here too we could organize a series of joint ventures for the production of video recorders with any of the western companies who mass-produce them. The aim would be to make one and a half or two million VCRs a year priced at 500–1,000 roubles without the television set. Such a measure would generate a substantial amount of turnover, as demand for videos would greatly increase demand for expensive colour television sets.

There is also an enormous market in the Soviet Union for personal computers, especially for children. We should be producing millions of computers a year at a price of 300–500 roubles for

27

a simple computer and 1,000 or more roubles for more complicated ones. Some of the factories in the defence industry could be switched to the production of videos and personal computers.

The potential for increasing the production of consumer durables is enormous. All we need is to interest people in light industry and other sectors of the national economy; that is to say, we should give the producers of the actual goods or components an incentive to produce them. At the moment, when a consumer product is sold for 100 roubles, the producers' costs are no more than 20 or 30 roubles (these are actual figures). So 70–80 roubles are available on the nation's books for financial manipulation. Part of this sum, say 10 roubles, could therefore be used to intensify their production. The state would lose nothing by this; on the contrary it would gain from increased turnover and profit. For the next few years we must ensure that the production of consumer durables is given more consideration and is seen to be more lucrative than heavy industrial production. Enterprises should strive to find some consumer product that is in demand and produce it. We should encourage the people making these products and the people making the parts for them. We are at present discussing a series of measures to improve incentives and make factories more interested in producing popular consumer goods. But we are a little late. These and other such measures ought to have been put into effect in 1985 or at the very latest 1986. It is now 1989 and we are still only at the discussion stage.

In the next two or three years we can considerably increase imports of consumer goods. In any case the process is reasonably profitable, as for every rouble we spend on the purchase of these goods we get several roubles back through the retail trade.

We must further allow those factories and enterprises that actually have foreign exchange earnings to spend this currency on more than simply capital equipment and raw materials. They should be allowed to buy consumer goods abroad for their workers and sub-contractors and for sale in their region or district: this would be an effective new way of bringing imported consumer goods into circulation. In 1987 manufactured consumer goods made up 13 per cent of Soviet imports (with machinery and equipment making up 41 per cent); this is down from 18 per cent in 1970. In my opinion, we could, in the next three years, double our imports of consumer goods. This would increase the retail trade figures by no less than 30 billion roubles.

However, we also have to avoid simply transferring money out of savings accounts into the purchase of goods. The best way would be to make people more interested in investing money in longer-term projects by giving worthwhile returns. Apart from reorganizing the existing types of savings on offer, we could develop the whole concept of state bonds – introduce share ownership. Shares in an enterprise would be sold primarily to the workers of that particular enterprise.

In order to facilitate the acquisition of consumer goods abroad for the use of our population, we could start selling foreign currency to the population, at the same time making the whole process of going abroad on tourist visas more democratic.

One recent social development is that an ever greater part of people's earnings is spent on holidays. In order to make the wage structure economic and to combine this with greater productivity we ought to make it easier for people to take days off without pay. On the other hand we must also improve leisure facilities. We must allow people to use their earnings to take more interesting holidays, to spend their free time in ways they enjoy. The amount of money invested is less than 10–15 per cent of total earnings. We should make it our aim to encourage people to spend half as much again on leisure in much improved conditions.

I have not yet touched on several aspects of financial balancing. In particular I have not yet discussed the thorny problem of the politics of retail pricing. This is deliberate, as I wish to devote a separate section of this book to it.

To conclude, I would re-emphasize that at this stage in perestroika the most important problem is balancing the national economy. If we can bring the market into balance, if we can satisfy demand by filling the market with a variety of good-quality consumer goods and services, we will have more or less solved half our problems. For a balanced market would mean a real increase in the standard of living, as people would be able to purchase what they chose, and it would also increase incentives to work and create a barrier against inflation. It would also strike a blow against black marketeering and other antisocial phenomena. A balanced market is the most important factor in the stable development of national economy. Without financial equilibrium as a basis we will not be able to introduce price reforms successfully. I shall now turn to that very subject.

Price reform and price formation

It is essential that we establish a correlation between the circulation of money and the circulation of goods and prevent surplus money being accumulated. However, this on its own will not balance the socialist market or create a direct relationship between production and demand. We have to use another important lever: prices. Prices are primal to all decisions within a balanced economic system. In such a system the producer, i.e. each enterprise, decides for itself what and how much it will produce, taking into account demand and profitability, both of which will depend directly on costs. If the product's cost gives a low profit or even no profit at all, the enterprise will not be over-anxious to produce it. If, on the other hand, the price of the product makes its production particularly profitable and there is a demand for it, an enterprise will want to use all its resources to produce it and will, furthermore, find it to its advantage to increase production.

We must set prices such that whatever is profitable to society will be profitable to the producer. In this fashion we can ensure that the national economy will acquire effectiveness and a sense of proportion.

The system of price regulation we have inherited from the old administrative economic system is unsatisfactory. Production was not regulated by the price system because the quantity and choice of product were centrally planned. If the prices did not ensure profitability, central government subsidized the production. If there was a certain, not very high, profit, there were subsidies for various other purposes. But if a particular product proved to be highly profitable, most of that profit was taken away for the national budget. So prices were part of the national accounting system and were not seen as decisive economic indices in the producer's development.

Now let us look at enterprises as consumers. Again price played no part in their orders, as they were not making purchases of capital goods or raw materials on an open market: their requirements were met by a centralized supply agency. But as if all this were not enough, here too prices were not formed in a market but were decided on centrally. So prices were doubly dependent on central policy, and the result was that price formation was also non-economic. Prices would be reviewed in isolation on a yearly

30

basis, never as part of a whole. Wholesale or retail prices for things as important as agricultural produce would be determined in accordance with extraneous principles. The whole system of price formation was smothered in historical layers. The idea of subsidized prices was far too widespread. Nobody thought it unusual to subsidize prices of important goods. As a result we had a curious situation whereby whole important branches of the economy, for instance coal mining, were considered to be of enormous significance to the state and were consequently nurtured at all times, even though production was actually proceeding at a loss. A great deal was invested in coal mining with a view to constantly increasing production. This obsession with quantity meant that as a rule there were only minimal differences in price for products of differing quality. As a result it was not particularly profitable to improve the quality.

Under the administrative economic system, a two-tier method of price formation grew up. On the one hand, raw materials prices were considerably lower than world prices. For instance, fuel prices in the Soviet Union are two or three times lower than world prices, the prices of other industrial raw materials are about half those of world prices, and the prices of agricultural produce about two or three times lower.

But when we look at manufactured goods, particularly certain polymers used in the chemical industry, we can see that a completely different level of pricing was created, a level that was in some ways deliberately set too high. The same is true of some products of the mechanical engineering industry, especially if we consider the consumer demand for them.

This price structure was based on incomplete or very primitive costing notions. No allowance was made for costs in the use of natural, labour or production resources: it was assumed that these resources were available to an enterprise for free. Capital investment costs were amortized at artificial rates which were always too low. The notional profit included in the price was not supposed to include provision for possible reconstruction or even for expansion of the enterprise. The ruling principle was that only running costs needed to be covered. To cap it all, about 60 per cent of the profit went straight into the national budget, while the capital for the development of an enterprise was allocated separately on the decision of a central agency. For a number of items (mostly consumer goods and petrochemicals) purchase tax

31

made up a large proportion of the retail price. In fact, under the old system the purchase tax usually exceeded the amount that went into the budget from the profit on the product.

To change over completely to an economic method of administration while such a system of price formation remains in existence is impossible. So the most important aspect of the restructuring of management must be a radical reform of prices and price formation. We plan to initiate this reform in 1990. First of all we intend to carry out a global review of prices and to reconstruct the whole system of price formation in the country. This new system will have to be based on a unified set of principles. We shall review wholesale prices in industry, agriculture and the building industry, including transport costs, and then we shall reassess the retail prices paid by the population for goods and services.

Prices should be formulated primarily with regard to socially essential spending. In fact we need to rethink our whole approach to expenditure. The new prices will have to take into account expenditure on all kinds of resources and on compensation for the pollution of the environment. They must also permit realistic profits to be made so that enterprises will be able to finance their own reconstruction, their expansion and also any social needs of their workers. All this will have to be achieved as part of the transition to a unified pricing system.

One of the difficulties of the projected price reform is the need at the very least to double the wholesale prices of fuel and raw materials. This will have to be done for two reasons. Firstly, a rise in prices will ensure that the branches of industry which produce these resources will be able to be self-financing. Secondly, it would force industries to be more careful with natural resources. Artificially low fuel and raw materials prices encourage the squandering of resources. For example fuel oil was used far too wastefully in ordinary boilers and even in thermal power stations. At the prices then being charged there was an appearance of profitability. Indeed, the prices on natural gas were so low that there was no reason for making the process of gas pumping more economical. Artificially low bread prices had a similar effect. Bread is so cheap that it is profitable to feed it to cattle.

Our intention is to change the price structure in industry. Prices of raw materials and fuel will probably double, while prices for semi-finished products will go up 1.3 or 1.5 times, and prices for finished products will hardly go up at all. At the same time the

32

prices of polymers and suchlike materials will even decrease. All in all we expect prices in industry to go up by an average of 15–20 per cent.

Clearly it is not enough just to reform the prices in industry. At the same time we shall have to introduce price differentials dependent on quality. This would encourage those enterprises that produce good-quality, competitive goods. If outdated products are priced centrally, it will be done in such a way as to make their manufacture unprofitable. This will provide an incentive for change to better, more efficient practices.

In reforming prices in industry and agriculture, we shall have to maintain a balance between goods and financing and between industry and agriculture. In particular, goods bought by the agricultural sector will have to be priced at a realistic level. We shall have to abolish subsidies on artificial fertilizers and certain kinds of agricultural technology. However, this abolition of subsidies will be taken into account when the prices are set. In agriculture too, prices will have to be changed and sharply differentiated in order to take quality into account.

This brings us to the most vexing aspect of price reform, because it is the one that will affect every member of the population most: retail prices. At present retail prices on bread, meat and dairy products in state shops are particularly low, since they are sold at less than cost. The approximate price in the state shops of a kilo of meat is 1 rouble 80 kopecks, and the state subsidy on that same kilo amounts to 3 roubles 50 kopecks. The total state subsidy in this branch of the food trade is more than 60 billion roubles a year out of a total state budget of 480 billion roubles.

The results of this artificial lowering of prices on food are obvious. There is waste in the use of food, while at the same time there is a shortage of meat and dairy products in the state shops. As a consequence more and more of these products have to be bought either in the co-operative shops, where prices are double those in the state shops, or on the peasants' markets, where prices are even higher: 2.5–3 times as much. But the capacity to produce varied and high-quality meat and dairy produce is far lower in co-operatives, in the kolkhozes (collective farms) and, particularly, in individual households than in the state food industry. And as meat and milk resources within the state food industry are limited and there are great shortages, there is, at the moment, no possibility of filling the market with the required amount or variety of meat and dairy products. Demand cannot be met in quantity, quality or variety.

People often argue that there are not just negative aspects to the artificially lowered prices on bread, meat and dairy products but also positive ones. It would appear at first sight obvious that lower prices should improve the diet of low-income families. This line of argument leads to the assertion that low prices are in fact a social advantage that our society possesses. But studies have shown that the subsidies on meat and dairy products primarily help high- rather than low-income families. This is connected with the fact that it is the higher-income families that consume more of the meat that is sold within the state system, often through the network of canteens or shops within enterprises. We have to face the fact that food subsidies are not simply uneconomic but socially unfair, as they widen the gap between higher-income and low-income families.

Moreover, the situation in the state meat and dairy-product trade varies enormously from region to region. In Moscow, for instance, several times more meat and dairy products are available than anywhere else. This means that Muscovites are secretly subsidized by the rest of the country. In a number of towns and cities in the Russian Federation there is in effect no state trade in meat products. The amounts of meat available to the state are so low that they barely cover canteens, factory shops, hospitals, kindergartens etc.

There are some people who oppose the raising of prices on meat and dairy products because they nurture an illusion that with increased efficiency in agriculture we could lower the cost of agricultural production to such an extent that these low prices would actually cover the cost without any subsidy. Their argument is very simple. They consider that raising prices is a way of encouraging the existing inefficiency and wastefulness of meat and dairy farming. I cannot understand these arguments. It is quite apparent to me that the prices of bread, meat and dairy products should be raised. Something else is apparent, and has been discussed many times at the highest party and state levels: that retail prices will have to be raised in such a way that there is no drop in the living standard of the population at large. This can be achieved if the people are compensated for the greater expenditure that will be the result of the higher prices by paying directly to them what would previously have gone in state subsidies.

We cannot raise prices on meat and dairy products sufficiently to balance the total present-day expenditure and abolish subsidies completely. Nor would such an action be advisable. First of all, there is a deal of justice in the claim that there is much inefficiency in the meat and dairy farming sectors. But under perestroika we have tried to introduce a new economic structure that for the first time in many years has achieved a lowering of production costs, and we can therefore expect some lowering of expenditure. We can think about raising prices sufficiently to reduce subsidies from 60 billion roubles to 15 billion roubles only. There is nothing unusual in subsidizing agriculture. It is done in Japan, in Sweden, and even to a certain extent in the United States, a country with far better conditions for agricultural productivity.

There is, however, another aspect to the question. Prices in the consumer co-operatives and on the peasant markets are different in different parts of the country. For instance in Omsk one can buy a kilo of meat on the market for 3 roubles 50 kopecks; but in other parts the price is 5–6 roubles a kilo. We cannot raise the price of meat above the market price in different parts of the country.

Let us now turn to the problem of compensating the population for higher food prices. We have to decide what form this compensation should take. If we simply include it in the salary, families with many children will suffer in comparison with single people. Besides, wages fluctuate from month to month, depending on the amount of work done, and we may create an impression that the compensation is incomplete or merely temporary. Therefore I believe that the compensation should take the form of a definite sum calculated for each person and paid out regularly. This was, incidentally, the way the 'bread addition' was paid out when rationing was ended after the war. The need for this additional payment later disappeared as wages increased and the sum in question simply became part of the regular wage packet.

From what we have already seen about the social effects of food subsidies, it will be people on a low income who will gain most from compensation calculated equally for each person. Those on higher incomes will gain proportionately less. However, if this is not enough, we can raise the compensation level for those on low wages to ensure that their living standards are maintained.

It must be said that, judging by the many letters received from workers by newspapers and journals, the above ideas about raising

35

prices on meat and dairy products will not be popular. Many people have grown used to and accepted the existing situation of shortages in the meat and dairy trade. They accept that the state shops offer an extremely small choice of goods. Many people have never known or even seen anything else, and they are quite understandably worried that prices may rise while their situation will remain the same. They are also worried that any compensation they may receive will not cover the extra they will have to pay out for food. Others are afraid that having raised prices on meat and dairy products we shall start a chain reaction that will raise other prices as well. We must devise a series of measures that will ensure that this does not happen.

I have to admit that there has not been any serious or extensive presentation of our case for the raising of meat and dairy prices. The problem is endlessly worried at by the press, but most of the letters published oppose our measure and so emotions win over understanding. We must decide immediately on a general approach to the whole problem and discussion of it before we even think of reforming the system of retail prices.

My own opinion is that we should examine possible measures for the reform of retail prices in a more general context of wider measures for the renewal of the consumer market and improving living standards. At the same time as we are changing the retail price structure we should raise pensions and child benefits. It would be even better if at the same time we increased the production of consumer goods.

So far I have talked about only one aspect of the price reform: the rises. The main result of the reform will be that price levels, both absolute and proportionate, will converge – inside the USSR and indeed globally. This in turn will ease our transition to a convertible rouble and the USSR's greater participation in international economic relations.

But it is not enough to see the price reform as simply a matter of a change in price levels. Even more important, perhaps, will be the change in the process of price formation itself. We shall have to make a big step forward in the decentralization and democratization of the process of price formation. We shall have to change noticeably the relative weight of floating and fixed prices in favour of the former. At present 80–90 per cent of prices are set centrally. But from the very earliest stages of perestroika we have been extending the proportion of floating and contractual prices. The practice of giving discounts or making additional charges has also extended, while the system for establishing new prices has in many cases been simplified.

Let us look in this context at retail prices. We see that the base prices, namely 'N' for new products and 'D' for fashion products, have been raised. These prices are now established by direct negotiation with the trade. Prices on imported goods have also been established in a different manner, in that the problem of supply and demand was taken into account far more than before. The freedom that co-operatives have been given in setting their own prices has increased the role of consumer co-operatives within the food trade. Now their prices are different in different parts of the country. Other changes have taken place: for instance, local councils have been given greater discretion in pricing fruit and vegetables according to the season or according to whether or not they are local produce.

One aspect of the price reform will be a considerable reduction of the number of prices fixed centrally. These will continue to apply to fuels and raw materials, to products of mass technology, to the most important necessities and to mass services. The role of republican and local organizations in price setting will increase. Finally, there will be a considerable increase in the number of floating and contractual prices for special quality products, for goods produced in small quantities or even individually, for imported goods, and so on. I rather think that as we carry out the price reform in 1990, the majority of prices will still be set centrally, since we will still be dealing with an underdeveloped market. As I see it, centrally fixed prices will constitute 60–70 per cent of all prices, the remaining 30–40 per cent being contractual. But during the next Five-year Plan we should aim at reducing the number of centrally set prices to 30 per cent of the total, while raising the proportion of floating and contractual prices to 70 per cent. However, we shall only be able to implement this if we master the economic methods of market regulation and the principles of socialist competition, and if we liquidate production and trade monopolies.

One of the problems is that the role of competition in socialist society is badly developed in theory and in practice. To make myself perfectly clear I have to say that for many years we were afraid of using the word 'competition' in connection with social economies because we connected it with such totally alien phenomena as unemployment, bankruptcy etc. But in the Law on State Enterprises we spoke of the need for enterprises to compete on the market. We called it 'economic competition', and by using this term we made an important step forward: we spoke openly about the need to abolish monopoly in production and trade, the need to achieve some competition between enterprises.

The next step in this development was taken in the Law on Co-operatives. Here we actually used the term 'economic competitiveness' in reference to the socialist market. A new question arose: what measures were required for the development of this competitiveness?

We have done a certain amount. For instance, we have taken the first steps in the development of pluralism in property ownership. Alongside state enterprises, we have created co-operatives and even encouraged the growth of individual labour activity, that is the growth of self-employment, as part of the economy. This is, of course, not enough. We need to think about competition between the various state enterprises. To achieve this we shall have to ensure that there are numerous enterprises producing similar goods. We shall have to break up or prune large inefficient conglomerates. In general we shall have to concentrate on the creation of middle- and small-scale enterprises even within the state sector. An important part will be played in this process by the authorities at the republican and local levels. Initiative there will be of great value. But first we intend to delegate responsibility for some of the middle- and small-scale enterprises from the central ministries to the republican ones and to local authorities. This will, naturally enough, lead to some reviews of their work within the enterprises themselves, as they will have to take demand and social need into account. We have given enterprises, associations, republican and local authorities, even central ministries the right to create new enterprises and new economic organizations. We must now stimulate the creation of these enterprises, particularly ones that gear their production to new demand. One way of doing so would be to exempt from taxation that part of their profits that is used on further investment.

We possess another tool for the encouragement of competition. We can and must encourage the growth of joint ventures with foreign firms. By 1 February 1989 there were only 200 such enterprises, and several hundred more were under consideration. But this is only the beginning. We shall acquire experience in this field and as we liberalize regulations concerning joint ventures and special economic zones economic activity in this area will grow. We only have to look at China to see how far one can go. There are almost 10,000 joint ventures in that country and the capital involved amounts to 20 billion dollars. The total capital in joint ventures in the Soviet Union has barely reached one billion dollars. But I believe that as we make our currency convertible and as we open our economy more and more, the pressure of external market forces will affect the competitiveness of our goods in both the social and world markets.

Moving to a market system in capital equipment

We are determined to establish a wholesale trade in capital equipment. To do this we must meet two important conditions: we must achieve financial-material equilibrium and we must reform prices.

We need to move away from the current system, and its centralized supply of materials and technical equipment, to a system based on wholesale trade. This may be hard but it is also a *sine qua non* of any radical reform in management. That it will be hard and that it is important both derive from the fact that the centralized system of supply is the very cornerstone of the administrative, 'compound' system of economics. The point is that orders from above under the old system touch mainly the most important categories of production and apply to very large units. If administrative management were to restrict itself to this, individual enterprises would still retain a fair amount of freedom in their choice of what to produce. But they issue more than just planning directives. In addition they specify more concrete tasks to do with material and technical supplies. These take the form of specific directives to the enterprises detailing what they should produce and for whom. These planning directives cover about ten times as much ground and detail as the actual state plan for production. Tnis is one side of the problem. Every enterprise is given a detailed plan telling it what kind of fuel, raw materials, parts, and so on it will receive and precisely how much will be due from each supplier. Working all this out in such detail for the

39

whole country is a Herculean task indeed, and to accomplish it a nationwide network of planning agencies specializing in material and technical supplies has been created. Each ministry and each department has a large section dealing with supplies. In addition Gossnab (the State Supply Agency) has its own network of offices with sections specializing in different products: Glavmetall deals with supplies of metals, Glavpribor deals with deliveries of equipment, and so on. Gossnab also has subdivisions dealing with material and technical supplies in various branches of industry.

Clearly the system of centralized supply ties an enterprise up with directives and leaves no room to manoeuvre. It has even reached the point where enterprises have been forbidden to sell or resell unwanted equipment or materials. All such activities have to be centralized and can only take place with permission from the ministry in question and the various planning agencies.

It is virtually impossible to live and work under such an inflexible administrative system. It is unwieldy in the extreme and at the same time it cannot actually ensure that enterprises get what they want when they need it. So what has happened is that each enterprise has created its own stockpile of raw materials, spare parts, equipment and so on as an insurance against breakdowns in the supply system, which are not just frequent but endemic. To cap this, the supply agencies, above the actual enterprises in the hierarchy, are not considered responsible for breakdowns in the supply system.

Therefore, in order to ensure that the right amounts of raw materials and parts were available, enterprises would engage in a number of semi-legal and even illegal operations. Whole networks were created on the 'you scratch my back and I'll scratch yours' principle. A huge black economy grew up. It functioned alongside the official economy with its centralized allocation of resources and developed with the tacit approval of the party and local authorities. After all, those same authorities demanded that enterprises should give material support to the country's agriculture, requiring them to use their own materials to build for social and productive purposes in the villages, to provide tools for the repair of agricultural machinery, pipes for providing running water and so on. In return the agricultural enterprises illegally lent their tractors for clearing snow on the factory's land, supplied food for use in the factory's canteen, and so on. Some idea of the importance of this sort of unofficial arrangement can be had from the following

40

isolated instance. In just one district the collective and state farms erected buildings to a value of 400 million roubles, while their allocation of metal, cement, building equipment, bricks and wood was sufficient for only 60 million roubles' worth of buildings. We are talking here about resources which are legally supposed to be planned and allocated only by centralized agencies. What this means in effect is that five-sixths of this region's agricultural building was achieved through illegal methods of direct exchange and barter with industrial, construction, transport and other enterprises. It also means that the local party and Soviet (council) were directly involved in this activity.

However, the worst consequence of our centralized supply system was the creation of a division between the producer and the consumer. The system can be compared to a wall between the producer enterprise and the consumer enterprise. The producers would hand over their products to the supply agencies, who would then share these out among the consumers. Under such a system there could be no question of consumers influencing producers or of adjusting production so that the goods produced were actually the best possible for the particular consumer's needs.

Let me quote one of many similar instances. The Chelyabinsk tractor factory comes under the Ministry of Agricultural Machinery and is a major producer of bulldozers. The factory, like any other enterprise, was judged by how much it produced a year and by the gross value of its output. In order to produce more bulldozers the factory decided not to bother with designing something new for a specific purpose and took an easier option. What they did, in fact, was to add a blade to a caterpillar tractor. And the tractor with the blade was proclaimed to be a bulldozer. Every year the factory turned over to our system of centralized supply tens of thousands of such bulldozers, mostly 130-horsepower ones, with a few 250-horsepower ones thrown in. All the bulldozers were identical, with no modifications for any particular consumer's needs. This meant, for example, that a few thousand, say, were taken every year to the Far North, to Magadan, Yakutia and other gold-mining areas where the bulldozer is the main tool of the trade. The bulldozer cuts the peat to bare a seam of gold-laden sand, which it lifts to special washing equipment which pans out the particles of gold.

Everyone knew that the Chelyabinsk bulldozers were unsuitable for heavy work in the Far North. In fact, as they stood, they were not suitable for work at all. So when the northern enterprises received a new consignment of bulldozers, they had to rebuild them, welding on reinforcements and strengthening them. Nevertheless, no bulldozer lasted even a season, and every year each one required a total overhaul costing several times more than the original purchase. So in the North, where labour costs three to five times as much as it does in Chelyabinsk, they have had to build eight large factories whose sole purpose is to mend and overhaul the inadequate bulldozers. I visited the Chelyabinsk factory and tried to discuss these problems with the designers and engineers there. Completely unabashed, they informed me that their bulldozers were not meant for that kind of work, and, anyway, this was the first they had heard of the whole problem. This is typical of a system where the consumer is kept away from the producer and has no say in what he does.

The evil of a centralized supply must be understood. We must appreciate that it is economically inefficient and ineffective. We have to understand that such a system leads inevitably to shortages and to the dictatorship of the producer over the consumer. If there is a balanced market where you freely buy the materials you need, there is no need for the producer to stockpile. Stockpiling is expensive and leads to losses, but if materials are distributed through a centralized agency, no one can manage without stockpiling. Let us examine how goods that in a free-market system would be readily available fall into short supply.

This is how a centralized supply system works. First comes the requisition campaign. The enterprises all submit written requisitions to the supply agencies. These, be it noted, are presented many months before the start of the planning period in question. On top of that, the materials requisitions go in about six months before the enterprise is told in detail what its centrally planned output is to be. So, without knowing what their plan will land them with, each enterprise puts in requisitions that would, if met, cover all possible contingencies. They also know from past experience that their request is unlikely to be met in full – they will be short-changed. So each enterprise puts in a requisition slightly greater than is absolutely necessary. Once all the requisitions are in, it becomes apparent that some materials have been requested in quantities far greater than can be produced. So the requisitions are trimmed back and the enterprises strive to stockpile the scarce material.

42

The negative effects ripple throughout the economy. On the one hand resources are stockpiled, that is, effectively go out of circulation. Our national income is something like 600 billion roubles. At the same time the goods hoarded by our factories, enterprises and departments are worth more than 460 billion roubles. This is at least twice as high as any rational stock level ought to be. Turnover slows down and the economy functions far less efficiently. At the same time the scarcity of a particular item puts the producer into a privileged position vis-à-vis the consumer. And so we get the rule of the producer under which contact is lost with the demands of the consumer and society. It is production for production's sake.

But back to Chelyabinsk and its tractor factory. If its customers had a direct say, it would have to improve drastically the quality of its bulldozers and ensure they met their needs. If that were done, fewer tractors would be needed and the factory would be able to economize its metal and labour and production costs. This would have a far-reaching effect on the economy. But when the producer rules, absolutely everything is done the wrong way round. The factory sees it as more profitable to increase the output, to mass-produce. Since the needs of the consumer are immaterial, the producer does not make enough spares for the bulldozers. Anyone who buys a Chelyabinsk bulldozer must produce spares for himself, overhaul the machinery himself, and so on. In the North-East, as I have mentioned, it is five to twelve times as expensive to produce spares as it is to buy them from Chelyabinsk, where a certain quantity is produced. This story is repeated in every branch of the automobile, shipbuilding and machine-tool industries.

Within an administrative system of management the producer's main aim is to get rid of his output. Out of sight – out of mind. How and where the product will be used and how long it will work are not the producer's worry. This leads to a paradoxical situation. If we look at the amount of money spent on the upkeep of a car or a tractor we can see that actually making it cost society only 2, 3 or 4 per cent of the total amount spent on it. From the point of view of the national economy it would be useful to halve or reduce still further the amount spent on a product during its lifetime. To achieve this we must reach a stage where the producer himself builds longevity and reliability into his goods and supplies spares for them. This might require new investments in the

43

production process, but any investment here would more than pay for itself. However, this approach is far too sensible for the existing administrative management system because it undermines the very foundation of that system – the centralized supply of materials and equipment, which itself causes the segregation of producer and consumer.

Finally, we must look at the obverse of the centralized distribution system coin – the physical supply of goods. The system guarantees the disposal of the product. It does not concern itself with such details as whether the enterprise designated as the consumer requires the product or has any money to pay for it. If the distribution plan says that such and such a state farm is to have ten tractors, then it will get ten tractors whether it wants to or not. Suppose, however, the state farm has no money. No matter. Money is considered to be of secondary importance in this scheme of things. It is goods that are important; money and financial considerations are a mere formality. If a sovkhoz (state farm) has no finances the bank will provide, even if the sovkhoz in question is known to be a loser and unlikely to pay it back. The bank does not care because it is not lending its own money – the bank has no such money – but funds provided by the state. The bank, in other words, is merely a transitional stage in this transaction.

All this leads to the complete divorce of production from society's needs. Let us look at a classic example – the production of tractors. The USSR produces 4.8 times as many tractors as the USA, although it lags behind in the quantity of cereals produced. If we bring this fact into the equation, it then works out that in the USSR we produce six times as many tractors as they do in the United States. Do we really need that many tractors? Were we to ask such a question under the old administrative system we would get an unequivocal answer: not only do we need all of them, we need still more. The fact is that in the USSR we produce neither powerful cultivator tractors nor sufficient small tractors of the type that could be used in smallholdings and allotments. The conclusion followed: build another multi-billion rouble tractor factory, and this was very nearly done in Yelabuga, not far from KAMAZ. Only combined protests by various scientists and social organizations prevented it, and instead a new factory is being built to produce 900,000 passenger cars for our people. At the same time we have begun the restructuring and expansion of already existing tractor factories. Had the administrative system continued we might quite possibly have reached a situation where we produced ten times as many tractors as the United States, tractors not needed by our agriculture. Now if they were bought with one's own money, if they were used rationally, economically, we should need two or three times fewer of them. Characteristically, two or three times fewer attachments are made for each tractor in the Soviet Union than in the United States. In other words, right from the very start our tractors are not intended for full use.

This kind of mass-production of tractors naturally affects their quality. So instead of lasting twelve or fifteen years a number of Soviet makes of tractor barely manage to last six, and for a considerable proportion of that time they are broken down or under repair.

Perestroika means the transition to a new economic system. Under perestroika the collective and state farms are to be self-financing. Furthermore banking credit policies have changed. No one now gives credit for the purchase of new technology without some sort of guarantee that the money will be returned. These two changes have had an immediate effect: there has been a considerable reduction in the number of requests for new tractors, combine harvesters and other pieces of agricultural technology, the production of which had in any case been divorced from the needs of society. But this is only the start. Agricultural enterprises that have adopted self-financing on an experimental basis have, on average, halved their purchases of agricultural machinery.

Another reason for this reduction in demand is the move by certain agricultural enterprises towards leasing. What happens here is that a brigade, a unit or a family negotiate with the collective or state farm to lease some land together with the necessary machinery. The lessees then sort out all their own finances from the profit they make on the produce from the leased land and machinery. Any residue becomes the farmer's personal income. In state and collective farms that have broken themselves into leaseholding collectives about 50–60 per cent of the existing machinery is not asked for. It is simply unnecessary, surplus stock.

We have noted one bad result of the segregation of producer and consumer in our country. There is a lot of surplus, and much is of too low a quality, too far removed from what is needed by the consumer. But there is another harmful consequence. A good deal of what is needed by the consumer is simply not being produced in the country. The production of more and more low-powered and low-quality bulldozers in Chelyabinsk suited the Ministry of Agricultural Machinery, and so the factory went on producing them. But in the building and mining industries, massively powerful bulldozers like Caterpillar or Komatsu are needed for jobs such as pipelaying and so on. Our country has not produced bulldozers like that for many years, despite the fact that we have the world's most extensive construction programme and largest mining industry. Any suggestion that the product range should be changed was blocked by the Ministry of Agricultural Machinery and the Chelyabinsk factory. For both of them such a change would have been very inconvenient. But they went further than just blocking change. When, under pressure from the various construction and mining ministries, a new factory was opened in Cheboksary to make more powerful bulldozers, designers from Chelyabinsk were asked for help in designing the new machinery. Billions of roubles were allocated for the new venture, but the Chelyabinsk designers, supposedly the most experienced in the field, produced a completely useless design for a completely useless new bulldozer. So every year we have to spend vast sums of money abroad on bulldozers and pipelayers.

The reason I have spent so much time discussing in detail the negative results of the centralized supply system is that I want to emphasize that they are an inevitable part of it, which is why the whole must be destroyed in favour of a market system of distribution. This we are planning to institute, concurrently with the price and banking reforms, in 1990.

It is absolutely vital that these three facets of the reform be interconnected. In order to achieve a balanced market in capital equipment, we have to do away with the channels through which excess money flows and establish a correlation between the circulation of money and of goods. If there is any more money than there are goods on the market, the results will be extremely unfavourable. The market will collapse and there will be shortages. We must remember that in the early stages of the reform many prices will still be centrally fixed. That is why any change to wholesale trade in capital equipment will have to be supported by a complete restructuring of the finance and banking system, since they too are involved in regulating the circulation of money.

On the other hand, a balanced market in capital goods can be established and developed only on the basis of a well-founded

46

pricing system. If, for instance, we maintain our artificially low prices on raw materials and fuel, then we shall find that these vital items will be in short supply and there will be no incentive to economize on them. Furthermore the market will maintain itself only if an ever-increasing proportion of products are bought and sold for free and contractual prices set by the market itself. So a reform of prices and price formation is an ineluctable part of the transition to widespread wholesale trading.

This is not the first time that the question of introducing wholesale trade in capital equipment has been raised in the USSR. It came up in the mid-sixties following the September Plenum of the Central Committee of the CPSU in 1965. Kosygin reported on the need to drop the centralized system of supply in favour of wholesale trade. Then, however, it was decided to move to wholesale trading gradually, as production developed and shortages disappeared. This approach was based on the view that shortages come about because various branches of industry are insufficiently developed. No one even suggested that shortages might be the inescapable result of an economic mechanism characterized by an administrative system of management and a centralized supply system. Under such a system shortages have nothing to do with the quantities produced. We have seen in the case of tractors that there can be and often are shortages even when production is actually in excess of need.

Experience proved very soon that the notion of developing wholesale trade only after production had increased was erroneous. During the 8th Five-year Plan (1966–70), which followed the proclamation of an economic reform, the tempo of economic development increased by half as much again. In terms of quantity, production grew faster than ever before. But still there were shortages, because there was no wholesale trade.

Some experiments conducted at that time demonstrated beyond any reasonable doubt that shortages were not caused by the volume of production but by the economic mechanism itself, the centralized system of resource distribution. One such experiment concerned the distribution of lubrication oils. These were always in short supply and distribution was severely centralized and subject to the strictest administrative control. Then four regions went over to wholesale trading in these oils. At first many of the consumers there tried to buy as much as possible – they did not believe that this kind of free trade would last. When they saw that

47

it would continue, they tried to get rid of the surplus lubricants they had acquired. Demand became lower than it had been under the centralized distribution system. Then demand became considerably lower. The results would have been even more spectacular if this particular experiment in wholesale trade had been accompanied by a well-founded increase in prices that would have taken the prices nearer to world prices and by a system of self-financing under which enterprises made purchases with their own money. Now we are approaching the problem of developing wholesale trade in capital equipment with the knowledge that we must go over to a system of complete self-financing and cost accounting and that we must reform wholesale prices.

I believe that in the vast majority of cases the shortages we experience are related to our underdeveloped economic mechanisms. We will only eliminate shortages when we go over to new economic conditions that include new prices, a new finance and credit system, all based on wholesale trade instead of administrative distribution. But it is true that to some extent the shortage of goods is connected with inadequate production, with the fact that it is divorced from the demands of the consumer. It will take some time for those particular branches of industry to develop, and we need to create the most economic conditions that will nurture them. We could offer particularly generous credit terms to those enterprises or perhaps invest in them from central funds or otherwise provide incentives to ensure that they improve faster. And while some items remain in short supply we shall have to retain a limited centralized distribution system. This would effect 10 or at most 20 per cent of total capital equipment turnover.

The 19th Party Conference emphasized the need to speed up the transition to wholesale trade in capital goods and the particular importance of this process to any radical management reform. We had previously assumed that by 1989 30 per cent of the trade in capital equipment would be done through wholesale trade, while 70 per cent would still be distributed in the old centralized, administrative fashion. By 1990 wholesale trade was to account for 60 per cent of turnover, while by 1992 this should be reaching 90 per cent. However, the Party Conference changed all that, and we have now been enjoined to be quite revolutionary, so that, by the end of this Five-year Plan, 80–90 per cent of capital equipment should be traded on the wholesale market. We can achieve this by restructuring prices and reforming the banking system.

At this point we should ask ourselves what we mean by whole-sale trade. This is not as easy a question as one might think. Some people believe that wholesale trade is simply a version of the old administrative distribution system. It is easy to see why. The Gossnab (State Supply Agency) apparatus is used to distributing and apportioning and wants to keep going in the same old way within the new economic forms that have developed under peres-troika. This also happened in 1988 with state purchase orders and economic rules and regulations, as I have already described.

In my opinion wholesale trade means just that – trade. And trade is the free, multifarious commercial intercourse of equal economic partners. Wholesale trade can take place only by means of direct contacts between the producer enterprise and the con-sumer enterprise, or through a middleman such as some sort of wholesale trading office or a distribution co-operative. We need to enlarge and democratize the whole process by which products are sold. If an enterprise so desires, it will handle its own sales, setting up its own sales department. But in many cases it will be more profitable to use an intermediary to buy its goods and then act as distributor. Suppose the goods are actually consumer goods. The producer will deal with a wholesale organization or directly with shops and department stores, with the whole retail network. These direct contacts between producers and retailers are growing all the time. Alternatively, an enterprise could use its own money to create its own network of shops and transform itself from an industrial enterprise into an industrial-trading enterprise. In our opinion no obstacles should be put in the way of this. Experiences in Estonia or with Russian industrial trade enterprises such as Kuban or Novomoskovskaya have shown that such enterprises can be very successful.

Developing the socialist market in the USSR – the next step

Today in the USSR we have in effect only one market, that of consumer goods and paid services, and even this is distorted and unbalanced. During perestroika it will be supplemented and overtaken by the market in capital goods. But matters will not stop there. A year or so ago we might have contented ourselves with developing only these two markets, but now we can see that this is not enough. We have witnessed a spontaneous surge of creativity from below. At the urging of their workers, several enterprises have taken the initiative and have begun issuing shares and bonds. This will lead inexorably to the formation of a new market – a market in commercial paper.

The first share issues were made by enterprises in Lvov. Recently I visited some of these enterprises to study this development. First I looked at the Konveyer conglomerate, which mainly produces overhead conveyors for the engineering industry. This enterprise issued shares which were distributed among its workers with assistance from the Lvov branch of the State Savings Bank, which opened a special office at the factory. Shares could be bought and sold there. Another of the region's enterprises, an agricultural machinery producer, also issued shares to its own workers in the same way. However, a third enterprise, Provisyen, chose a different route: it made various other enterprises and economic organizations in and around Lvov its shareholders. In return for their investment, Provisyen, a specialist producer of hothouse vegetables, supplies its shareholders with vegetables for their canteens and shops, and further investment income is to be used for enlarging its area under glass. In addition to this payment in kind, shareholders will be entitled to a dividend on their shares. Provisyen is now considering a second issue of shares to be sold to its own workers and those of the enterprises that have already invested in it. In all these cases the actual purchase of shares by workers is limited, in some cases quite severely. Nobody is allowed to invest more than three months' earnings. In other cases there is an absolute limit on the sum that may be invested, say 5 or 10 thousand roubles. The dividends are also paid out in different ways. In some enterprises these are limited to 5–7 per cent a year. (In parenthesis let us note that the State Savings Bank pays out 2–3 per cent, depending on the kind of account held.) The dividends can be much higher in those places where investments can amount to no more than two or three months' salary.

One feature of these first attempts at issuing shares is that dividends do not depend on the profit made by the enterprise; they are more likely to be a fixed amount, thus making the shares more like bonds. The shareholders are a section of the workforce. They meet periodically to hear the managers' reports on the way

50

the shares have been distributed and how investment income has been used. The shareholders discuss possible further sources of profit, how to make the enterprise more efficient, and how the capital invested by shareholders should be used. In other words it is assumed that shareholders will take a more active part in their enterprise's life. For the time being, however, there is no market in shares; they can be acquired only in an organized, centralized fashion. Shareholders cannot sell their shares to each other or to outsiders. It is not possible for outsiders to hold shares in an enterprise.

Obviously we are talking only of the early stages of what will lead to a financial market. But it is important to remember that the process has started in the country and that a chain reaction should ensue. Scores of enterprises have decided to issue shares for their workers. Some of these, such as the Sverdlov chemical engineering conglomerate, are quite large. They are proceeding according to the ever more widely applied principle that anything not actually forbidden is permitted. And, of course, we have no laws or regulations forbidding the issue and sale of shares and bonds.

The recently adopted Law on Co-operatives, which is considerably more progressive than the Law on State Enterprises in the allowances it makes, includes a section specifically enabling co-operatives to issue shares. There are no limitations on such issues.

The USSR's financial agencies are examining very carefully these first attempts to issue shares in the Soviet Union. They intend to formulate a basic law to govern these activities. Senior officials at the Ministry of Finance have made it clear in an interview that they are not against enterprises issuing shares, but that they want to have a law to regulate these matters.

I believe that issues of shares and bonds by enterprises and other economic organizations will develop very rapidly. After all, there will be something for everyone in this. The self-financing enterprise will have an additional source of income, under conditions more favourable than a loan from a bank would be. Shareholders, that is workers in the enterprise, will receive a higher interest on their investment than they would if they simply kept the money in the State Savings Bank. Some people have expressed the fear that widespread investment in shares would draw resources away from the State Savings Bank. That is true, but we have to remember that because of the low interest paid by the bank many people keep their savings at home anyway. The first experiments in Lvov show that people are more likely to use money that is kept outside the Savings Bank to buy shares.

Another benefit of the shareholding system is that it will draw the worker-shareholders into the management of their enterprise. Efficiency will naturally increase, since any worker who has invested money is likely to work better to increase production and his dividends. To make the system more effective, the payment of dividends should depend on results rather than being fixed in advance to an amount, say 5 per cent. On the other hand the number of shares any worker can hold should have an upper limit. This limit could be quite high but should not exceed the amount that might reasonably be bought from the holder's earnings.

There remains, however, another and more vexing problem. We have to reach a decision on our approach to the sale of shares to people who have no real connection with the issuing enterprise. Some fear that if we allow free trading in shares, people will acquire enough to become rich simply by owning shares and will live off unearned income. Clearly shares and bonds can bring one quite a considerable additional income. If outsiders buy shares, their income will not be earned, since they will not be involved in the production of the particular enterprise. Therefore, I think the issue of shares will at first have to be limited to the workers of the particular enterprise.

The situation is different with bonds and certificates issued by the state, various ministries and other economic and industrial organizations. These have a specific aim. I have already written about the possible issue of certificates on new passenger cars, which would guarantee that anyone who invested a certain sum would be given priority in the purchase of the car. Similar shares or bonds could be issued by organizations concerned with communications. Families could thus acquire priority rights in getting a telephone. This would be important while there are shortages in this field. Incidentally I have used the example of the communications industry because this has been done in Hungary, to considerable effect. In these instances the purchase of shares cannot be viewed as the acquisition of wealth. The bonds issued would have a specific purpose such as the provision of some material service or the acquisition of some stated thing, like a flat, car or telephone, for which demand exceeds supply.

Obviously our ideas about the way share and bond ownership should develop in the USSR are still at a very early stage. In fact, we are still at what one might call the embryo stage and cannot foresee in detail how the process is likely to develop. But I shall go so far as to predict a market in commercial paper in the Soviet Union, a market that will consist of organizations and individuals. While individual participation in such a market is likely to be limited, ownership of and trade in each other's shares by various enterprises should be quite active. Some enterprises whose production is particularly profitable will own shares in other enterprises. Whether this will lead to a share market on special stock exchanges or not is hard to say. We shall have to watch developments carefully and try to predict the tendencies.

To me, a market in commercial paper means the movement of funds from one branch of the economy to another, from one enterprise to another. Naturally this is not the only way such movement can take place. A market in commercial paper is inconceivable without a credit market, as the two together constitute the financial market.

One other aspect of financial development needs to be examined. Eventually we shall have a currency market on which the exchange rate of various currencies and the rouble will be quoted. We have stated our intention of making the rouble convertible, and this development will therefore be of great importance.

Let us now turn to a problem that will arise as the socialist market develops, that of the labour 'market'. I have put the word market in this sense in quotation marks because the relationship here between hired worker and the hiring institution, whether it is a co-operative or a state enterprise, is radically different from that between a hired worker in bourgeois society (where he does not own the means of production) and his employer, a capitalist or group of capitalists owning those means of production. In our socialist society every worker is co-owner of the national property. When he seeks employment he does so not as a hired hand in the capitalist sense but as the co-manager and co-owner of a given enterprise. This is seen most clearly with co-operatives, where the members are, so to speak, hired by themselves to work for themselves and to be owners of the co-operative simultaneously.

At the same time every worker is free to choose his place of work. It is in this process of choosing a place of work that we can see all the known elements of a market. We have supply in the shape of the workers, who want to take jobs, and demand on the part of the enterprises and organizations, who need workers. Price is obviously the salary and other social benefits that are offered to the workers by the enterprises and organizations. There is also a clear division between the possessor of the working ability and the body that provides him with work. So employment is regulated by a contract, and both sides have certain material obligations based on the agreed rules. We therefore do already have a labour market of sorts, functioning through supply and demand and with freedom of choice, but radically different, nevertheless, from capitalism's labour market.

Under capitalism the labour market is fed from the large army of unemployed. But there is no unemployment under socialism, since the state, as representative of society, is obliged to find work for anyone willing to work. Under the earlier, administrative system of management, there was a shortage of labour, as of everything else. In almost every branch of the economy there were unfilled positions, numbering several million countrywide.

Several bourgeois specialists have argued that we do in fact have unemployment, but this is because they label people who are between jobs as being unemployed. Every worker in the USSR can leave his job at two weeks' notice. He then has the unrestricted right to compete for other jobs. Inevitably a certain amount of time passes between his leaving one job and beginning in another. Sometimes this time is longer than is absolutely necessary: one worker may want a holiday, and another may find that taking up the new position involves the additional difficulty of moving with his family to another town. Such breaks in one's working life are therefore to be viewed as voluntary. They are created by the workers themselves, who cannot, therefore, be called unemployed. On average 10–15 per cent of the workforce is between jobs. In 1987 the number of working people in the USSR was 131 million. So in other words 15–20 million people change jobs every year, and the average interval between them was three or four weeks.

Both absolute and relative figures show the high level of employment in the Soviet Union. With a population in 1987 of around 283 million, the total number of employed people – blue- and white-collar workers, collective farmers and self-employed – stood at a little over 131 million, so we can see that more than 46 per cent of the population was in employment. But if we look at the able-bodied section of the population, then 92 per cent of it is in

54

full-time employment or studying. The remaining 8 per cent is composed mainly of women who are housewives because they have very young children or because their families are particularly large. Of the capitalist countries, only one comes anywhere near the Soviet Union in this matter: Sweden, where the unemployment level is only 1.7 per cent. In other capitalist countries the proportion of those in employment to the whole of the population varies between 30 and 40 per cent. According to the official figures, unemployment in Japan is 3 per cent, in the United States over 6 per cent, in West Germany 9 per cent, in France and Great Britain over 11 per cent, in Italy and the Netherlands 12 per cent, and in Spain 22 per cent.

Behind the average figures for a country as large and as diverse in economic activity and nationality as the Soviet Union, we inevitably find enormous regional differences. The Baltic region, Byelorussia and most areas of the Russian Federation have a shortage of labour, with innumerable unfilled jobs in many branches of the economy: meanwhile, in Azerbaijan and Central Asia there is a surplus of labour, and new jobs have to be created for those who are coming up to working age. Therefore, there are differences in employment policies across the country. In areas where there is a surplus of labour we encourage the cultivation of seed crops by means of irrigation and the development of labour-intensive agriculture such as the growing of fruit, vegetables, cotton and so on. Industries from outside the region are encouraged to set up subsidiaries there, and, after training courses, these enterprises employ mainly locals.

Let us now sum up what is meant by the extension and intensification of the socialist market. We can safely say that the market will encompass the key sections of the economy and will play a very important, indeed crucial, role in the further development of our country's economy. It will be in the market place that the goods and services produced by enterprises to satisfy money-backed demand will acquire their social value. It will be the market that balances production and demand in the country. And it will be through the market that production will start to depend more on consumer demand and will begin to satisfy social needs.

Naturally, as I have written elsewhere, the socialist market will be limited and regulated. The limitations we shall place on the market will relate to the fact that, unlike in the West, not everything can be bought and sold in our country. Land, mineral

55

wealth, certain cultural treasures of national value are not for the market place; they cannot be bought or sold, although the presence of a market and the realities of the relationship between goods and money in the country will have a certain effect on them. All property in a country acquires a certain monetary value that needs to be taken into account in economic calculations or when land or other natural resources are used for special purposes. Thus land and other natural resources do have a certain value which, although not a market price, is nevertheless the value used, say, to calculate lease charges for land or other material goods.

Our market will be a regulated market influenced by the state. The state can also influence purchasing power through a system of economic rules and regulations, or by encouraging or discouraging production in a particular field, or by taxation. It is one of the state's duties to control the money supply. As Gosbank, the State Bank of the USSR, is in charge of the credit policy of the country, the market will also be regulated by state purchase orders, which ought to account for 20–30 per cent of the total volume of production. State methods of price formation are another powerful means of influencing the market. This will include centralized price setting for the most important goods, though I do not think this will apply to more than about a third of what we produce. All other prices will be set freely or by contract. The state will also regulate prices by establishing the working rules for free and contractual pricing. We shall want to avoid deliberate and unnecessary price rises leading to extortionist profits. After we introduce state duty tariffs and liberalize imports, world market pressures on internal prices will inevitably ensue.

In connection with these restrictive and regulatory aspects of the socialist market, we need to look yet again at the problem of possible inflation in the USSR when the price reform is carried out and the market is extended and intensified, that is to say when the economic system of management begins. It is quite clear that there will be inflationary pressures because enterprises will consider profit and costs to be of paramount importance, and both of these depend directly on prices. A price increase of 1 per cent at the point of sale will increase industry's income by 3 per cent, as its share in the price is about 35 per cent. At the same time profits will go up by at least 6 per cent, as they make up about 15 per cent of the price. Therefore, unless we take anti-inflationary measures there is bound to be a great deal of pressure on prices from enterprises, co-operatives and individual producers.

Inflation is likely to grow because of the financial imbalance we have inherited. Our economy is unbalanced, money is in excess supply, and its circulation is completely divorced from the circulation of goods. The forthcoming major industrial changes in the economy are intended to speed up technical developments and reorientate the whole economic system towards more social goals, while improvements in efficiency and quality will also have a serious effect on the relationship between money and goods.

And, of course, the freedom we intend to give enterprises under the new economic system of management in their choice of how much and what to produce, together with the freedom to set or negotiate prices, will aid the inflationary process.

It should be noted, however, that there already is inflation under the administrative system of management, and even centralized price fixing does not prevent it. Inflation occurs as the cheaper goods in a particular range disappear and are replaced by more expensive ones. In other words, the average price of a particular product rises and there is a shift in the range of goods available. At the same time the concrete, centrally established price of any given product remains, as a rule, unchanged. This kind of inflation is caused by a deformed market, by shortages, and by a lack of financial balance. As far as consumer goods are concerned, inflation would appear to be in the region of 3 per cent per annum.

Some capital goods are subject to even higher inflation. For instance, when ordinary machine tools are scrapped in favour of new computerized ones, efficiency and productivity increases roughly double. They frequently cost, however, five to eight times as much. Therefore the average price of a single item of consumer technology rises on average by 4 per cent a year because of the increased price of the new machinery and equipment needed to make it. Price rises in building projects have been even greater, since each one is individually costed. The annual growth in construction costs (on a per-unit basis) has been 5–7 per cent.

There was another reason why producers found it useful to exaggerate prices, thus increasing inflation under the administrative system of management. Under Gosplan special emphasis was laid on the volume of wholesale production. Using hidden price increases, it was easier to fulfil and overfulfil the plan. So, for example, a timely price increase would boost the apparent volume of work in the building industry and thus enable workers and managers to be given bonuses or other incentives. And while the producer ruled, there was nothing to prevent him from increasing prices endlessly. Only a central administrative ruling could stop that. The consumer was powerless. Moreover, since the consumer enterprise was in any case reimbursed, it was not going to worry about the price of the product.

Under an economic system of management, the situation is going to be completely different. On the one hand, as we have already noted, inflationary tendencies may increase, but on the other certain factors will appear to counteract this. The importance of the consumer as customer will increase, and the customer is likely to protest against increased prices. The existence of a market will mean that there is competition and that the customer will have a choice of products. As I have already said, we intend to bring in quite severe measures to achieve a balance on the market. Purchasing power will be economically but severely regulated, and a balance will be achieved between supply and demand. This will make it more difficult in conditions of cost accounting and self-financing for enterprises to pay higher prices, and this tendency will be reinforced by equally severe economic controls on the credit system.

Naturally this will not on its own stop inflation. We shall have to elaborate measures to dissuade enterprises from increasing their profits by jacking up prices. In particular, we may introduce a progressive tax on profits to redirect some of the money into the ministry's centralized funds. We may introduce a progressive tax on that part of the profit that is to be directed into the wages fund, in order to deter workers from demanding unnecessary price rises. At the same time we could abolish tax on profits allocated to the reconstruction and extension of production; or we could make that tax a unitary one, and a modest one at that. Then more popular goods will actually be offered on the market. When that happens, pressure on the whole price structure will result, and prices will not be able to go up unnecessarily.

To develop and understand fully how to operate anti-inflationary mechanisms in the socialist market will be quite a test. Various socialist countries have failed in this for a number of reasons. Poland, Hungary and recently China experienced quite serious inflation connected with their transition to an economic method of management. It is true that while Hungary was developing normally without a large foreign debt, inflation, even though the economic system was well developed, was quite moderate, 4–6 per cent per annum, and was under state control. Incomes grew faster than prices, and the standard of living rose steadily. At the same time the market was well balanced, and consumer goods were in plentiful supply. In other countries, such as East Germany and Czechoslovakia, anti-inflationary policies were put into effect through severe state control of prices and there was a very high level of economic discipline. Yugoslavia is the one socialist country that has an open market with capitalist countries, and recent economic development there has been notable for ever worse inflation. In the past it was kept at a relatively acceptable level, while income grew and welfare in the country increased. But in more recent years, as the economy became less stable as a result of a large foreign debt, inflation has escaped government control. In 1987, for instance, prices doubled in just one year. At the moment the Yugoslav government is trying to work out a new stabilizing programme, whose primary aim is to control inflation and bring it back to some kind of manageable rate.

In China the rate of inflation on consumer goods was 20 per cent in 1988. In my opinion this high level is the result of an 'overheating' in the economy caused by the sudden large expansion of major construction work and large-scale capital investment. This boom in investment has taken place in a very free way, with decisions frequently made at the provincial level without reference to the centre. Many of the Chinese comrades feel that too much initiative has devolved to the regions. For instance, China's banks have no independence at all and are totally controlled by the regional governments. A number of regional organizations have the right to decide how part of an enterprise's profits may be used, or, in other words, they have the right to appropriate them. Under this kind of management, many provinces fund their investments very largely by such unbudgeted means. And with the banks ever ready to extend credit, purchasing power is growing faster than production. The Chinese government is now trying to introduce an anti-inflationary programme, the main drive of which will be for a considerable reduction in the volume of capital investment and a lowering of expenditure by enterprises and organizations on consumer goods, since such spending can accelerate out of proportion.

I was in China in December 1988 and studied these processes. My meetings with Chinese leaders, economists and scientists provided a number of useful lessons based on their experience for the furthering of our own reform. In particular I discussed the following topics: the efficiency of long-term land leases as part of an agrarian reform, the need to maintain a balance between town and village, the need to balance rights and duties between local and central authorities, because of the danger of giving too much to one or the other, the need to liberate pricing and to make price formation dependent on the market, the need to make banks independent (particularly from local authorities), the efficient working of special open zones and much more.

It can be seen from the above that in our efforts to find ways to develop the market we have looked at all the positive and negative aspects of market development in the socialist countries which began the process before us.

We also looked at developments in capitalist countries, seeking to use their experiences (or some of them) here. Two, in some ways contradictory, aspects of the workings of capitalism gain one's attention straight away. The first is the concept developed by the Chicago school of economists and a number of other scientists, chief among them being the Nobel Prizewinner Milton Friedman. This concept of the free market denies that there is any need for the state to interfere in market and pre-monetary relations. Furthermore, they claim that any such interference is completely ineffective. When visiting San Francisco, I had the good fortune of being the guest of Milton and Rose Friedman. Like every economist I had read Milton's works on the theory of prices, on humanitarian problems in the United States, his book on inflation and, naturally, the two studies he wrote together with his wife: *Capitalism and Freedom* and *Freedom of Choice*, which Milton presented me with. But the printed word is no substitute for personal discussion with a great thinker, which is what I consider Milton Friedman to be. I was astonished by his fantastic faith in private property, a faith that excluded the possibility of any other kind of property ownership such as that which exists in the socialist countries. In Friedman's opinion, well-being can be reached only through private ownership of property, a free market and the existence of banks completely independent from the state and serving that free market. To support his point of view he cites examples of unwise interference by the state in market and financial dealings. In his opinion the world stock exchange crash of October 1987 was caused by incorrect state policies. The great depression of 1929–33 was also, in his opinion, the fault of the state. And so on.

But if we move away from conceptual problems to the concrete theories advanced by Milton Friedman in his studies, we find that many of them can be of great use to us. In a number of cases Friedman points to examples of financial misjudgement by the state in increasing expenditure, printing excess money and so on. And while I do not accept his view that the socialist countries should transfer property into private ownership, I nevertheless listened with great interest to his explanations of the present inflation in China, which he had recently visited, and in other socialist countries. Unfortunately, Friedman's works have not been translated into Russian and are unknown to the economic community of our country. I think something should be done about this; we should publish the works of western economists.

Friedman's theories in some ways contradict the Keynesian approach, which is actually better known in our country, since the major works of Maynard Keynes himself and his ideas as interpreted in the works of his followers have been translated into Russian. The best-known of all these is Paul Samuelson's textbook. Apart from its marvellous form and astonishing use of language, this substantial book is useful in that it gives a systematic exposition of the views of many western authors on the structural development of economics. The book does not quite form an integral whole, as the author's opinions are clearly eclectic, one point of view borrowed from one economist, and another from another. Nevertheless the book does in some senses give a global impression. Undoubtedly this is a very fine example of what an economics textbook should be like; unfortunately there is nothing like it in our country. It is my ambition to free myself from administrative duties for a few years and to write something similar, but covering a whole economics course.

Economic studies here seem backward when compared to other disciplines, particularly the sciences. Splendid mathematics textbooks have been written in our country. These are well-known in the West. One example is *Differential and Integral Calculus* by Fikhtengoltz. There is also Academician Smirnov's textbook on higher mathematics, and an even better-known six-volume physics textbook by Landau and Livshitz. But there is nothing even remotely like these in economics. Our economics textbooks were mostly written by committees. Thus a group of people who do not necessarily see eye to eye 'cook up' a book, with one person writing one chapter, another writing another. Such an approach is sometimes inevitable, but it is not likely to produce good textbooks.

We are particularly interested in the work of those western economists who show up the limitations of the free market, its darker side, so to speak. The best-known to Soviet readers is the American scientist and writer J. K. Galbraith, who at a recent general meeting of the Academy of Sciences was, together with the American economist Vassily Leontyev, elected a foreign associate member of the Academy. The two were proposed by me as the Head of the Economics Section of the Academy of Sciences and seconded by Ye. Primakov as the Head of the International Affairs and International Economics Section. Many economists were particularly impressed by the translation of one of Galbraith's best books, *The New Industrial Society*, which contained a very sharp critique of the limitations of the market. Recently Galbraith has spoken and written much about the convergence between capitalist and socialist economies, underlining their similarities. When Mikhail Gorbachev was in Washington in December 1987 he met a number of leading American intellectuals, including Galbraith and Leontyev. Galbraith asked Gorbachev directly: 'Why are you afraid of the word convergence?' To this Gorbachev replied: 'I am not afraid of that word.' As everyone knows, in our new political strategy, perestroika, we have allowed for common human characteristics to reign above narrow class and group interests. We have accepted that many economic processes are common to both socialist and capitalist countries. This has shown us that we need to study the experience of all the advanced countries, and we are doing so very diligently.

Let me give a small example. In the 13th Five-year Plan, we are considering changing our tax system. First of all we want to introduce new taxes on the profits and income of state enterprises and co-operatives, after which we want to design a system of taxes for the whole population. This is something in which we have no experience, so the government commission for the development and planning of the economic mechanism decided to form several groups of specialists and send them to various countries to study taxation systems there. Some of these groups recently returned home. I was particularly interested in Canada's and Sweden's tax systems and talked to people who had been to those countries to find out which aspects of what they had seen could, in their opinion, be applied to our country. There are many ways for the state to regulate the economy, one of the prime ones being taxation, which, in some capitalist countries, generates a considerable part of the national budget. Others are state purchase orders, the regulating function of the central bank, and state regulation of the market in stocks and shares and of currency exchange. In a number of cases state regulation in these areas has been very successful, particularly when a country needed to be extricated from a difficult economic situation.

We need only remember the example of the 'economic experiment' in West Germany after the war under the guidance of that exceptional economist and politician Erhardt. Recently when Chancellor Kohl and Vice-Chancellor Genscher were in the Soviet Union, I had breakfast with them. Naturally enough we talked most about the economic reforms in the USSR, the problems we were encountering, possible extensions of our economic links with the Federal Republic, and about the further development of our scientific and technical co-operation. As we were talking I suddenly remembered and mentioned Erhardt, whom I greatly respect, and the post-war economic reform in Germany, which is, I think, a classic example of a highly regulated economy. I was astonished when Kohl showed great interest and talked a lot about Erhardt, quoting him extensively. On leaving, he presented me with a newly published copy of Erhardt's selected works, which he autographed.

The state's regulating role in the post-war economic development of Japan was equally important and effective. When I visited Japan in 1987 at the invitation of the Foreign Minister, I was given the opportunity to study the work of the Ministry of Industry and Foreign Trade, which played a key role in the development of Japan's export productivity and speeding up scientific and technological developments.

There is a term which has been widely used and widely practised in several capitalist countries in recent years. This is *privatization*, which is of great importance in any discussion of the free market and state intervention in the capitalist economy.

The widest possibilities implied by the term privatization are discussed in a book by the American economist Professor Savas.

I was fortunate enough to have a discussion with Professor Savas and Umberto Agnelli, one of the leaders of FIAT, at a specialized seminar organized by the International Labour Organization, which was represented at the seminar by its General Secretary.

First of all I should point out that the process of privatization does not mean handing state property over to private ownership, as some people think. It is really a search for new, decentralized forms for the management of state property in capitalist countries. Therefore the significance of this phenomenon, as Professor Savas and I agreed, becomes ever greater, and the term privatization is actually inadequate to describe this complicated process. It might in fact be more accurate to call the process *socialization*. This is what it occurred to me to call it, since the process is one of advancing property to people, of liquidating the alienation of people from their property.

State ownership is now well accepted in capitalist countries. I have in front of me a table that gives data for eighteen different advanced capitalist countries, showing the proportion of private property in each. In most cases, the post, telecommunications, electricity, gas and railways are more than two-thirds state-owned. For instance, in thirteen of the eighteen countries, that is the case for electricity supply, while in one country the state controls 50 per cent of the industry and in the remaining ones 25 per cent. The main airline is state-owned in ten out of the eighteen countries, while in two of them the state owns a 50-per-cent share. The oil and shipbuilding industries are state-owned in four and five of the eighteen countries respectively.

The most consistent privatization policy has been followed in Britain under Margaret Thatcher. But even there, in the ten years of her premiership only about a third of state-owned companies have been privatized. But it would not be right to attribute Britain's recent, mostly successful economic development solely to the one factor of privatization. The Conservative government has received a certain amount of benefit from North Sea oil, but the most important stimulus for the economic revival was the removal of various government limits on banking activity. This allowed Britain to recover its position as one of the world centres for banking and stock exchange activity. Lowering taxes provided a further stimulus which led to new technical developments: British goods were once again in demand. This in turn created new jobs, especially in the south of the country, and unemployment was

64

reduced. As the market was saturated with goods and the financial position became more balanced, inflation went down. But the most important factor is that for the last ten years economic development in Britain has been even and dynamic, without recessions or crises. At the same time we have to note that the unemployment level is very high – 9 out of every 100 able-bodied individuals are unemployed. There has been a considerable increase in income differentials, with the northern areas lagging particularly. I have been able to see this for myself during my visits.

Britain's economic growth has been to a great extent connected with the extension of the service sector and of banking. Following the sharp rise in capital in circulation, the speed with which financial operations grew was far greater than that of production. This process helped to stimulate the growth of finance capital, and the break between pure financial transactions and the circulation of goods and money caused the crash of 1987 on the London Stock Exchange.

If I were asked my opinion of the new policies of the Conservative government, often labelled Thatcherism, I would generally have to give them quite high marks. During my first visit to Great Britain, in November 1987, I had a conversation lasting an hour and a half with Margaret Thatcher. She is undoubtedly a strong leader who makes an unforgettable impression. Mrs Thatcher questioned me about the economic reforms in the USSR, proceeding in fact at quite a pace, putting one question after another. Each required a definite and precise answer. When I subsequently analysed the system behind the questions I realized that Mrs Thatcher had thought them through very carefully and arranged them in such a way as to extract maximum information in a fairly rapid, dynamic conversation. Although our conversation appeared easy, I was kept on my toes, because the way the questions were asked meant that I had to answer them rapidly, briefly and fully at the same time. I have met a number of political leaders in my time, but I do not recall holding a conversation about economics with them that was quite so difficult for me. Only one other conversation – with Raymond Barre, one of the three presidential candidates in France – was remotely similar, but Barre is a leading economist and his questions were hard to answer because they were professional ones. During my conversation with Mrs Thatcher, it seemed to me that she discussed quite openly the difficulties of the reconstruction, the perestroika, so to speak, of Britain's economy. She emphasized that difficulties and disappointments are inevitable and that success comes only after determined and consistent hard work. She also talked about the advisability of having a small, well-qualified, hard-working inner cabinet which implemented measures and checked they were done.

Talking about economic reform, Mrs Thatcher emphasized the importance of raising the qualifications of managers, and offered her country's services in organizing training for our managers with some of Britain's leading companies. She particularly recommended that I should visit and study Marks & Spencer. As it happened, I had already planned to pay them a visit and I learnt a great deal from my discussions with that company.

Incidentally it was while I was there that Mrs Thatcher turned to Ambassador Zamyatin with a request, which she repeated to me, to invite Mikhail Gorbachev to visit Great Britain on his way to the United States to see President Reagan. As we know, Gorbachev accepted the invitation, landed in Britain on his way to the United States and had a meeting with Mrs Thatcher at the airport.

How can we make people care about their work? Will we have to supply extra stimuli through moderate unemployment?

This is perhaps the central problem of the new economic system: how to make people care about the results of their work, how to inculcate, as part of the economic reform, feelings of personal responsibility. Since human beings are the most important of all the productive forces, much depends on their attitude to work. This influences productivity, the efficient use of resources, and the quality of the final product. And the role of each individual in the development of a country's productivity grows greater and greater as science and technology develop. This is, first, because people affect scientific and technological progress in vital ways. Higher technologies provide the clearest examples: information technology, for instance. Fifteen or twenty years ago, up to 80 per cent of all expenditure in the computer industry went on the hardware. Today 80 per cent of our spending is on the writing of new programs, on software, since it is on the quality of that that the whole progress of information technology depends.

On the other hand, manual work nowadays involves very high levels of technology. One worker can operate machinery that produces the equivalent of 50, 100 or more horsepower. In other words this work is amplified a hundredfold, and results depend to a great extent on a single worker's activity, on the quality of his work.

One other matter needs to be taken into account. Recent developments in technology and the organization of production have made labour more and more of a collective affair. This means that the work of one individual affects the work of a whole group of people involved in the productive process.

Let us compare, for example, the work of a navvy in the past and the operator of a powerful excavator. The navvy worked on his own. At most his labour affected the transportation of earth on a wheelbarrow, if there was one. The powerful excavator is served by a fleet of trucks that take the earth away, by a bulldozer that smooths the earth in its wake and so on.

Obviously an interruption of the navvy's work is not going to have an enormous effect on the final result, because there are dozens or even hundreds of other navvies working with him. But what happens if there is an interruption in the work of the powerful excavator? Immediately the work of the dump trucks is in disarray. Furthermore, if work on the foundation is not completed in time, the whole job may be disrupted.

These considerations are all common to the related problems of motivation, care about one's work, incentives and individual responsibility, which have become central to theoretical economics and practical economy.

This problem has become particularly acute in our own country. The reason is that the distortions introduced by the previous period and the nature of the administrative system of management reduced individuals to the status of cogs in the huge state machinery. This made us unable to make good use of human potential. According to theory, our socialist system, in which there is no exploitation, no discrimination and no unemployment, should inspire each worker to work better and produce more than a worker under capitalism. In practice, even when we possess the same technology and the same technical knowledge, we require more workers to complete the same amount of work. In addition our products are of lower quality. What happens when we acquire a factory from a western firm? We inevitably employ 300 or even 400 people when in the West they need only 200. According to western calculations the factory is ready to start operating from day one, but we invent assimilation periods that can be as long as a year or even two before the factory is ready to function. All this assimilation is largely connected with the quality of our workforce.

Sometimes, though not very often, the process is reversed. We might, for instance, build an enriching factory using our technology abroad, in Finland, for example. According to our norms, an assimilation period of two years is needed and the factory cannot function with fewer than 400 people. The Finns put in 280 people and the factory works at full blast from the very first year.

The reason for all this is that we have not found the mechanism to ensure that people would be highly motivated in socialist conditions. We have not even been able to motivate people to acquire further skills or further education. We do not even need to look to the West to understand how great the possibilities are. When we manage to interest people in their work, productivity invariably goes up many times over.

I shall cite only two examples. In the Novosibirsk region the output of one agricultural worker is worth 10 or 12 thousand roubles a year. This figure is a steady one and quite usual. Three years ago, a group of specialists and particularly good workers proposed that we should set up collectives to engage in high-intensity work. As a rule these were small collectives which were given large tracts of arable land or farms for animal husbandry. They leased the machinery and paid with their own money for all materials and services. The collectives were paid in accordance with the quantity and quality of the final produce.

Dozens, even hundreds, of such small collectives were formed. Their members had all previously been members of collective farms with the standard technology. The difference lay in the organization of labour and its rewards. Members of these collectives felt they were the masters. Their reward depended on their work. And what happened was a miracle: on average these collectives achieved a productivity many times greater than before.

68

Each worker now produced the equivalent of 100 thousand or even more roubles.

Let me quote another example, concerning the gold panning practised in many parts of the USSR, particularly Siberia and the Far East. I spent almost a quarter of a century working in Siberia, where I used to visit gold mines, and became interested in the problem. I became particularly well acquainted with the work of one team in Northern Yakutia. This team consisted of 280 people, and every year they panned about a ton and a half of gold. Next to where this brigade worked, there was a state-controlled gold mine. Its work was exactly the same. In fact, the area it was working was richer. It too produced a ton and a half of gold a year. But it employed 1,200 people.

So what was the problem? Quite simply, the members of the prospecting team were paid in direct proportion to the amount of gold they produced, so each extra person meant loss of money for the others. Therefore on that mine there was no director, no deputy, no special technician. All that was done by one of the bulldozer operators, who was the team leader. Nor did they need people to overhaul the bulldozers or operate the pumps, because the other workers, bulldozer operators and pump operators, could cope with that kind of work too.

In the state mine, on the other hand, each worker was paid according to his grade and not according to the amount produced. A bulldozer operator was paid for the amount of sand he dug up, the overhauler for the amount of overhauling he did, and so on. That was why that mine needed three or four times as many people.

As may be seen from the examples above, our backwardness in productivity, in efficiency, in quality of output, as compared to the developed capitalist countries is caused to a great extent by faults in the organization and payment of labour. In other words we do not have an effective system of individual incentive and responsibility.

This is not the only reason for our backwardness; in many industries we have fallen behind in our levels of technology. However, I deliberately stress the human factor, the role of labour organization, because we must not blame lack of technology for everything. Times have changed and we now live in a different world in which the human element in economic development has become all-important.

In our attempts to radically reform the economy and restructure our administration we have accepted that these problems are of primary importance. We are faced with the immense problem of how to involve people more in the productive process, how to make them feel that they are in charge of that process, how to create effective incentives.

We have kept this in mind in our careful study of the situation in the capitalist countries. Superficially it might seem that the greatest incentive to good work there is high unemployment. Nobody wants to be unemployed, so everybody works like a horse hoping that the high quality of his work will keep him his job. Certain economists in the Soviet Union and in other countries have expressed the idea that it might be useful to have 'controlled' unemployment in the socialist countries as a kind of stimulus for better work. Even so well-known an economist and writer as Nikolai Shmelyov, whose two very sharp articles in *Novy Mir*, 'Loans and Debts' and 'Our Worries', are widely quoted, has succumbed to this temptation. He supported this point of view in the first of these articles.

Personally I doubt whether unemployment could provide such an incentive. Such information as I have does not appear to prove that unemployment's effect on work quality is particularly positive. In Yugoslavia, for instance, unemployment is quite high, especially among young people. But this has not had an appreciable effect on the quality of production. On the other hand, in Sweden there is virtually no unemployment. The proportion of unemployed in the able-bodied population is 1.6 per cent, and even this is due mostly to unemployment in the northern regions of the country. In the south and the central regions, where most of Sweden's industry is situated, there is no unemployment to speak of. Yet productivity in that country is one and a half times higher than in Britain, where unemployment stands at 11 per cent.

That is not the only reason why I do not agree with the idea of having 'controlled' unemployment in the USSR. These are not even the most important of my considerations. In the USSR we consider unemployment a social evil, a cause of unhappiness. As a country where power is in the hands of the workers, it is natural that we should want to have no unemployment. The fact that in our socialist society there has not been any unemployment for many years is in our opinion an important achievement

70

of our social and economic system. Since perestroika is be carried out in the interest of the people, since its success is to lead to improvements in the lives of the Soviet people, we cannot and must not give up any of our achievements. On the contrary, in the course of perestroika we must strengthen the advantages and social achievements that are part of our socialist society. It would therefore be extremely ill-advised for us to allow unemployment.

The problem of unemployment during perestroika is not an easy one to solve. Perestroika will see a speeding up of the economic process. There will be major technological and structural changes in the development of socialist productivity, with great cut-backs in the production of raw materials, in agriculture, in construction and in the transport system. In general the number of people employed in raw-material production will decrease, and people will be transferred to the service sections of industry.

According to our calculations, in the next few years and up to the year 2000 we shall lose 1–1.5 million jobs every year. A certain number of people will be re-employed within the same industries in newly created jobs made possible by the new, more progressive direction of the economy. But this will not be possible everywhere, and there will be an inevitable problem with retraining and the redeployment of people to different enterprises.

Foreseeing that these processes will accelerate, the government passed a regulation about a year ago on the subject of effective employment. This regulation will give more importance to employment agencies and will lead to the creation of new self-financing retraining centres in every town and every region. These centres will work alongside the various enterprises and will not charge the workers themselves. The state guarantees employment in accordance with the relevant articles of the Soviet Constitution.

I should also point out that the whole question of employment will be decided in the near future against the background of the serious demographic changes that have been taking place since the war. The generation about to reach maturity will be the children of those born during the war, when the birthrate was very low. Therefore the labour force will not be quite as large as previously, although it will grow again later.

At the same time the number of old people has increased. There are more pensioners. This is because in the previous generation fewer men became pensioners, so many having been killed in the

71

war. But the generation now of pensionable age did not fight in the war and is therefore more numerous.

So the numbers joining the working population are decreasing, while those leaving it are increasing. The middle section of the population will grow relatively slowly, therefore, while there will be a marked increase in the proportion of children and adolescents on the one hand and elderly people on the other.

Usually the working section of the population in the USSR increases by 10–11 million in the course of a five-year period. During the period of the 12th Five-year Plan it will increase only by 3 million. In the course of the next couple of five-year plans there will be a certain growth in the working population, but we shall still not yet return to the normal level of replacement.

This will ease the task of redeploying people who lose their jobs in connection with structural changes.

During my visits to the West I was often asked whether the necessarily common phenomenon of enterprises closing because of inefficiency will not lead to unemployment in the Soviet Union as part of the transition to an economic system of management.

We have in fact included a number of articles about the closure of unprofitable enterprises in the Law on State Enterprises and Conglomerates, but we have not as yet gone into great detail about the possible bankruptcy of enterprises, as has been done in Hungary, Poland and China. I do hope, however, that after the price reform we are planning to carry out in 1990 we shall start disbanding certain unprofitable enterprises.

All the same, I do not think that the closure of enterprises which will oblige their workers to seek other employment will ever become a widespread process. It will happen to scores, maybe a few hundred, enterprises a year. Most likely what will happen is that some enterprises will be redirected, or rather included in other, flourishing ones. Furthermore, the enterprise's own workers and the organizations immediately above it will take measures to prevent bankruptcy. After all, ministries and local councils under whom the enterprises will function do have certain funds at their disposal, and they will be able to offer temporary assistance while ensuring that the enterprise starts to work better.

Of course there will always be some 'hopeless' enterprises which it will be easier to close than to try to reform. Mostly these are mining concerns where the geological and social conditions for the mining of raw materials have become much worse. Some of

72

these are closing down even now, although others are often kept going artificially.

As we intend to reorientate the entire production of raw materials, with a view to ensuring a much-needed economy of resources and a reduction in the growth of industry, we shall be particularly severe in this branch of the economy. We shall have to liquidate loss-making mines and lumber concerns.

Turning to agriculture, we can see that about fifteen hundred collective farms are irredeemably loss-making. These are the farms that have not been able to stop making losses since the raising of purchase prices after the acceptance of the Provisioning Programme in 1982, and this in spite of the fact that they have been given time and a number of good seasons. On the contrary, their debt to the state has only grown. These farms will have to be disbanded, and in their place it will be best to organize teams of leaseholders, co-operatives, or family leaseholding farms. Naturally, this will have to be with the willing co-operation of the farmers. Some will probably want to leave the area, either for a town or another, more profitable farm.

It is my own personal opinion that more jobs will disappear as a result of technological progress and structural shifts than as a result of the closure of inefficient enterprises. But the redeployment process will be the same in both cases.

There is a legal requirement that six months' notice has to be given to anyone who is to lose his job because either the job or the whole enterprise is to disappear. He is also to be paid an extra three months' salary. If the worker cannot or will not find a job for himself he can call on the services of the employment agencies that guarantee employment.

Our country is very large and varied. Working conditions vary in the different regions. So when we discuss this problem we have to differentiate between the areas that have a surplus of labour and those that have a shortage of labour.

The areas where there is a shortage of labour are the Russian Federation, large parts of the Ukraine, Byelorussia and the Baltic regions. Here there are numbers of unfilled jobs, as the birthrate is low and the demographic consequences of the war are particularly in evidence.

The areas where there is a surplus of labour are above all Central Asia and Azerbaijan. In these regions the birthrate has remained high because of ethnic and national considerations. In

73

fact, it is three or four times higher than the birthrate in the areas discussed above. The demographic consequences of the war are also less obvious, as these areas were further away from the front line. Here we shall have to make considerably greater efforts to create additional jobs for the ever-growing population.

For instance, in the last nine years the population of Uzbekistan has gone up from 15.4 million to 19.6 million people, a rise of 4.2 million. At the same time the Ukraine, with a population of 50 million, grew by only 1.6 million. Over the same period the population of Azerbaijan increased by 900,000, that of Turkmenia by 700,000, while in Byelorussia, which has over twice the population, the increase was a mere 600,000. The population of Latvia, which is as high as that of Kirghizia and Tadzhikistan and higher than that of Turkmenia, went up by only 300,000.

One way to create more jobs in Central Asia and Azerbaijan is to develop labour-intensive agriculture, such as market gardening. Another is to set up a large number of subsidiaries of already existing enterprises and organizations and to create new enterprises to use the local produce.

Having established that in our socialist conditions unemployment cannot become an incentive to labour, how then are we to stimulate good work in conditions of full employment? First, we must apply consistently the socialist principle of distribution according to work. This principle, which Marx and Engels called the basic principle of socialism, is: 'From each according to his abilities, to each according to his work'. Marx and Engels gave this principle a firm intellectual grounding in their *Critique of the Gotha Programme*. Distribution according to work is profoundly rooted in socialist conditions. If all property is owned by society, with all working people owning it collectively, then each may take as much out of the common fund as he is entitled to by his work, by the amount he has put in.

However, before anyone can rightly claim his share of consumer goods from the fund of manufactured goods, we have to restore into the production chain the material resources consumed, to direct part of the means towards reserves, to create funds to provide free or subsidized welfare necessities such as the health service, education, pensions etc. A certain amount must also be put aside for defence and government. The principle of distribution according to work seems the fairest in a society that has not reached the stage of plenty in material goods. All members of

74

society become equal in that each receives according to his work, that is in accordance with the amount he has put in.

What do we mean by work? We have to take into account the quality as well as the quantity of invested labour, for, as Marx said, highly qualified work is ordinary work multiplied. To be completely fair in this distribution according to the quantity and quality of labour put in, people have to be given the opportunity to work in accordance with their own abilities. This is allowed for in the first part of the distribution equation: 'From each according to his abilities'. It is not all that easy to put this part of the principle into practice, since in order to ensure that everyone is working according to his abilities, those abilities must be developed. This is where education becomes a decisive factor. Every individual must have free access to education and must receive the education he or she wants and is capable of absorbing.

As part of the process of perestroika we are at present carrying out a programme of reform which will touch every aspect of the educational system, from schools right on up to professional education, higher education and on-the-job training. Our task is to incorporate within the education given in schools ideas that will instil the habit of productive work, to give the children a general educational foundation to which they can add further professional training.

In the past the scope of professional training, including the training given by specialist colleges, has been very narrow and specialized. This is no longer enough, because the speed of modern advances results in constant structural shifts which mean that people have to retrain all the time. As a result, people need a wider educational base.

Today we take a new view of professional training and higher education. It is now assumed that we need specialists with wider training who will be able to combine several professions. They will continue with their own education and, if necessary, acquire further qualifications and adapt themselves to various specializations.

One example of an institution which does give this kind of wide scientific and technical education is the Institute of Physics and Technology, founded in the late forties with the express purpose of educating specialists for the new sciences and technologies such as atomic energy, laser technology, radiation chemistry etc. What makes this institute special is its close connection with the most

75

advanced organizations for scientific research and production, organizations which are in the vanguard of those particular branches for which the students are being prepared. Naturally enough, many of the graduates of this institute now head large scientific, design and technological organizations. They are the successful ones in industrial research and are in the forefront of science and technology.

Another useful incentive for the full realization of potential is the availability of jobs which are not simply attractive to a young person just beginning his or her career but which will also oblige that young person to continue with training and improving his or her qualifications.

The present-day job structure in the USSR is backward, and the reasons for this lie in the backwardness of our economy, in our hypertrophied traditional industries and raw-material producers. Meanwhile the development of those branches of industry that need scientific research has been as inadequate as the development of our service industry. So advanced branches of mass technology that ought to attract hundreds of thousands of people to work in them have yet to be established. I am talking about the development of information technology, of flexible manufacture, of new materials production, of biotechnology and other such industries.

The backwardness of our job structure is the result of a one-sided development that placed too much emphasis on basic production, leaving auxiliary and ancillary work to be handled in the old way. Because we have not paid attention to specialization and the development of co-operatives, 40 and even 50 per cent of workers in some industries are employed in these auxiliary and ancillary jobs, many of which are still done in a primitive fashion. As a consequence the proportion of frequently heavy, monotonous and always unqualified manual labour is very high.

Our new investment policy has a view to a radical reconstruction of all branches of the national economy on the basis of the very latest technology. This should lead to a rearrangement of the job structure. In particular we intend to reduce the number of manual workers in production from currently about 50 per cent of the workforce to about 15–20 per cent by the year 2000. Technological progress and the re-equipment of industry with microelectronics will change the way we work. Where work has been mechanized, it will become more creative, more interesting, more attractive.

Recent developments in Soviet industry mean that robotics, processing centres and even flexible production systems are becoming more widespread. The same applies to rotors and rotor-conveyors and to new technology controlled by up-to-date computers in the chemical and metallurgical industries.

We can see that young people are drawn to these new technological processes, that they are fascinated by the work. I think that soon more and more fields of work will show progress.

So far we have looked at the first part of the formula: 'From each according to his abilities'. But the most important part is the second one: 'to each according to the quantity and quality of his work'. How do we get people to work better and harder? How do we get people in state enterprises and co-operatives to work as well as if they were working for themselves, maybe even better? It has to be better because, as Marx foresaw, working together with one's comrades should produce 'the additional productive force of collective labour', as he called it.

The crux here is to convert the factory worker into the boss. Under administrative managerial methods, when work was done to orders from above, the worker gradually became alienated from the ownership of the means of production. Property was supposed to belong to the whole people but in reality belonged to the state. State departments made the decisions. And although in theory this was the workers' and peasants' state, representing those very workers and peasants, no formula was found to make the real interests of individual workers or working collectives coincide with the interests of society as represented by the state. In an individual enterprise social ownership appeared to be no ownership at all. Whether matters there were handled well or badly had little effect on the workers' wages. So over the last thirty years less and less was put into the economy as a whole, even such important branches as industry and agriculture.

In other words the country's production apparatus worked ever less efficiently. Each rouble invested in industry produced an ever-decreasing return. In each of the five-year-plan periods from 1970 up to 1985, returns decreased by about 3 per cent per year (15 per cent overall).

Let us say that the volume of production increased on average by 3–4 per cent. To achieve this, the main production funds had to be increased by 6–7 per cent. Accordingly every rouble invested brought in less income. There were more and more unfinished buildings, and for one reason or another the technology we introduced was for many years under-used.

Workers displayed indifference to the use of raw materials and other supplies. But waste again has no effect on workers' wages. So in the last twenty years we have fallen far behind other developed countries in our production of energy, metals and raw materials. We consume about as much fuel and raw materials as the United States to produce half as much in goods and services. For example, each cubic metre of timber in our country is converted into one-third the value that the Americans achieve. We produce twice as much steel as they do, but we use it to produce considerably less equipment and fewer cars (this is true if we do not compare the relative weights of the cars and machinery, since by weight we do produce more). However, what we need to look at is productivity and efficiency.

Even after the recent energy and raw-material crisis, when world prices for oil, other fuels and raw materials went up suddenly and sharply, and the whole world began to worry about economizing on resources, we did not make much progress in that respect.

This kind of uneconomic attitude towards supplies gradually spread to the work done with them. In the past, while the old traditions remained alive, we always respected fine work that produced goods of high quality. Of course, given the backward conditions in our country, our possibilities were not all that great. For instance, we did not have paints as beautiful, or packaging as attractive, as the West did, and therefore our goods never looked as attractive as theirs. But if we look at what we produced thirty or forty years ago, not to mention earlier still, we have to admit that the goods then were durable and of good quality. I remember our first television sets. They functioned without breaking down for ten or fifteen years. In the fifties the TV repairman was virtually unknown. ZIL refrigerators made by the Likhachevsky factory in Moscow worked for twenty years without once breaking down. I still have one of those early refrigerators in my dacha. For my thirtieth birthday, my friends clubbed together and bought me a watch. This was a new Soviet watch – a very ordinary, mass-produced one. They had the watch inscribed and presented it to me so that I would not oversleep and would get to my doctoral viva in time. Two years later I had my viva and was granted my doctorate, but my watch went on without once breaking down for the next fifteen years and could probably go on in the same way for another fifteen. But all that is in the past, unfortunately.

Gradually, in the period of stagnation, the prestige attached to high-quality work was lost. People's attitudes to their work became worse and worse. Despite the fact that we had a large number of inspectors, quality went down. Of course, one can say that the new products are more complicated and it is harder to make them as good and as reliable as the old ones. True, but then our technology has improved as well, and so too has the workers' education.

It is practically impossible now to buy a television set that will not break down at least once before the guarantee on it has expired. The Ministry of Trade has decreed that a television set may be exchanged for another if it has had three major breakdowns during the guarantee period, and in no other circumstances. This says something about the quality of those sets and the lack of concern for consumers' rights.

Watches, too, have become less accurate, though more attractive to look at. The plain old analog watches were more or less accurate. Of the new ones, or at least of those that have come my way (I try to wear only domestic products), we can safely say that they go faster than the watches of any other country in the world. One in every fifteen or twenty refrigerators needs servicing in the first year of use.

All this is the result of the workers' alienation from their work. They have lost the feeling that they are the masters, and they do not particularly care about the final product or its quality.

This is the most complicated and at the same time the most crucial task of the reform: we must get rid of this feeling of alienation, we must make people feel that they are in charge of the means of production, we must make them care about the quality of what they produce. And we shall persevere in our efforts to find the ways and means to achieve those results.

The task is complicated because it requires a multilateral approach. We must involve the entire workforce of a factory or an enterprise in the work they do, but at the same time we must also involve the individual teams or sections in each factory and enterprise, and finally we must involve each individual worker.

Actually our entire reform – the transition to an economic system of management and all the separate parts of that transition

– is all about solving this problem. When an enterprise goes over to full cost accounting, self-financing and self-management, it is creating the necessary conditions for involving its workforce in production.

In the new economic conditions the workforce will have to use the enterprise's income to meet all expenses. This is precisely what we mean by full cost accounting and self-financing. After covering all expenses, paying taxes, contributing to the various funds of higher organizations, and settling accounts with banks and clients, the enterprise is left with its residual income. This, according to the Law on State Enterprises, is to be shared out by the collective itself. Part of this residual income will become the wage fund, and part will be shared out between various incentive funds, such as the general development fund, the social development fund, and the material incentives fund. Usually more than three-quarters of the residual income will be used for the welfare of the workforce either through the wage fund or the social development fund which will provide for children's organizations, pioneer summer camps, factory canteens, accommodation and other socially necessary buildings. As for the general development fund, this is to be used first of all for technical re-equipment. This will improve working conditions and increase efficiency, thus increasing the enterprise's income.

We can see even from such a schematic description of the new conditions under an economic managerial system that a direct connection between the workforce's income and the results of its activity has been achieved.

Of course the results of this work and the full extent of an enterprise's costs can be established properly only when prices and the amount paid for materials have been correctly set. The present price system, formed under the administrative system of management, relies too much on spending, so that its effect on the nation's economic efficiency and on necessary labour costs is distorted. Thus any calculation of results and expenditure is inevitably distorted. Our system of individual economic norms and state subsidies to loss-making enterprises was devised to correct these distortions.

As we carry through our reform of prices and price formation in the Soviet Union, we shall also introduce payment for all resources. This will provide some basis for a better-founded system of valuation, expenses and results. After the introduction of the

80

new price system, the cost accounting income will reflect more accurately and more objectively the workforce's contribution to the social income.

The wage fund will be the part of the costed income that is of the greatest concern to the workers. In accordance with the Law on State Enterprises, this fund can be formed in one of two ways. Under the cost accounting system, it will be possible to establish the wage fund according to strict economic rules. A formula will establish the relationship between the size of the wage fund and the volume of production expressed by various indices: commodity output, conditional net production or net production. At the moment we generally use two indices: commodity output and conditional net production. Neither of these provides enough stimulus towards economizing on material resources, as they do not influence each other much. We have therefore begun to pay more and more attention to the third index – real net production – because this one increases if there is a decrease in the material capacity of the production and is therefore better at encouraging economies to be made. In any case, using the net production index in the petrol and petrochemical industries has brought positive results, stimulating better processing and savings in energy, raw materials, and so on. Because of these results we intend to use the net production index more widely in other branches of the economy.

The wage calculation formula can be established either as an incremental index or as a share index. In the first the fund value is derived from the previous year's base fund. To this one adds the wage fund, which is calculated according to an incremental formula (for instance 0.4 per cent increase in the wage fund for every 1 per cent increase in output).

This approach would evidently not be the recommended one for an enterprise that had in the past used its resources fully for growth, but it would be advantageous for the inefficient enterprise with more resources which it could use to achieve production increases.

Another approach is possible. This would be based on a formula that would set the wage fund relative to conditional net production. If the index were set at 0.6 per cent, then the wage fund would be allocated 60 per cent of the conditional net production.

Once the wage fund has been calculated, the remainder is residual profit for distribution to the incentive funds. By acting in this way, the total package for workers will be made up of the wage fund plus the material incentive fund.

Now let us look at another way cost accounting might operate. In this method, the wage fund will be residual or resultative. Enterprises taking this route will first distribute money into the various development funds, while the residue goes into a wage fund.

In this form of cost accounting the economic incentives will be stronger, since any increase in efficiency will have a direct effect on the wage fund, that is, on each worker's wage packet. In the first version of cost accounting, any savings or waste will affect profits and will affect the payment fund only indirectly through the material incentives fund, which will absorb a proportion of any economies or waste. The greater part of any economies or waste will be reflected in the enterprise's contribution to the budget and also in the size of the largest incentive fund, the one set aside for productive, scientific and technical development.

The fact that the second type of cost accounting uses a single fund to make the relationship between work and its reward simpler and more comprehensible is an added bonus. This is not so with the system that calculates the wage fund according to one formula and uses a completely different one for calculating the material incentives fund.

When the transition to the new economic forms began in 1988, the first method of cost accounting, which decided on the wage fund according to some previously fixed formula, prevailed. Each enterprise separately established its formula for each year of the 12th Five-year Plan and the tasks that the plan allocated to it. Results in 1988 show that the creation of a wage fund according to this method does not achieve the intended aim, that is to say it does not ensure that people start to care about economizing on resources or using production funds better.

However, for understandable reasons this method of cost accounting did increase incentives for higher productivity. The wage fund and the material incentives fund are shared out among the workforce, and the fewer people there are in that force, the larger each individual share will be. If an enterprise manages to reduce the numbers employed, the average income will rise, and vice versa.

In 1988 those enterprises which adopted the new administrative

82

measures increased their productivity by 6.4 per cent, while the remainder increased theirs by only 4.2 per cent. This increase in productivity is significant, since in 1987 the figure was only 3.6 per cent.

Only about 1,000 enterprises, mostly electronics and light engineering plants in Byelorussia, adopted the second method of cost accounting. Labour productivity in these enterprises rose by 11.4 per cent, compared with 7.5 per cent in enterprises in the same branch of industry which opted for the first system.

Some production conglomerates under the Ministry of Geology were converted to the second method of cost accounting, and their productivity increase was positively explosive – 25 per cent – while other indices improved greatly as well.

With the second method of cost accounting, the incentive to economize on resources is greater and the production funds are used better. The conclusion cannot be denied: the second method of cost accounting is more efficient that the first and provides workers with greater incentives.

That being so, why is it not more widespread? Fewer than 200 enterprises have taken it up, while 30,000 in industry alone have accepted the first method of cost accounting. The second method is more risky for the workforce, and results depend to a great extent on the prices being soundly based. As we are still only in the preparatory stages of price reform, people have expressed fears that some new prices may create difficulties for a workforce which has adopted the second method of cost accounting. The first method may not provide such great incentives but is safer.

We must also remember that the formulas were originally worked out on the basis of the first method, because that was considered to be the main one. It was also difficult to adopt the second method, because it did not always have previously established taxation levels or formulas for calculating contributions to the various development funds. But both cost accounting methods are greatly affected by the introduction of the notion of payment for the use of resources.

Usually an enterprise pays about 6 per cent of its value for physical resources and about 300 roubles per person per annum for labour resources (this last figure is somewhat lower in those areas where there is a superabundance of labour). In the price reform and the transition to the new prices we shall introduce the concept of paying for such resources as the land, water, and so on. If these are badly used, that is, if production is low, then the cost of these resources per unit of production becomes very high. This decreases profitability and consequently the wage fund. If, on the other hand, the collective uses its resources well, if its production increases, then each unit of production has lower resources costs and profitability increases, leading to a rise in the wage fund. As the resources actually distributed between the enterprises belong to the state, one could regard payment for them as a kind of lease payment for their use by the workforce.

So far we have talked of the need to arouse the interest of the workforce as a whole. But an enterprise is a sizeable unit: there are usually between 600 and 800 people in an industrial enterprise and between 400 and 600 in an agricultural one such as a collective or a state farm. This faces us with the problem of how to balance the interests of a large workforce with the interests of smaller units.

An effective answer was found by the workers themselves – collective leaseholding. A collective may be anything from just several people to a hundred or more workers. The collective signs an agreement with the administration for the performance of a job. It is better if this job is a process that results in something tangible, like a completed house or the production of some kind of goods. The collective is given the capital equipment, raw materials and anything else they may require. They are also provided with the necessary utilities. On completion, the two parties to the agreement settle according to its terms.

This sort of collective leaseholding could cover merely the use of some resources, or it could involve a complex, full agreement based on cost accounting. The simplest form of collective lease-holding occurs when a collective is paid for a certain amount of work according to a price structure. For instance, in a shoe factory a collective produces clogs and is paid according to the price fixed for clogs. On completion, the leasehold collective is paid the contractual amount and divides it between its members according to its own democratic principles.

Collective leaseholding could be improved by the inclusion of costings for fuel, raw materials, and other resources in the agreement. The collective could 'buy' these resources, and if it managed to produce the required output without using all of them up, its earnings would increase by the amount of money it had managed to save. Here we can see the beginnings of a properly costed system and so the ordinary leasholding collective becomes one based on its own cost accounting.

Such an idea could be developed further to include payments for the machinery and equipment needed by the collective in the lease. If the collective then consumes less by increasing its efficiency, its income will increase still further.

The highest form of contract agreement is the full leaseholding arrangement. In these the collectives pay for the use of all the means of production and cover all their expenses, including any outside services, and distribute their own income. It is very important that the organization and stimulation of labour in these micro-collectives should match the cost accounting agreements and wage fund formulas agreed by the whole workforce of a factory or conglomerate. In this connection we can see that the second system of cost accounting is virtually a collective contract for a whole factory. Under this system it is easy to connect the contract made by groups or teams with the general economic state of the whole enterprise. With the first system of cost accounting it would be more difficult to form such a connection, because the previously set formulas for calculating the wage fund may come into conflict with the amount decided on by the various subsections of that enterprise.

I have already said that the highest form of contract agreement is the lease agreement, because only then do the means of production definitely pass over into the possession, use and management of the workforce. In return the workers will pay rent for these means. So the actual owners of the means will be the workers who will be using them – with one proviso: they will not be full owners, merely the managers, and will not be able to sell them and share the proceeds. However, this will not greatly affect the economic interests of the workers, who will be the virtual owners of the means of production.

Leaseholding first began to develop in our country in the agricultural sector, where various teams began to lease land, agricultural machinery and farms so that their income was decided on the basis of their actual results. The leaseholding collectives used their income to pay a rent which was usually decided beforehand rather than being on a sliding scale; they also paid for whatever means of production they used, and they contracted for materials and services they needed from outside their own group, and so on. Any residue was income. Usually this income was shared out in proportion to participation in the work or results, taking into account various qualifications and anything else that seemed necessary. Part of the income was often set aside to cover unexpected expenses and other contingencies. Not only large collectives but even families became leaseholders. This was the beginning of family holdings.

Conditions in our country vary enormously. In the Baltic region, for instance, agriculture was based in the past on the family as a unit. In Russia the situation was always different. Here peasants have long lived in villages, and the agricultural working unit was often not the family but the *artel*, a small group of people. So even now the leaseholding collectives in Russia are more likely to be larger units, with family holdings subordinate to them. However, there are regions with their own traditions, and some family holdings are important. Naturally we do not consider this to be wrong.

We look upon the idea of leaseholding in agriculture as the way to improve the whole agricultural sector of the country's economy. It is very important that the leaseholders should not consider themselves to be only temporarily in charge; they should make longer-term agreements. Therefore, leaseholding agreements on land are now made for ten, fifteen or even twenty years. This ensures that those who work the land will not simply try to get as much as possible out of it in the shortest possible time but will ensure that the land is cared for and becomes more fertile and productive.

Gradually the notion of rental agreements has spread to other parts of the economy. In the Moscow region, for example, a transition to a contract system was initiated by the Butovo building materials factory. The factory was a loss-maker and in a pitiful state. The workforce suggested that it should sign an agreement with the central Moscow agency for building materials, the organization immediately above it. The collective agreed that it would pay a moderate rent and would not receive any subsidy to cover losses as it had in the past. All the money, less various expenses, was managed by the workforce.

Once this contract was signed, people began to work differently, more intensively, and paid more attention to the quality of their work. They felt that they were the masters in their own workplace, responsible people. Output increased sharply and income began to rise. In a single year the loss-making enterprise became profitable.

Labour productivity in that year went up by almost 150 per cent, and wages increased by a third.

When they saw how this enterprise had flourished, others in the Moscow region decided that they too wanted to have contractual agreements. Several hundred factories in the Moscow region alone are planning to take the same plunge next year. The whole system of rent contracts is developing rapidly, giving rise to a number of questions such as the legal aspects of the process, which have fallen behind. At present there are no legal guarantees for the independence of leaseholding collectives, but something is being done about this and work has begun on a law covering rent contracts and leases.

However, the family holding and leaseholding in general are encountering difficulties. Clearly the better workers, those with more initiative, want to go over to contract agreements. They have faith in themselves and know they can produce better work. They want to become masters of the situation and exert pressure from below for the creation of more leaseholding agreements. There is, however, a great deal of resistance to this pressure.

On the other hand there are the highly qualified workers who appear to be indispensable and are therefore paid a high wage. They are loners, who often hide tools they have designed themselves from their colleagues and refuse to share the secrets of their trade. They are not greatly liked by their fellows but are tolerated because it is hard to do without them. Workers like this do not want to change over to the team system because they fear a levelling of incomes and are anxious that their special qualifications will not be appreciated sufficiently.

Then again there is the large section of relatively weak workers, shirkers and drunkards for whom work is not the most important thing and who try to do only as little as they can get away with. Better workers try not to take people like that into their teams because they are no use.

All this creates a number of conflicts among the workers themselves in the formation of working collectives.

The use of specialists is even more complicated. In our country, the engineer has been much devalued as a specialist. An engineer is anybody who has a higher education and works in an industrial enterprise. Most of them are not in reality engineers, in that the work they do is mostly clerical. These engineers are specialists in labour and planning. There are even engineers whose speciality is socialist competition. As a result of this kind of attitude the number of engineers in every enterprise has gone up considerably. In the USSR there are five times as many engineers in industry as there are in the United States, although the volume of production there is several times higher.

There are a number, one might even say a large number, of specialists working in our enterprises at the moment whose labour is not productive and who would not really be needed if these enterprises were organized sensibly. I have already quoted the example of a gold-panning team of 280 people whose productivity was the same as that of a 1,200-strong industrial mine. In the state enterprise the director had three deputies, there was a personnel section, a planning section, a production section, a separate appointments section and many, many others. In the gold-panning team the leader did his own job as well as that of all his non-existent deputies, the production section, planning section, personnel section and even the job of interviewer. Apart from the chairman, the management consisted of an accountant, an engineer and a storeman. Everybody else was involved in the actual production. And in fact, when supplies arrived and men were needed to unload them, all these administrative workers would turn out with the storeman. Naturally enough, the team chief had no secretary – he telephoned people himself – and no driver – he drove his own car. This sort of arrangement was necessary because every extra person would have had to be paid by the members of the *artel* out of their wage packets.

In the state mine things were different. It made no odds to anybody's wages whether the director had a secretary or not. Nor did it matter whether there were a hundred people in the management or only fifty; everybody received his salary, independently of anyone else, and all at the state's expense. The situation was the same in many other enterprises.

Leaseholding collectives are formed and function in the same way as the gold-panners. Every worker has to be accounted for. They may take on engineers, but only if they will be worth their wages or, better still, bring in extra profits for the whole collective.

When I was working in Novosibirsk I was friendly with a number of directors and even organized a directors' club. We met regularly in their various enterprises and discussed problems of general interest. Several of the directors were interested in research. My colleagues in the Institute of Economics and I assisted them in their economics studies and in getting their dissertations accepted. In particular I took to a young but nevertheless very experienced man who was at the time general director of the *Ob* shoe and leather goods factory; in fact I became Stanislav Zverev's supervisor. A progressive director, always looking to improve things, he was one of the first to introduce the idea of contract agreements and changed a large part of the production of fashion shoes over to that system.

The workforce on that particular assembly line included several engineers, a foreman and a technician. They asked for a designer. The designer was asked to create several prototypes of new shoes that would be not only of high quality but also less labour-intensive in production and thus easier to make. The inclusion of a designer in the team proved to be very effective; the example had a good influence in the factory, and a number of subsections with contract agreements were formed. It worked very well.

When you look at a shoe-making assembly line, your immediate impression is that there is nothing to improve, that everyone is working at full speed and without distractions, that nothing could go any faster. Then the assembly line goes over to a contractual arrangement. The workers get rid of those whose work is not up to the mark and help those who are trying but have not yet learnt the best way to do things. They organize production better, think of improvements. And immediately productivity goes up. At the fashion shoe assembly line, for example, productivity went up by almost 30 per cent, although there was no change in personnel or equipment. This is the result of genuine involvement, of feeling that you are the master of your own workplace.

Further difficulties arise between the workers who want to move over to a contractual system and the enterprise's management. This is because the collectives have to sign an agreement with the management and both parties have to accept certain obligations. The management takes it upon itself to pay for the work done and also to supply the collective with materials and many other things without delays or interruptions. This puts a certain obligation on the management. If the contract is drawn up properly, the management is responsible for any failure to meet its obligations. Not every manager likes this, particularly as under the old system there was no such concept as being responsible to the working collective for your mistakes and wrong decisions.

There is another side to this problem, perhaps the most serious aspect. It is not in the manager's direct interest to move sections of his workforce over to a system of contract agreements. If the teams work well, the workers will receive more money. But the managers receive nothing extra, though the new system brings them more work, because they have to ensure the conditions for better work, they must rearrange their plans so that they will fit in with the contract system, and they must make sure that supplies keep coming in smoothly. In fact, the administration will be worse off, since under the new system, if there is a miscalculation or if some undertaking has not been fulfilled, the collectives, who lose part of their income as a result, are justifiably angry with the management and make this felt. Moreover, it is important to ensure that the economic conditions under which the enterprise functions agree with the independent productive functioning of the collectives under contract.

Let us take as an example a collective farm. If all the arable land is divided up between the various teams, then they are the ones who make decisions about it. Each team decides for itself what to sow and when, what to harvest, and so on. If the collective farm is also independent and can decide such matters for itself, then the needs of the two can be accommodated. But what happens if the kolkhoz is under the rule of the regional authorities and it is they who decide when the grain should be delivered, how much land should be ploughed, what should be sown where, what sort of cattle they should acquire and so on? The contract teams do not know anything about these requirements. They have undertaken to produce something, say milk, with the proviso that they can decide how many cows they should have. So their aim will be to produce as much milk as possible, and it may be that they choose to reduce the number of cows in order to increase yield and to use fodder more effectively.

Even though we are moving over to complete cost accounting and self-financing, this is still a transitional period, and the administrative style of management has to a very great degree been retained. The various enterprises, the collective and state farms are not yet sufficiently independent to change all their production to a contract system or to introduce leaseholding on a wide scale. They may have one or two such teams, and maybe they will manage to organize a few more, but for the most part the workforce will go on working as before, according to instructions from above, from the organizations that still direct these enterprises and collective farms.

In the future, as organizations change over completely to methods of cost accounting and self-financing, it will become possible for more and more contract teams and leaseholding collectives to be set up. What we shall have to solve is the problem of how to encourage the chairman of the kolkhoz and the whole administration to establish contract teams and to have more leaseholders.

Next there is the important problem of how to interest each individual worker in the quality of his work. It is one thing to talk about the labour collective, a leaseholding team, but it is quite another to deal with the individual members of that team. How can one define each one's personal involvement and responsibilities, and how should one combine these with the interests of the whole team?

In the years before perestroika, each worker's labour was assessed individually and wages were paid on an individual basis. Most of the workers had individual agreements for which individual formulas and methods of valuation were drawn up. Wages were paid according to whether the agreed norm had been fulfilled. In a number of cases there were clauses about bonuses. A large section of the workers and practically all the engineers were paid on the so-called temporal system; in other words they were paid for the amount of time they worked, and in addition there were frequent extra payments decided according to some other index of activity.

This method of payment did not unite the interests of all the members of one workforce, although they jointly produced something or other. Each person's labour was separated from the actual production, the final result of all the work. Under the system of individual agreements, each worker's salary depended on reaching set production norms. But these were set by special norm setters who often did so with one eye on the size of the wage. This meant that there was no particular reason for the worker to overfulfil his norm. On the contrary, if he did so, the norms would be raised. And those who were paid for the time they put in, that is simply for turning up at work, had no feeling of involvement at all.

Under perestroika, we want to develop contract teams, and we aim to put more emphasis on the leaseholding system.

In these cases all the workers are in one way or another involved in the final result of their team's work. Within the team, money is divided democratically, either by a general meeting of the whole collective, if it is small enough, or by a council elected by the members.

What often happens is that a co-efficient of involvement is determined for each worker. This reflects the amount of work put in by each individual as evaluated by an expert or by his colleagues at work. Everybody works harder, both to achieve a higher wage fund from which everybody's salary will be paid and to achieve a higher co-efficient of involvement. In such cost-accounting collectives workers usually have intermediate professions, they help each other, change to other types of work if needed, stay on longer at work, and so on.

If a well-organized team goes over to cost accounting there is usually an immediate growth in productivity of 20–30 per cent or even more. There have been not a few cases where productivity doubled or even tripled.

The involvement co-efficient is applied to the whole wage packet by some collectives; others apply it only to an agreed portion with the main wage based on the worker's qualifications or profession. Under the system of individual agreed wages, workers depended directly on the norm setter, on the foreman or on the head of section who decided the norm and the valuation. Under the collective organization and payment system the collective's income is better founded because it is more likely to be based on established prices. When a collective is in control, even an increased norm is easier to establish than a number of individual norms, which are in any case constantly under review because of modifications and improvements in the products.

Anyone who works as part of a leaseholding team can raise his income not simply by improving his work but by better organization, by reducing the number of redundant workers, by better use of equipment, by improving the quality of the product if there are payments for better quality, and so on.

Obviously each worker thus has far more choices, and it is easier for everyone to realize his potential. So we can take it as read that collective labour creates additional possibilities for raising the efficiency of labour. The question is really how to organize collective labour in such a way that each individual member of the collective can best utilize his particular talents.

When I was in Washington as special adviser to Mikhail Gorbachev during his talks with President Reagan, I had breakfast with the well-known Chicago businessman Joseph Ricci, head of the Chicago Research and Trade Company, a company active on the Chicago and other stock exchanges.

On my next visit to the United States I paid a special visit to Chicago because I wanted to see for myself how the members of that company – from director to junior – worked. I was interested in their new approach to the organization of and payment for work. Joe Ricci is a fervent advocate of the new system, and he was particularly anxious to prove that its starting point was the collective. He paid a great deal of attention to the compatibility of workers in each subsection, comparing it to the family, where there is a head and other members who love each other and work well together. To organize subsections on that basis, Joe Ricci maintained, one has to be selective and hire only people with open minds. He maintained that to a great extent the company managed to achieve its results thanks to the joint collective labour that was a counterbalance to individual competition within the collective.

The 600 members of his company deal on the stock exchanges of the world to the tune of 3–5 billion dollars. They make up an extremely effective company with a productivity 3–5 times higher than that of their competitors doing similar kinds of work but with more traditional methods of organization and payment.

Actually it was not easy for me to judge whether the company's very high level of efficiency was the result of the collective form of labour or whether it had more to do with the fact that it was particularly well supplied with up-to-date computer technology and special programs that allowed staff to select and close deals immediately.

I noticed that many workers had up to three VDUs, mostly colour ones, and all displaying graphically the results of the various stock exchange deals. Presumably both these aspects of the company's work play a part in its high efficiency.

Even a few hours in the company's workroom showed me that there really was a marked feeling of compatibility in the subsections. I was highly impressed by the planning of the work-place. The computers of one group were arranged in a semicircle, with a table in the middle where people could have coffee while they discussed their work.

93

In the course of that trip I came to the same conclusion I had reached when examining the work of the leaseholding collectives at home: there are huge unused possibilities, an enormous potential, in people who, if well organized, will produce very good work. I am convinced that our research into collective and family leaseholding, cost accounting and other forms of contractual relationship are all moves in the right direction.

There is another marvellous thing about a working leaseholding collective: it is a splendid school for democracy and self-government, a school for social education. Everything in these collectives is decided on a democratic basis. Their very existence depends on free individual choices, not on force. Any member of the collective can leave it at any time he wants to. The collective chooses its leader, and if it is a large one then it chooses a council to deal with organizational problems. Usually these collectives have a great deal of self-discipline; action follows words and there is precision in the organization.

In my visits to the gold-panning *artel*s I noticed that they worked 'dry'; getting drunk was considered one of the most serious breaches of their discipline. In the state mine next to it there were many drunkards, and discipline was at a far lower level.

The school of democracy and self-government that workers learn from in their collectives helps them to deal with the larger problems of the enterprise as a whole. In accordance with the Law on State Enterprises each working collective has extensive rights and responsibilities. The collective chooses its own council, approves its plan, decides on ways of using its income and selects its director.

This process will draw the workers into real management, giving them a say in the use of the social property allocated to the team. This is an essential part of socialist motivation in work. Together with the organization and stimulation of collective labour, it is participation in the organization of his plot of land, factory section or enterprise that will make a worker feel he is the master in his own workplace. He will see that he is participating in all the decisions of the collective, that his word has some importance in the use made of state property by the collective. Because of his participation in management, he will understand clearly how the final result of the collective's activity affects the lives of all its members, and in particular how it will affect his life. He will know what his income is likely to be and how he and

94

his family will benefit from the development of the country's welfare.

So far we have talked only of material considerations and have concentrated mostly on pay. But money – wages – is only the intermediate link, the means whereby the workers can acquire the things they need to live. There is a point to working hard to get more money if that money can be exchanged for goods or services. So the problem of supplies to balance purchasing power becomes part of the same problem of material interest, incentive, motivation.

In the developed capitalist countries there is a wide choice of goods and services, and that is of course a powerful stimulus to raising one's earnings. But saturating the market with consumer goods and services is not the only noticeable aspect of these countries' economies. Two more factors must be noted. Firstly, life becomes ever more expensive. In the sixties and seventies it became more expensive by something like 5–10 per cent a year. By the early eighties inflation was contained, and with some exceptions the annual increase in prices of goods and services remains at 3–7 per cent. In these conditions every worker must strive to ensure that his wages go up, for rises in wages are not automatic. Otherwise the real value of his labour decreases.

The second reason why every worker is interested in increasing his pay by improving his labour is that in the West each family and each individual lives to a certain extent on credit. One can be given credit for several decades when one is buying a house or flat. One can use credit to buy cars, television sets and videos, furniture, consumer goods, anything. Recently people have started running their household accounts with the aid of credit cards. In other words, at any given time, everybody is in debt, and so must work harder and harder to pay back the money they have borrowed. But the more people earn, the greater the possibilities for which they need yet more credit. People live within this circle practically throughout their entire working life.

In our socialist conditions, these incentives are not well utilized. Consumer credit is only in its infancy, and most of our families do not owe anything to anyone. It is only recently that there has been any possibility at all of getting some kind of credit for individual building work or for the purchase of a co-operative flat; and this touches only a small percentage of families.

95

In the future, as our market becomes saturated with goods, we shall have to attract money from the population for home building, for better recreation facilities and for the acquisition of cars, garages and other long-term consumer goods. Recently the State Bank of the USSR signed an agreement with a European credit card company which would allow such cards to be issued in the Soviet Union. I am sure that eventually we too will begin to use credit cards more widely.

As for the inflationary stimulus, that virtually does not affect us at all. It does not do so because our price system is still an administrative, centralized system that is not flexible and does not take fluctuations in supply and demand into account. For many years prices have remained virtually unchanged.

However, even in our conditions of severely centralized price formation, there is hidden inflation through changes in the goods that are put up for sale. Fewer and fewer cheap goods are on offer, and their place is taken by more expensive ones in the same range. But this kind of hidden inflation clearly does not provide an adequate spur, because it always seems to be possible to buy cheaper goods. Indeed, cheap goods are available, but not in sufficient quantities to satisfy demand.

Above all the state of the market in consumer goods leaves much to be desired: it is greatly distorted, many goods are in short supply, and demand for them cannot be satisfied; there are long queues in shops. All this diminishes the real choice we have in goods. Worse still is the fact that in our present conditions, where the producers rule, the range is very limited. This leads to a severe deformation of material incentives. It is not the amount of money one can earn that decides what one can buy, but the kind of friends one has, what one's position is at work, where one lives and other considerations that have no direct connections with work.

When there are severe shortages nobody is anxious to work harder to earn more. This applies particularly to agricultural areas, where the choice of consumer goods available in local shops is small. The population in these areas has accumulated quite a lot of money. Many would like to buy cars, motorbikes, modern furniture, power tools for work in their homes and on their allotments. But none of these is available on the open market. Goods can only be acquired with help from friends, and even then there is no certainty that they can be got when wanted. In other

96

words, there is no connection between the amount one earns and the consumer goods one can acquire.

The financial renewal of the economy and the saturation of the consumer market with a choice of goods and services are therefore all-important in our efforts to involve people in their work and provide them with material incentives.

From backroom politics to democratic decisions in economics

Under the old administrative system of management all the main decisions were taken centrally by the higher organs of management, either the ministries or the local authorities. Enterprises were allowed only the absolute minimum of independence in this process, and usually all decisions were taken on the basis of the government plan.

Government plans are made for a five-year period, and their details are based on the *Main Trends* of the country's economic and social policy for the following five years, as confirmed first by the relevant party congress and then by the ensuing session of the Supreme Soviet.

The five-year plan determined the annual plans which actually regulated the country's economic existence. An annual plan would be presented in dozens of volumes in which all the immediate tasks were described under something like 60,000 headings. There were headings for volume of production in cost and kind divided according to ministries, departments and republics. There were headings on labour and wages and on lowering production costs. Several volumes were devoted to programmes for large building projects. These included detailed lists of all the main projects, together with the amount of capital invested, setting the actual volume of construction work. Each ministry that was at all concerned with construction would get its own programme, together with instructions on how each enterprise was to be involved.

There were other volumes devoted to agriculture, transport, geological prospecting work, developments in various branches of the economy and in the non-productive sectors. Yet another part of the plan was about the provision of adequate material resources.

97

In the first place, Gosplan shared the resources out according to the main headings. Then came the turn of Gossnab. The main headings consisted of more than 2,000 items; Gossnab would give more detailed instructions about supplies to ministries and departments. This list consisted of about 20,000 items.

Then there would be a separate volume of the plan devoted to the deployment and productive resources and the development of the republics and regions and the most important territorial production units.

This whole voluminous plan was introduced by a thin notebook with a summary table of headings for the national economy. These included headings on national income, the productivity of social labour, the numerical strength of the blue-collar and white-collar sections, general data on productivity, agriculture, the growth in average individual incomes, in commodity circulation, and profits in the whole of the national economy, and many more.

Finance had a separate section of the plan devoted to it, distributing various tasks according to expected profits, the taxes deducted from them, the volume of tax expected from commodity circulation and so on. The annual plan also included plans for the amount of credit to be used and for money circulation. A whole volume was devoted to international trade.

Several volumes of the state plan were devoted to the development of science and technology. These would list the most important items of research and development to be done, along with timings for them and indications of the financial allocations they were to receive and so on.

One of the most important sections of the plan was the section on trade turnover which issued recommendations to the Ministry of Trade on the volume of sales to be achieved in the given year, in terms of both cost and sales.

The government would in the course of the year pass up to one thousand amendments and addenda to the plan.

A special volume of the plan would be devoted to important measures on environmental and ecological protection.

All these sums and figures – the plan – added up to the implementation of many economic decisions on new construction projects, the expansion of production, reforms, decisions to manufacture new products, and so on. Any resolutions on major long-term problems would be issued jointly by the Central Committee of the CPSU and the USSR Council of Ministers. If the resolutions touched on matters such as labour resources, pay, or standards of living, then they would also be issued in the name of the VTsSPS, the central organ of the trade unions of the USSR.

The plan therefore included a very great variety of resolutions, ranging from the development over the next five to fifteen years of individual branches of industry or parts of the country to the solution of particular economic tasks, such as, for example, opening up new oil- and gas-bearing regions of Western Siberia. There would also be separate resolutions on the development of science, technology, and various social matters.

In preparing the annual plan, Gosplan tried to take into account all the tasks under the headings allowed. However, in real life the main work headings set by official resolutions were quite at odds with the actual resources at the state's disposal and it was therefore impossible to ensure that all the tasks were included in the detailed plan. So, apart from the full plan, there is usually another volume that listed tasks which should have been included in the actual plan.

This duality between the plan and the official decisions it was supposed to be implementing caused a number of difficulties, arguments and mistakes. It was the cause of contention between those who tried to ensure that the central edicts were fulfilled and those organizations like Gosplan, the Finance Ministry, and Gossnab which tried to ensure some kind of balanced development, knowing that they did not have enough resources to satisfy everybody.

With the transition to economic methods of management the rights of enterprises and separate organizations have become much wider. They can now adopt their own plans, and these do not have to be ratified by any higher authority. They can decide for themselves how to share out their earnings and can determine the other uses to which their resources are to be put. They have to make their own agreements with other organizations, obtain credits from the bank, and conduct other such business. There has been a sizeable redistribution of resources in the individual enterprises' favour, because in the new economic system they will have to run their affairs on the basis of full cost accounting and self-financing. In other words, they themselves will have to cover their expenses out of their earnings.

Under this new system of management, the centralized plan has lost much of its importance and its aims have changed considerably. The immediate difference is to be seen in the number of headings used in the central plan; from around 60,000, these have shrunk to something like 8,000 in the 1989 plan.

We are in the transitional period between the old administrative system of management and the new, largely economic one. At the moment both the old and the new forms and approaches co-exist. State purchase orders still play a large part in the country's economic life, and wholesale trade has not yet taken the place of the distribution of resources from a central fund. Much of this stems from the fact that we have not yet carried out the price reform we have planned for 1989. One must also take into account that the tasks set by the 12th Five-year Plan, for the period 1986–90, are still current. These tasks, broken up for each year of the period, were set under the old system. That is why the state plan for, let us say, 1989 has a certain transitional aspect. The new stage in planning will not be reached until we start work on the 13th Five-year Plan, for the years 1991–5. This will be developed on a completely new basis. We must start the five-year plan with a completely new economic system that will include the new prices and a system of wholesale trade and in which all the enterprises and organizations in the country will operate on the basis of cost accounting, self-financing and self-management.

Once this is a fact, there will necessarily be fewer headings in the centrally formulated plan, a few thousand of them at most. But even more important than the number of headings will be the actual content; this will be completely different from what we were used to under the administrative system of management.

What the plan will now consist of will be general headings of economic development, and these will merely act as a guide to planning departments and other agencies concerned with the solution of social and economic problems. They will not be headings that instruct directly. The other section of the plan will concern itself with the now limited nomenclature of state purchase orders, which will take up something like 20 or 30 per cent of the volume of production. State orders will involve the defence industry and the production of parts for construction projects that are the concern of the country as a whole. An example of the latter is the construction and supply of reactors for atomic power stations. Then there will be state purchase orders for goods which the Soviet Union exports. It is possible that state orders will extend to the production of certain vital fuel and other products which need state involvement. One example that springs to mind is children's clothing, which is sold in our country at less than cost and therefore needs subsidizing by the state. But on the whole state orders will consist of only a few hundred headings and these will include building jobs of All-Union significance financed from central funds and orders for some major new technological developments which will also be at least partly financed by the state.

Naturally enough, the plan will pay attention to those objectives and directions that can be realized only with the help of the state budget. By this I mean particularly the development of social welfare, above all the large-scale construction of housing, using government funds. Then there are the programmes that involve the country as a whole, one such being the plan to speed up the development of the Far Eastern USSR adopted in 1987. But for the most part, production in all its variety will not be part of the centralized state plan. What should be produced and in what quantities will be decided through contracts between suppliers and consumers in a decentralized manner, on the markets for capital and consumer goods.

As each enterprise and each conglomerate will now decide for itself such matters as its expenses, number of employees, and how to reduce its costs, the central plan will no longer have headings divided up for ministries and labour productivity departments, and covering such matters as price formation, cost reduction, wages, profits, incentives to be paid from enterprises' profits, and so on. Decisions on these matters will be taken by the workforces themselves.

Some aspects of the plan will be new. For instance the state will establish economic rules and regulations for the enterprises to work to, and these will be included in the central plan. By rules and regulations I mean here the amount to be paid for all kinds of resources, production funds, labour resources, natural resources and so on. Other rules will apply to the amount and proportion of the tax to be paid on profits and the formula for the formation of the wages fund. Where applicable, there will also be rules about the amount of hard currency to be deducted from the budget.

These rules and regulations will be established for the whole five-year period, which will ensure long-term stability.

Enterprises will work out their plans on the basis of orders from consumers that will include state orders and on the basis of the established economic rules and regulations.

This transition to the new planning system based predominantly on economic methods of management will change radically the nature of centrally taken decisions. The centre of gravity will no longer lie in the directives given to branches of the economy or to individual enterprises, but in a system of economic advantages and privileges, in additional incentives to encourage the development of certain aspects of the economy. Decisions will also have to be taken about the way budgetary resources are to be used.

Certain decisions of the first kind are already being discussed. I can mention a few of them: the new Law on Quality, the new Law on Inventions, a planned Law on Shares and Bonds and another for transferring banks to a system of cost accounting and self-financing. We have discussed reforming wholesale, purchase and retail prices, and a Law on Leaseholding is being drafted. Many other laws and regulations of this kind are still at the discussion stage.

Decisions of the second kind could concern the need to develop the regional economy and the gas and oil resources of the Caspian area; plans to build large factories for the production of passenger cars, or the decision to build the Volga–Chogray canal as well as the decision to cancel the project.

Let us look at how these decisions will be considered and taken.

Under the administrative system of management, decisions were normally taken in secret by a small group of people from the government apparat. When a large project was being discussed, experts were sometimes consulted. One of the secondary sections of Gosplan was its group of experts. The government apparat was all-powerful because the experts were hired and fired by the apparat, and in any case the decision was to a great extent taken by the apparat itself. Those experts who showed any kind of stubbornness when this or that decision was being discussed were not included in the next commission. So if the apparat particularly wanted a decision to be carried out, it would be, as the expert commission would always support it.

Let me cite as an example the story of how the 'decision of the century', as it is called, was taken – the decision to partially re-route the flow of the Siberian rivers to Central Asia.

In Central Asia agriculture is based for the most part on a

system of irrigation. The volume of river water that flows into the Aral Sea amounts to 138 cubic kilometres a year. Most of that flow is already in use for irrigation, but the methods employed are the old-fashioned, uneconomical ones by which less than 50 per cent of the water taken from the rivers actually gets to irrigate the land. This water was distributed free, so it was freely used and abused. Hardly anyone thought of constructing drainage systems. This resulted in a rise in the underground water level. The underground water is mostly salty, and the rise in its level meant that in many parts the soil became salty. Extra costs were now incurred for desalination, and the quality of the water became worse and worse because it became saltier and saltier.

One must also bear in mind that agriculture in Central Asia, particularly in Uzbekistan, developed unevenly. It was a monocultural agriculture, based almost entirely on cotton, and mostly fibrous, second-rate cotton at that, which required a great deal of watering. The amount of land under cotton was enlarged all the time, and what with that and the worsening of the water quality as well as waste, the Central Asian republics began to have water shortages in drier years.

Furthermore, irrigation was practised with no consideration for any kind of ecological consequences. The lower reaches of the Syr-Darya and Amu-Darya rivers were frequently dammed, and less and less of the water reached the Aral Sea. Water that had been used for irrigation was then poured into large trenches with no outlets. A paradoxical situation developed. On the one hand the Aral Sea was drying out because the rivers that were supposed to flow into it no longer did so adequately, while on the other hand the sea was surrounded by a great deal of accumulated water in trenches that had no outlets. These could be seen with the naked eye from a helicopter, and the water in these trenches was evaporating, leaving a residue of salt on the bottom.

The Central Asian leadership under Sh. Rashidov, recently unmasked as a major bribe-taker who had spread corruption in his republic, therefore decided to use state resources to divert part of the flow of Siberia's rivers into Central Asia. As irrigation in the Soviet Union was historically best developed in Central Asia, many important officials in the Ministry of Land Reclamation and Water were closely connected with the Central Asian leadership. Furthermore the Ministry rather liked the idea of diverting Siberian rivers, because they felt that this would increase their work and their share of the state budget.

By various underhand methods, assertions of the need for such a diversion and points about how to set it up were inserted into the decisions of party congresses and plenums. There was a complicated multi-stage plan for the first steps to divert the rivers. It involved the building of a dam in the middle of the Irtysh, the main tributary of the river Ob. However, the Irtysh by itself could not send enough water to Central Asia. So it was decided to divert some of the water from the river Ob into the Irtysh. In other words they were going to reverse the flow of the rivers. Instead of the Irtysh being a tributary of the Ob, the Ob would become a tributary of the Irtysh. The plan was then to build several dams across the Irtysh and to pump the water up into the Tobolsk reservoir, or, alternatively, to build a canal parallel to the Irtysh, as a sort of anti-Irtysh that was to take water from the Ob in the opposite direction, from north to south. This canal would be 380 kilometres long. Then, from the Tobolsk reservoir 28 billion cubic metres of water a year would be raised by powerful pumps that had yet to be designed 110 metres to a watershed, and would then be sent along an artificial watercourse in the Turgay hollow towards Central Asia. This canal was going to be about 150 metres wide and 15–20 metres deep, with buffered water reservoirs along the way. Altogether the water was to travel about 2,380 kilometres before flowing into the Syr-Darya and Amu-Darya.

In order to build this canal, 3 billion cubic metres of soil would have to be moved, tens of millions of tons of reinforced concrete poured, and something like 200,000 builders employed. The project was going to require the most powerful excavating and other equipment, much of which was not available in this country. In other words large amounts of money would have had to be spent abroad.

Almost 100 million roubles were spent on all kinds of preparatory work, research, payments to 200 institutes subcontracting parts of the work and so on. There was a huge propaganda campaign in the press about the 'construction project of the century' and about the benefits the project would bring to the whole country's agriculture. The canal was described as the best solution to the food problem, as a powerful demonstration of the country's economic strength, and as a symbol of friendship between the people of Russia and Central Asia.

Public opinion was against the project. Many writers, scientists, experts, party and soviet workers in Siberia and elsewhere spoke out against it, saying that it would disrupt the country's ecology, that it was not particularly effective, that a great deal of water would be lost on the way, that the project would not only fail to solve the food problem but would actually waste money that could be used to solve it. The whole project was to cost 15–20 billion roubles, although its supporters tried to lower the estimates, saying that it would cost only 8–12 billion.

In order to make use of this water, further work was needed. Irrigated fields would have had to be created in the middle of a desert; these in turn would have needed roads, towns, housing and utilities. According to my calculations, the entire project would have required immediate expenses in the region of 100 billion roubles. This is a stunning amount, even for the Soviet Union, where we go in for gigantic construction projects. The scheme would have required the entire allocated growth of the construction and road industries in the whole of the USSR. We would have had to redeploy tens of thousands of builders from current projects to this one. And after all that, the new irrigated areas would have generated only a small percentage rise in the country's agricultural output. Each cubic metre of water reaching Central Asia in this fashion would have cost the country one rouble. We could have used the same money to get a great deal of agricultural produce without diverting the rivers.

Supporters of the diversion made sure that their opponents' articles did not appear in the more popular press. Not wanting to excite public opinion too much, every article against the project was severely censored; most of them never saw the light of day.

Finally we came to the state expert commission. The country's leadership was basically in favour of the project but had certain doubts, mostly due to the astronomical figures involved. At this time money for vital necessities was in short supply. So the commission was specially chosen by the supporters of the diversion project so that its positive report could be used to prove to the government that the project had scientific backing.

The Ministry of Land Reclamation and Water and the Central Asian leaders managed to get all the previous directors of Gosplan, the President of the Soviet Academy of Sciences and various other important people on their side. But the Siberian section of the Academy, where I was working at the time as head of the Economics Institute, voted unanimously against the whole project. The commission of experts became a battleground. Supporters of the diversion falsified all the data whenever there was any opposition. They set up hand-picked committees, and despite the protests of one part of the commission and of many experts, despite the fact that the Department of Economics and the Department of Earth Sciences in the Academy were both against it, supporters of the project managed to push it through the State Commission of Experts and Gosplan.

They next decided to deal with those who had spoken out against the project. The old leadership of Uzbekistan, under the First Secretary of the Central Committee of the Uzbek Communist Party, wrote a letter to the Chairman of the Council of Ministers of the USSR which denounced me as an enemy of friendship between Soviet nationalities, saying that I wanted to sow discord between Russia and Central Asia, that I wanted to deprive the region of water or, according to them, of life, and so on. The letter demanded that severe sanctions should be applied to those who spoke up against the party's policies, identifying the building of the canal with party policy.

The most unpleasant aspect of this was that the letter was accompanied by another one, no less nasty, from a number of Central Asian scientists who denounced me on other grounds, declaring that I knew nothing about economics, that I was incapable of calculating efficiency, that I misused my facts and so on and so forth.

Gosplan was instructed to deal with me. Fortunately, by this time the leadership of the party had changed and Mikhail Gorbachev had become General Secretary of the Party Central Committee. During the 1985 April Plenum of the Central Committee a new course was decided on, old ideas were reviewed, and the question that had apparently been decided reappeared on the agenda.

Even to begin perestroika, the country needed large capital investments for the technical re-equipment of the entire economy and to solve immediate social problems. The new leaders were also very sensitive about ecological issues, and a whole series of decisions was taken that required more stringent rules for dealing with the environment. All this worked against the plan for the diversion of the Siberian rivers.

Nevertheless the supporters of the diversion managed to push a resolution about the need to begin work on the project into the Central Committee's plan entitled *Main Trends for Economic and Social Developments in the Soviet Union for 1986–90 and the Years up to the Year 2000*. This discussion paper was presented to the Party's 27th Congress and was then opened to public discussion. By this time censorship had become weaker, and I, together with the Vice-President of the Academy Alexander Yashin and other colleagues, managed to publish a long article in *Pravda* against the whole plan of diverting rivers and against the way the Ministry of Land Reclamation and Water conducted its affairs. We were actively supported by many writers and led by the Siberian writer Sergey Zalygin, who had moved to Moscow and become the editor of the journal *Novy Mir*.

As a result of these renewed discussions, the Central Committee and the government decided to remove the resolution on the need to start work on this project from the general documents presented to the Congress and to discuss the whole problem separately.

There followed a series of more balanced discussions, and I ended up attending them and even speaking at all of them.

I recall a particularly dramatic discussion at the Presidium of the Council of Ministers, conducted by the Prime Minister, Comrade Nikolai Ryzhkov. Supporters of the project put up bright posters, mobilized their forces and filled a large part of the room. They spoke at length, supporting each other, trying to convince everyone of the rightness of their case; but their speeches were dogmatic rather than convincing. The huge figures given for the outlay and the relatively low figures for the results were more effective than words could be. Academician Yashin and I spoke resolutely against diverting rivers, and a number of colleagues supported us.

The members of the Presidium realized that Ryzhkov did not support diversion and therefore came up with compromises. For instance, they spoke against diverting Siberian rivers, since this was a particularly unpopular idea, but supported the partial diversion of the flow of European rivers into the Volga.

The meeting went on for many hours. Twenty, maybe thirty, people spoke at it. Finally the decision was taken to stop all work on diverting rivers and to write off the 100 million roubles already spent on the Siberian project and not return to the question again. Shortly afterwards the decision was published in the newspapers.

That was not the end of the matter, however. Opponents of the plan took their revenge. Both *Novy Mir* and *Nash Sovremennik* published selections of articles that told the truth, sometimes in a slightly emotional way, about the harm which that kind of river diversion could cause and about the people whose idea it was. Supporters of the project demanded that their replies, often very harshly worded, should also be published. They fought for yet another special high commission, which discussed the whole problem and decided once more that rivers should not be diverted. I headed the economic sections in this commission.

Nowadays nobody speaks directly about plans for diverting rivers. These people are looking for devious methods that would in time allow them to return to the old ideas.

The point is that by diverting part of the northern rivers of the European part of the country into the Volga, we should increase the flow of the Volga. This is needed for the canal that would direct the water into the Don as the second section of the Volga–Don canal is being built. It would also direct the waters of the Volga towards the Kalmyk steppes and the Stavropol region, to make irrigation in these areas possible. This would have been the purpose of the Volga–Chogray canal.

There are also discussions about redirecting part of the Volga's flow eastward into the river Ural, whose waters have been used up by numerous industrial enterprises, worsening conditions for fish of the sturgeon family. These spawn in the Volga delta and also in the Ural delta, which has become far too shallow.

Although all work on the diversion of part of the northern rivers' flow into the Volga has been stopped, the canals are still being constructed. This is an important point, since the construction of the canals was always intended to be connected with river diversion. The Volga–Don canal is being built at full speed. A certain amount of preparatory work has been done on the Volga –Chogray canal, although the final decision has not been taken and scientists and public figures have spoken out against it.

Recently the USSR Council of Ministers has noted popular feeling on the subject and decided to call a temporary halt to work on the Volga-Chogray canal pending the preparation of a new technical and economic examination of the need for it. In the end the Volga's waters will run dry and its delta will become even shallower, having already suffered in that respect after the construction of the dams for the hydroelectric power stations. The effect on the fish population, particularly in the lower parts of the river affected by the Volgograd hydroelectric power station, has been appalling. When the waters of the Volga disappear into the new canals, the situation in the delta will worsen still further, becoming catastrophic in drier years. We can expect reduced supplies of fish and an absolute lowering in the volume of large-scale agriculture which is conducted in the lower parts of the Volga. Then we shall once again be faced with the 'need' to feed the Volga with the waters of the northern rivers.

This is how I understand the arguments of the supporters of the river diversion scheme. And they intend to get their way, by hook or by crook.

However, if the costs were not to be borne by the state, if the regions that wanted this water had to pay for the construction out of their own budget, the whole scheme would die a natural death.

In reality, the situation is completely different. Every regional leader would like to get this water free, at the state's expense. Gradually, this sort of attitude will cease. In principle the decision has been taken to make users pay for water from the beginning of the next five-year plan. Another idea is being discussed: money advanced from the budget for large-scale building work is to be paid back in the future. But until this rule has been introduced we shall not see the end of people who want to get money from the state budget.

On the whole, perestroika has made and is making great changes in the way economic decisions are discussed and actually taken. The most important of these is the democratization of the whole process, the acceptance of the need for publicity in discussions and decision making. But, as I have already stated, we are still in the transitional stage between the old and new methods. We have begun the process of democratization and have achieved a great deal. But a great deal still needs to be done in connection with the resolutions of the 19th Party Conference on the reform of the political and legal systems, on the development of glasnost and on the need to fight bureaucratism. The fact that we are in transition may be seen from the decision-making and decision-taking process. While there are many examples of decisions being publicly discussed, there are many other examples of the old approach, with decisions taken in secret behind closed doors. This applies even to important problems.

Now I shall describe how things happen in reality.

Before a matter is discussed, let alone a decision taken, there have to be cogent reasons why that matter should be raised at all. On the large scale, the reason might be a complete change in economic policy, like the new economic policy adopted at the April Plenum of the Central Committee of the CPSU. A resolution like that would need a whole series of lesser ones to implement the new social policy and radical reform of management, to bring about the changes in investment and structural politics, and to find new approaches to international trade and economic relations.

In the previous sections I have described to the best of my ability how the concept of perestroika came into being, what factors led to it, and how it came into existence. What concerns me here is how an economic decision is reached after the need for it has manifested itself. Under the old administrative system, as I have already described, decisions were reached by the apparat and its members made sure that not even members of the scientific community, let alone members of the public at large, came anywhere near the decision-making process.

The situation is changing. The new leadership under Mikhail Gorbachev encourages scientists and public opinion in general to take part in the preparation and discussion of important decisions. Special organizations have been set up to ensure that this continues. For instance, decisions concerning various aspects of the restructuring of management are taken within the framework of the government Commission on Management, which is headed by the First Deputy Chairman of the Council of Ministers and President of Gosplan, Yuri Maslyukov.

The Commission includes the leaders of the central economic departments: three other Deputy Chairmen of the Council of Ministers – from the State Committee for Supplies, the State Committee for Science and Technology and the State Committee for International Trade Relations. Other members of the Commission on Management are the Finance Minister, the Chairman of the Committee for Labour and Social Affairs, the Chairman of Gosbank, the Chairman of the Committee for Prices, the Secretary of the All-Union Trade Union Council, representatives of permanent departments in the Council of Ministers, representatives of the economics department, representatives of the management department of the Council of Ministers and many other leading figures in economics and management.

At the same time there are other, equally important members

of the Commission. These are all practical or theoretical economists. I have been given the task of heading this group, and am
chairman of the scientific section of the Commission. Any particularly important decisions regarding the restructuring of management and requiring some scientific basis are first examined by the
scientific section according to a plan approved by the Commission.
When the Commission meets, it hears reports from the particular
economic section leader and from the chairman of the scientific
section or his deputy (at present Leonid Abalkin, the Director of
the Economics Institute of the Academy of Sciences).

Problems investigated by the scientific commission include the
reform of the banking system in the USSR; proposals for legislation
on shares and bonds; cost accounting in the republics and regions,
and how these should be related to the central organs; leasing
out industrial enterprises to working collectives; and preliminary
conclusions about the new economic system and industrial conglomerates. The scientific section is also reviewing the whole
question of economic reforms in other countries and the best way
of applying their experiences to the Soviet Union.

The scientific section consists of scientists who study problems
of management and economic mechanisms, and it unites scientific
institutes regardless of which department they come under. The
meetings of the scientific section are usually attended by one of
the directors of Gosplan and by representatives of the central
economic departments, who are often the speakers presenting the
papers. For instance if the Commission is discussing the question
of reforming the banking system, the introductory report will be
presented by one or more of the directors of Soviet banks. And so
on.

Having discussed the problem, the scientific section sets up its
own commissions to prepare the actual recommendations.

Important economic decisions are prepared in our country by
the group method. Commissions or working parties are set up and
given the task of discussing the proposal. If it is a particularly
important proposal, like the Law on Co-operatives, then the
working party leaves Moscow and takes up temporary residence
in a government dacha. They have the right to summon anyone
they wish for further consultation, but the main work is done
away from all distractions.

Once the proposal has been put together it is discussed at
several levels and before different kinds of audience. If it is a

proposal to do with management, then the first discussions take place at the meeting of the state commission on management. Copies of important proposals are usually sent out to the ministries and departments involved, to the Academy of Sciences and to the republics, and comments solicited. If the proposal concerns enterprises, copies of it may well be sent to a certain number of them.

Sometimes members of the government commission or of the scientific section, together with researchers from the management apparatus or from the central economic departments, take one of the projects to the regions and the republics. This happened when the Law on Enterprises was being discussed. The projected law is then put before representatives of regional and local authorities and enterprises and discussed on the spot. Proposals are adopted only after a great many amendments and additions.

Recently the Council of Ministers started holding extended meetings to discuss important projects. These are attended not only by members of the government but by specially invited specialists and even representatives of the public. For instance, when the proposal for a provisional law on state purchase orders for the years 1988–90 was discussed on two occasions by the Council of Ministers I was present on both.

The first of these sessions involved representatives of ministries and scientists, and although it lasted for six hours, the draft was not accepted. It was decided that directors of enterprises ought to be consulted and that they would be invited to the next meeting.

About six weeks later, early in August 1988, 100–150 people were invited to attend the next discussion in the Sverdlov Hall in the Kremlin, where there was plenty of space for everyone. Among those invited were many directors of enterprises from all over the country and other specialists. More than thirty people spoke. Everyone had received a copy of the draft before the meeting, and this time, despite a number of very important objections, the majority was in favour of it and it was accepted.

The draft was published in the Economic Gazette and became the regulation according to which state purchase orders were formulated for the years 1989 and 1990. This is completely different from what happened in 1983, when responsibility for the state purchase orders was handed over to the ministries, which turned the whole system into a virtual copy of the old directed distribution of tasks. They included 80–100 per cent of industry's entire nomenclature in the state purchase order, thus usurping the enterprises' power. In 1989 the volume of state purchase orders was sharply reduced; I reckon that only 50–60 per cent of the entire national economy's production will be taken up by them. In the manufacturing section the figure will be even lower – about 40 per cent. Ministries have been deprived of their right to decide state purchase orders, which will now be issued for the government by Gosplan and decided on centrally by government agencies.

When the decisions to be taken are strategic ones and involve the national interest, nationwide discussions are organized. Examples of such discussions were the ones that followed the early publication of the draft Laws on Enterprises, Co-operatives and Individual Labour Activity. This draft was discussed for five months and about 140,000 amendments were submitted. The commission took all of these into account and the amended draft went to the Plenum of the Central Committee of the CPSU.

After discussion at the Plenum, a few additional amendments were made and the completed draft was presented for discussion by the Supreme Soviet. The amendments had already been discussed by commissions of deputies. At the end of June 1987 the Supreme Soviet passed the Law on State Enterprises.

It has already been announced that there will be national discussions on the reform of pensions and retail prices. It is generally assumed that in future all major changes that concern the people directly will be taken only after nationwide discussions, such as the one proposed on the subject of health, improving the nation's health and the radical reform of the health service. Naturally enough, proposals for the next five-year plan are also to be discussed widely, and indeed we already have precedents for doing this.

At the same time we must note that members of our legislative assembly, the Supreme Soviet, can take part in this work only for short periods of time, since the sessions of the Soviet are not long. Shortly before each session, commissions of deputies get together but they only have time for a few meetings. Deputies have their own jobs to do as well as their duties as deputy, and they have very little time to delve deeply into the documents to be discussed at the sessions. That is why in the past discussions of draft laws have been a mere formality and voting was always unanimous.

This situation will change in the wake of the proposed political reforms whose main tenets were discussed and accepted at the

19th Party Conference. The basic aim of the reform is to return independent rights to the Soviets, the organs of national power. The highest organ will then be the Congress of People's Deputies. Delegates to this Congress will be elected by the people directly in electoral regions and also by meetings of various organizations. The rules for these elections will be established by the government.

The Congress of People's Deputies will elect the Supreme Soviet of the USSR, but this body will be smaller than in the past. Members of the government and other high officials cannot be elected to the Supreme Soviet, which is to wield all legislative power. The intention is that members of the Supreme Soviet will treat that membership as their main occupation. Therefore they will be either partially or completely freed from their previous occupations and will be able to devote adequate time and attention to the debates at the sessions.

The Supreme Soviet will set up a number of commissions to discuss thoroughly all projects, including ones that concern the national economy. These commissions will also be able to initiate new economic and other decisions.

The Supreme Soviet will elect the executive branch of the government, in the shape of the Council of Ministers, which will be wholly responsible to its electors. The same system will be adopted by all the republics and some of the regions.

We must not in future departmentalize major economic decisions but should rather discuss them collectively from the point of view of the entire economy. In the past the preparation of a project was entrusted to those people for whom the project was actually intended; for instance, the apparat of Gosbank prepared the draft Law on State Banking. Naturally the people who worked on it made sure the most important functions were reserved for Gosbank, that the State Bank was kept high above the others and had more rights and fewer obligations than other banks.

In the same way the drafting of a statute about the Ministry of Finance was entrusted to officials from that Ministry. They, naturally enough, included such matters as the regulation of the banking system by the Ministry of Finance. They too tried to place themselves above everyone else, to give themselves special rights and special powers.

Of course, a draft is only a first step. It is then discussed more widely, first of all by the government Commission on Management. In the course of these discussions working parties are formed whose task it is to take into account the various comments made and to change what was originally a departmental document into one that will be relevant to the whole economy. But they are not always successful, because everyone who works on a draft is influenced by the original text.

This situation has changed in one respect at least. Often, nowadays, the working parties that prepare the original document include scientists and other experts on the subject. They are given sufficient time to study the problem carefully and to prepare their proposals meticulously. Alas, even so, they are affected by the time limits. And these changes in the composition of the preparatory discussion groups are still only half-hearted. It is still the apparat of the particular department that plays the largest part in the preparation of the draft, and they will try to retain their powers and privileges. So far no adequate antidote to the efforts of the apparat has been devised. Only scientists and social scientists speak up against them and, in cases that concern the environment, the public at large.

Once the draft has been prepared it is submitted for discussion, and at this stage every effort is made to draw in the widest possible circle of people, in order for the best possible variant to be adopted. And, indeed, many valuable amendments are made during these discussions. However, to be completely honest it must be admitted that scientific commissions are quite often unprepared when called upon for advice and do not know how to argue for changes in such drafts or how to present more balanced and effective counter-proposals. There are historical reasons for this relative ineffectiveness of science in contrast to administration. The situation is an excellent illustration of the tenet that science becomes weaker if there is no demand for its findings, as was the case during the period of stagnation. Not only was there no demand for their findings but scientists were actually persecuted for having new ideas or bold thoughts and were encouraged to submit to all official decisions.

Now, thank God, the period of stagnation is over. We have quite definitely started out on the road of glasnost and democracy. We are in the middle of the process of perestroika. But, as Mikhail Gorbachev pointed out quite recently, we are still restructuring ourselves – we have not yet done so.

In this transitional period we can still find the old approaches in some places. Under the administrative system, the rule of bureaucracy was complete – the bureaucrats were all-powerful. They made all the decisions and signed them off, not worrying too much about the legal aspect. Lawyers were the people who had to make laws to fit what had been decided. Theirs was not to take part in the decision making. Unfortunately, to some extent this attitude to the legal profession is still with us. The government Commission on Management, whose task it is to prepare various decisions, has twenty members, not one of whom is a lawyer. In the same way, when a draft law is discussed, say by the Council of Ministers, lawyers may be asked for references but never for their opinions.

It is easy to see in our new rules and regulations, for example the ones referring to the organization of joint enterprises, that qualified lawyers were not involved in the formulation of those documents. The wording is often imprecise and capable of several interpretations, while some articles even contradict others. This is of immense advantage to those bureaucrats in the apparat who wish to retain their powers and privileges. They revel in these contradictions and spend their time searching for all those resolutions, points and sub-points which speak in their favour and distort all the others.

This kind of disdainful attitude to the legal aspect of the new documents is reflected in our all-pervasive legal nihilism. Legal education is badly provided for in the USSR. Even the College of Economics had for years no compulsory law course. Even when there was one, it was very short and disorganized. Nobody recognized the fact that a proper knowledge of law and legality was essential if one was to make serious economic decisions.

To some extent this shortcoming has been recognized. A legal reform is under preparation. The immediate task is the restructuring of our state as a legal one. This means that in the future the law will reign supreme, that all citizens' rights will be protected and the principle of equality before the law will be firmly fixed. This transition to the rule of law will, without doubt, allow us to improve the legal quality of our major economic decisions.

IS PERESTROIKA IRREVERSIBLE?

*Is it legitimate to use historical analogies in an
analysis of economic reforms?*

Whenever one answers questions on the subject of reforms in the
Soviet Union, whenever one gives interviews, one is inevitably
faced with this question: has perestroika reached a point when it
can be said to be irreversible? Usually people who ask this question
add: 'We remember, after all, other reforms, other perestroikas,
in your country, and look what happened to them.'

The New Economic Policy proclaimed by Lenin lasted only
eight or nine years. Then the management and market mechanism
was replaced by 'diktat', a semi-military economy linked to Stalin's
repressions. Then came the thaw under Khrushchev. In 1953–4
there was a sudden move towards economic methods, especially
in agriculture, and retail trade began to develop. The standard of
living rose. After a mere six years, there came another change.
We were back with arbitrary decisions, administrative methods
of management, and endless reorganizations. The whole process
ended unhappily with a worsening standard of living in the first
half of the sixties and price rises for meat and dairy products.
Finally in 1964–5 came the so-called economic reform of agriculture and industry, involving economic methods of management,

talks about caring and material incentives, about reviving the economic system and making noticeable improvements in people's lives. But after five or six years, we regressed to the administrative methods, all independent initiatives were cut short, cost accounting was abandoned and enterprise was suppressed. The inevitable result was a deceleration, until, by the end of the seventies, the country was in a state of stagnation and very near to a crisis.

So now we have something new: the perestroika of 1985. Why should we think that this one will be irreversible, that the changes will be long-term, that this reform will not share the fate of all the preceding ones? This is a very serious question: we might even say that it is the absolute crux of the matter, never to be dismissed, laughed off, or answered with a witticism. It is the question we must answer.

Just like everyone else involved in perestroika, I have thought about what we must do to make sure that the process becomes irreversible. After all, this is not some simple question of polemics, of propaganda. We are talking about our very lives, about the fate of our country. As I write in mid-1988, I have to admit quite honestly that in the three years that have elapsed since the new economic strategy was proclaimed by Mikhail Gorbachev at the April Plenum of the Central Committee of the CPSU, we have not managed to reach the stage of being able to say that perestroika is irreversible. This was honestly acknowledged at the 19th Party Conference in June 1988. After all, the main purpose of this conference was to work out a series of further measures that would ensure the irreversibility of perestroika.

Let us review this problem together, and discuss the various arguments.

All the above questions rely on historical analogy. Undoubtedly history teaches us much about life. That is why the great Russian historian Karamzin called history 'the sacred book of the people'. But all the same we must first ask ourselves whether a historical analogy is in fact legitimate. Does our perestroika look exactly like all those other economic reforms attempted in the Soviet Union?

I have to admit: yes, in many ways, it does. There is a certain logic in all the twists and turns of NEP, the immediate post-Stalin period, and the economic reforms of the mid-sixties. First of all, these policies always sought to redirect the economy and always aimed to improve people's lives. During the NEP we put an end

118

to famine, and workers' real incomes actually overtook those of before the revolution and the First World War. Towards the end of the NEP there was no unemployment and the workers had acquired a certain standard of living. Every one of these achievements was destroyed during the forcible collectivization of agriculture and the arbitrary redirection of the economy towards industrial growth during the 1st Five-year Plan. As a result there were once again famine, deaths, a return to rationing, and a marked worsening of people's lives.

The years 1954–9 were ones of large-scale market development and improved standards of living. During those six years, production of food increased by 60 per cent, and there was a radical improvement in the quality of the Soviet people's nutrition. People also started dressing better. You could feel the change. I entered the Economics Institute in 1950. Most of the boys wore hand-me-down military shirts from their fathers, worn old trousers, dilapidated boots. Even when we went out in the evening we had nothing else to wear. Everyone was poor. In the Moscow State Economics Institute our dinners cost us 2 roubles (now 20 kopecks since the currency reform), but there was no meat either in the soup or in the main course. Mostly it was buckwheat and boiled potatoes, which were a delicacy to us. You could also have a special dinner for 3 roubles (30 kopecks). This allegedly had meat in one of the courses, but it needed a miracle to find it. I remember the great excitement towards the end of my studies when bread was simply put out on the table and everyone could take as much as they wanted. The supply of accommodation was no better. I knew many people, but not one of them lived with his family in a separate flat, although there must have been people who did. My uncle, a distinguished doctor and director of a large hospital, lived modestly: his family of three lived in an airy 20-square-metre room in a communal flat. A professor from Moscow University lived with his family in one of the other rooms and a well-known doctor in another. Altogether there were six or seven families sharing the flat's facilities. My uncle managed to be allocated a second room in that flat, an unheard-of privilege. The only consumer durables that the richest people had were old wireless sets and hand-operated sewing machines. No one had television sets, refrigerators or cars.

Everything changed over the next six years, and we left that poverty-stricken life behind. Consumer durables such as refrigerators, television sets, washing machines, electric sewing machines, bicycles and so on were produced in large quantities. There were passenger cars for people to buy, and modern trade began to develop. This was the time when GUM (the State Department Store) and Detsky Mir (the Children's Department Store) were opened in Moscow and when new restaurants and cafés opened every month. New housing sprang up and families began to move into their own separate flats with all modern conveniences.

In the immediate post-war years there were many beggars who just sat in the streets or wandered up and down suburban trains asking for money. This ceased in the fifties. The minimum wage was increased sharply. In 1956 a new law on pensions was passed, setting high pension levels of 60 per cent of salary and a pensionable age which was the lowest in the world – 55 for women and 60 for men. The figures show that average real incomes went up in the period 1954–9 by 39 per cent.

There then followed a return to arbitrary methods of management. Agricultural production ceased to grow. Since incomes continued to rise, this meant there were immediate food shortages. Suddenly flour was rationed. In 1962–3 there were even bread shortages, and the quality of goods went down. In 1962 prices of meat and dairy products in state shops went up. But this did not affect the shortages, so that even sugar could sometimes be acquired only with great difficulty. Life had become so much better in the previous period that it was difficult to reconcile oneself to the endless queues, shortages, and ever higher prices in the kolkhoz (collective farm) markets. It was in 1963 that the Soviet Union for the first time bought grain instead of selling it.

After Khrushchev's overthrow the immediate difficulties of stagnation were quickly solved. Within a few months there came radical proposals for increasing agricultural production by the use of economic incentives and more economic methods of management. So food production once again rose phenomenally, by 4 per cent or more a year. Meat and milk immediately reappeared in the shops; bread improved. The building programme continued and 10 million people a year moved into better accommodation. During the Five-year Plan of 1966–70, production of consumer goods went up by half as much again, and there was a serious attempt to involve heavy industrial and defence industry enterprises in solving the consumer goods problem. But, alas, this improvement in the standard of living was short-lived. From the early seventies onwards, the situation worsened, till in 1979–82 we reached a position where there was an actual lowering of standards. The social spheres were now financed on the remainder principle, and there was a noticeable reduction in spending on education and health.

And now we have the new, modern perestroika – new social policies, new spending on the social sphere, a breakaway from stagnation in the provision of housing and socially necessary buildings, much greater expenditure on health and education, redoubled growth of food production, triple growth in the services section, and vast capital and currency investments in the development of light industry.

Of course, at every stage of socialist development there were specific problems connected with social welfare to be solved. Our standard of living now is immeasurably higher than it was in earlier periods. Nevertheless, we should note one common factor: every progressive economic strategy is primarily connected with a move in the national economy towards the well-being of the people, or, in other words, with the social re-orientation of economic policy.

This is natural, since to develop one's economy one must rely on people as the main productive force and instrument of progress. And experience here as well as in other socialist countries has demonstrated that this turn towards the people at historically important moments inevitably results in greater productive and social activity, more efficient work, and greater social productivity – in other words, greater national wealth and economic might.

Now in the USSR agriculture plays a particularly important part in the economy. Up to two-thirds of all consumer goods are produced in the agricultural sector – foods, products made from natural materials, leather, and so on. There are thousands of invisible ties between the countryside and the city, since the majority of our city dwellers are from the villages. Therefore, every move in our economic policies is directly connected with the way agriculture is run, with a change in attitude towards agriculture, with the search for ways to encourage it to develop and to make it democratic. Symbolically, these moves always seem to start with Plenums of the Central Committee of the CPSU devoted to agriculture.

Let us consider the NEP, although Lenin's famous proposal

that the food tax should be replaced by food distribution was addressed directly to the peasant. The post-Stalin changes began with the September 1953 Plenum, which discussed possible measures for the development of agriculture. The economic reform of the mid-sixties started at the March 1965 Plenum on agriculture.

During the present reforms the first management reorganizations and the first innovations in the economic mechanism were introduced in the agricultural sector. The old economic system based on agricultural departments was liquidated; instead, the new Gosagroprom (State Agriculture and Industry Organization) was set up on a territorial principle. Private allotments were encouraged, as were gardening and vegetable growing. The idea of family holdings was widely canvassed. Recently higher forms of renting based on leaseholding have been encouraged. State and collective farms have been granted greater independence in the matter of unplanned production. Many other new ideas have been tried out, including the formation of a special Agro-Industrial Bank to serve the agricultural sector and related branches of the economy.

The reason I mention this is that I have noticed that whenever I talk to Sovietologists, that is people who study and understand developments in our country, they always return to the same question – why did we not do as in previous reforms and start our perestroika with agriculture? Then they always add: look at China; they started their perestroika with agrarian reforms and achieved immediate results. Since 1978, when the reforms began, agricultural production in China has doubled, and the country now produces 400 million tons of grain – more than the USA does. This has noticeably improved people's lives. Usually I reply that in fact we too began perestroika by restructuring management in agriculture. However, that was right at the beginning, and at the time we did not have a wide concept of the new system. The forces of inertia were still very strong and we still thought we could somehow combine administrative and economic methods of management. Also the measures we passed for improving agricultural management were not discussed as openly as, say, the recent Law on Co-operatives, because we had not yet developed glasnost either. We did not even organize a congress of collective farmers to discuss the reforms in the management of agriculture.

Looking back at the whole process from the position we have achieved today, it would seem that the measures we took to reform agriculture were not revolutionary enough. For example, we did not get rid of the administrative tyranny of the various local party authorities over the state and collective farms. With the benefit of hindsight, it is clear we ought to have done more.

The most striking example of a change from 'diktat' economics to economic management was the introduction of the New Economic Policy in place of War Communism. Under War Communism a large part of the peasant's produce was confiscated without payment or compensation to its producer. This was called the food tax, and it left the peasant and his family the barest minimum to survive on. The New Economic Policy, as Lenin proclaimed, substituted food distribution for food tax. In other words the peasant surrendered a smaller part of his produce than before to the state and was paid for this according to firmly established state prices. The remainder, which was in fact the larger part, stayed in the peasant's possession for him to sell on the market. This new system greatly strengthened the incentive to work. Harvests improved at once and the marked increase in agricultural production gave a push to factories, which now had to produce machinery for the peasantry so as to get food in return. Commodity circulation between town and village livened up and led to the growth of the whole economy during the NEP. As the peasant now had surplus produce which he was allowed to sell on the market, a wide market was created and the relationship between goods and money became more productive. There was an equivalent relationship between town and village within the commodity circulation and this meant that both peasants and workers had an incentive to improve efficiency.

While the new market developed in the years after the October Revolution enterprises and conglomerates were also put on to a cost accounting system. In other words they were expected to pay their way out of their own profit. There were discussions about how to ensure that wages stimulated production. With the help of its planning activities and financial credit policy the state learnt to control the market and to regulate it indirectly. Instead of the economic blockade and the virtual absence of any kind of economic relationship with the outside world, as had been the case during the Civil War, the NEP years saw a gradual revival of economic relations between the Soviet Union and the rest of the world. The first steps towards achieving this were made under Lenin, who welcomed this development.

How the science of economics was uprooted under Stalin

The twenties were an exceptionally interesting period in our country's economic history, as they saw the establishment of peace-time socialist economics, that is to say the birth of the economic practice of socialism and the testing of theories by that practice. It was a period of noisy debates and discussions about ways for our country to develop.

At that time our country had a fair number of talented economists who were brought up in the zemstvo* statistics departments, a world-famous school of socialist science. Those involved in the discussions included the most important ideologists and economists of that time, people like Bukharin, author of a well-known book about the economics of the transitional period; Preobrazhensky; Kondratyev, who developed the famous theory of waiting cycles in economics; Chayanov, a leading specialist on the development of co-operatives; and many, many others. Quite a few journals on the theory and practice of economics were published in the country. Dozens and even hundreds of books on statistics and economic analysis were also published. All the discussions were conducted openly and were much commented on in the press.

The gradual growth of Stalin's cult of personality and the repressions which started about then fell in the first place on the ideologists and economists. Hardly any of them survived. Bukharin, Preobrazhensky, Chayanov, Kondratyev and many others were liquidated. Economic journals were closed down *en masse*. Economics institutes like the Institute of Theoretical Economics, the Central Institute of Labour Studies, and the Red Professors' Institute, where many of the discussions had been conducted, were disbanded. Statistics were first distorted, then simply abolished. In many important spheres statistical data were no longer published. It became a particularly heinous crime even to attempt to compare or contrast. For instance the well-known Professor Kubanin's attempt to compare tractor parks in the USSR and the United States in an article on economic problems resulted in the author's arrest, the closure of the journal and the arrest of several members of its editorial staff. Stalin and his clique

* Zemstovs were organs of regional government in tsarist days.

were particularly impatient with any new theory, any new word on any subject. When one of our best-known economists, one of the ideologists of Gosplan, Academician Strumilin, began to work on various ways of balancing the national economy of the Soviet Union, he was immediately forced to stop. The leading journal *Bolshevik* published an article about him under the title 'A Balancing of Monstrous Mistakes'. He was sacked, and although he was not persecuted, he could not publish anything for the rest of Stalin's reign. He was forced to study the history of metallurgy in Russia and wrote an outstanding work on the subject. Later, after Stalin's death, he was quite rightly awarded the Lenin Prize for it.

It pains me to write of these matters, because when I was beginning my work in economics in the fifties I became genuinely close to a number of older economists who had been young in the twenties and had done serious research but were subsequently arrested and spent time in prisons and labour camps. Only in the fifties, after Stalin's cult of personality had been condemned, were they released and allowed to take up their work again. I recall with sympathy a friend of Academician Strumilin, Lev Mints. I was fortunate enough to be his opponent when he was defending his doctoral dissertation. I was quite astonished to discover that all his work on statistics and labour problems had been done either in the twenties or in the late fifties. In between, he had been, as we say, not a million miles from home. His dissertation was extremely good and we voted for it unanimously. Apart from doing enormous amounts of research, Mints took on a great deal of serious organizational duties. He worked in the Moscow Scientists' Club and was actively involved in the organization of conferences and seminars. And all this he did as an unpaid volunteer. I remember visiting him once at home. He had a small room and lived alone, as his wife had not waited for his release. He cooked for himself, and his entire life was in his work.

Another of our outstanding economists, Albert Weinstein, took up a leading position in economics immediately on coming out of prison. He was a man of exceptionally wide knowledge and understanding, and a brilliant polemicist. In an incredibly short time he wrote his master's dissertation on Russia's national income. This dissertation was so professional, showed such a profundity of understanding and knowledge of sources, including materials that were unique, that someone suggested that

Weinstein should be awarded a PhD for it. This was approved unanimously, an extremely rare occurrence. Albert Weinstein told me that he was one of the first to be arrested at the beginning of the period of repressions, because he was supposed to belong to the banned 'industrialist party', which was alleged to be opposed to the Communist Party. Preobrazhensky and many others were tried at the same time. In reality, as Weinstein told me, he merely liked beautiful women and courted them assiduously. As he was chasing Preobrazhensky's wife, he got himself noticed by the secret police and subsequently found himself behind bars. He was an extremely witty man. When he was asked whether it was true that he had had many wives he replied with a smile that only savages said 'many' after they had run out of fingers to count on. After he had been awarded his PhD there was, as usual, a banquet. Someone asked him: 'How can it be that you spent twenty years in camp, then came out, and immediately wrote your dissertation? Could you study in camp? Did you have books there?' 'Goodness me, no,' he replied. 'I was grateful that I managed to become a stoker for a while in the camp I was in. Of course I regressed as a scientist in that time, but then economics did not stay in one place either. It regressed too. So we caught up with each other.'

There was a great deal of truth in that bitter remark. Under Stalin, economics did indeed move backwards. It became mere quotation-mongering and dogmatism; it lost any connection with real life and statistics, and in fact declined into mere apologetics and propaganda. It had lost its true meaning as the guideline for socialist development. What incredible abilities and moral strength the economists of the twenties must have had if the leading ones were destroyed; after all the ones who survived had been relatively young, in their late twenties, at the time of their arrest. And having been through all the torments of hell and returned, they did not simply resume productive work but very quickly became the leading economists of the country. They amazed younger people with their irrepressible energy, their capacity for work and their profound knowledge.

To take one example: I had the most profound respect for our well-known statistician Yakov Kvasha. When I worked in Siberia I often visited the Magadan region, the Kolyma road, and when I came to Moscow I always went to see Kvasha, who invariably asked me whether I had been to the gold mine in the Valley of the Four Marshals on the Kolyma river. That was what the valley had been called before Marshals Tukhachevsky, Yakir and others were liquidated, and that is what it is still called, though officially it has a different name. I specially visited the mine, but all that remained of the old buildings were a few of the foundations and pillars where the prisoners' barracks had been. Nothing else was left of what had once been a large labour camp, one of whose nameless, numbered inmates was Yakov Kvasha.

Kvasha was a statistician, a man of fine intellect and sensibility. He loved to repeat the *bon mot* of the nineteenth-century British prime minister Disraeli, that there were three kinds of lies: lies, damned lies and statistics. I well remember his marvellous work on levels of mechanization and manual labour in the USSR. Although I had worked on these problems for several years in the economic section of the Labour Committee attached to the Council of Ministers (1955–61), I was still astonished at the backwardness of our country at the time; I could not reconcile myself to the fact that even after industrialization more than half our workers, even in industry, were employed as manual labourers. Our published percentages of mechanization distorted the picture, because they did not calculate labour but units of work.

Our best specialist on the efficiency of capital investment and the economic problems of the building industry is Victor Krasovsky, who spent many years in a labour camp in the Norilsk region. When he was a little younger he spent many years as head of the capital investments section of Gosplan's Institute of Economic Research, transferring later to the equivalent section of the USSR Academy of Sciences' Institute of Economics, where he worked with Academician Tigran Khachaturov. I was constantly amazed by the depth of his understanding of his subject. Like all the members of the old guard of economists, he knew and loved statistics. He based his decisions on the summation of enormous amounts of factual material, took an active part in various expert discussions, and was one of the first to work on the problems of timed capital investment for the solution of our economic difficulties. He is still one of the directors of the very active Special Council of the Academy of Sciences that deals with capital investments.

Among our close family friends is Semyon Heynman, at over eighty still one of our foremost economists. His major works on the structure of our production, its organization, specialization, the problems of mechanical construction, and trends in scientific and technological development are still consulted by economists.

His own productivity is astonishing. He is constantly publishing fascinating new articles, carefully reads all reports about new equipment in the USA, studies all newly published books on economics, and is always full of new ideas and new approaches. The other day he called me on the telephone and said: 'Let's write a book about our country and call it *Spendthrift Economics* – there was a book with that title about America in the twenties, but we have our own brand of extravagance, our own reasons for it, and our own way of fighting it.' When I started a new, extremely popular economics journal, *EKO* (the first three letters of the word 'economics' in Russian), I invited Semyon Heynman to join the editorial board. This was a very good move; although he was almost twice as old as most of us, he became the life and soul of the board. He hardly ever missed a meeting, visiting Novosibirsk very frequently, and was always full of new ideas, new suggestions for articles. Our beginnings were quite modest – a mere 8,000 copies in the first year. Then we doubled the number of copies every year and the journal itself became larger. Now it is published in more than 160,000 copies. To a great extent this growth is the achievement of Semyon Heynman. Unfortunately both he and I have recently had to leave the journal, because the Academy of Sciences decided that no one should remain as editor or on the editorial board for more than two terms, and we had both worked for three, from 1970 to 1985.

I have told these stories about people close to me not simply because I wish to describe the role they played in my development as an economist but because I want the reader to understand in full the harm done to our society by Stalin's cult of personality, by the repressions. This small example of how Stalin dealt with our economists shows how much we lost because we did not have the specialists of the twenties with us in the difficult thirties and forties.

Immediately after the war, when our enormous victory caused a certain social uplift and people for a time breathed more freely, many economists came back from the front hardened and inspired by victory. They took an active part in scientific research and tried to understand economic ideas from the rest of the world. There was great interest at that time in the role played by economics in the West.

But Stalin was in no way about to relinquish his supremacy in the social sciences, including economics. In 1948 he and Zhdanov launched a campaign against the so-called 'cosmopolitanism' of the intelligentsia. Scientists were accused of worshipping foreign idols, and an era of mass denunciations began. The dogmatists and Stalin's and Zhdanov's henchmen called all progressive scientists 'restorers of capitalism'. One of my teachers, whose works I consider to be seminal, Professor Victor Novozhilov, dared to suggest at a discussion on the effectiveness of capital investment that we should establish efficiency norms. There was a huge outcry. He was accused of wanting the return of capitalism, where norms are set for profits, interest on investment, and so on. In the end Novozhilov, though a professor at the Leningrad Polytechnic, was kicked out. For a while he survived on occasional earnings, but he was not published any more.

Another of my teachers, the outstanding economist and statistician Academician Vasili Nemchinov, was also deprived of his job for a long time. He had begun his career in the old zemstvo statistics office and was an outstanding specialist in agricultural statistics. He was also the rector of the Timiryazev Agricultural Academy, which stood up against Lysenko, the man who destroyed all progressive science in his fight against what he called 'Weismannism' and reaction, that is to say, scientific genetics. This tragedy for Soviet agriculture and ideology was compounded in 1948 when scientists were harried at political meetings devoted to this question. Only a few of those criticized in quite unprintable language by Lysenko in the name of the Central Committee dared to speak up and defend their own and their colleagues' point of view. Among these was the unforgettable Vasili Nemchinov. He spoke twice of the scientific foundations of Mendel's and Weismann's teaching. He was of course sacked, and for a time nothing he wrote was published. Yet both Novozhilov and Nemchinov contributed a great deal to the study of economics, a fact which became clear only in the last years of their lives. In the sixties Novozhilov managed to publish his study which became world-famous: *How to Measure Outlay and Reserves in the Socialist Economy*. With this he, together with his friend, the Nobel Prizewinner Leonid Kantorovich, laid the foundations of the theory of optima in socialist economics. Nemchinov was one of the first Soviet economists to evaluate correctly the importance of the optimal approach and of the use of mathematical models and computers in economics research and planning.

When Nemchinov was fired from the Timiryazev Academy,

where he had been rector and head of the department of statistics, he began work at the Academy of Sciences. It is to the Academy's credit that the majority of its members always spoke up against Lysenko and gave support to the real scientists he persecuted. Lysenko therefore hated the 'Big Academy', wrote endless denunciations of it in the various party organs and was always trying to get his own supporters elected to membership. Quite often the Academy refused. One of Lysenko's allies, Nuzhdin, was vociferously rejected when put up for election in 1964. Academician Andrei Sakharov spoke up against him – an unheard-of thing at the time, since he was, if one chose to view it that way, speaking against the recommendation of the party. I became a corresponding member in 1964 and so was not present at that meeting, but I heard about it from the older academicians, who also told me that Lysenko complained to Khrushchev, saying amongst other things that the Academy of Sciences was a survival from the tsarist system and ought to be closed down. They also told me that in the last few months of his rule Khrushchev did seriously think about disbanding the Academy. This was the period when he did nothing but reorganize: he divided the regional party organizations into agricultural and industrial sections, changed the number of classes in schools, abolished Gosplan, and introduced many other reforms of that nature.

Khrushchev's and Kosygin's economic reforms – the forerunners of perestroika

A new age began with the death of Stalin. As I have already said, there was a major shift in economic strategy. The crucial September 1953 Plenum of the Central Committee of the CPSU undermined the 'diktat' system of management in agriculture, made an important move towards the introduction of economic methods of management, and revived the collective farms' interest in the results of their labour. It would not be an exaggeration to compare the decisions of this Plenum in importance with the decision to substitute food distribution for food tax. It is against the latter that we measure the introduction of economic methods in the management of agriculture. Stalinism damaged agriculture most of all. When Stalin acquired almost unlimited power in the late twenties, he ferociously demolished all Lenin's plans for the co-operatives. The NEP was developed in Lenin's last years. He witnessed the revival of the economy that had been buried under the debris of the First World War. In 1921 famine had killed millions of people. Following that, the country had managed to rise to general prosperity. As we know, Lenin was very ill in the last few years before his death and was not politically active. With all his remaining strength he concentrated on thinking and planning for the future. When his condition worsened and it became clear that he would not live much longer, he could no longer write or even think of detailed studies, but he did dictate brief articles, notes and letters which together make up his political testament.

Lenin selected a few of the enormous number of questions facing the country and dealt with them. The question of co-operatives was central among these, and he dictated a whole article on the subject. Lenin's opinion was that Russia's peasant millions would reach socialism through the co-operatives. In his private library in the Kremlin apartment there are about 200 books about co-operatives. Many bear Lenin's own annotations: one such is the famous book by Chayanov, the economist I mentioned above. Lenin particularly insisted that co-operatives must be voluntary and said that they need to come in many shapes and sizes. The first ones, he thought, should be supply and trading co-operatives, as these would be easier to set up and more likely to bring the peasants immediate profits. Only then, always taking into account people's wishes, should farming co-operatives – collective farms – be organized. Stalin ignored this recommendation of Lenin's, though it was a particularly important one. It was decided that peasants must be forced to join co-operatives, and only one kind was permitted – collective farms, the kolkhozes. The peasants were deprived of their animals, the tools of their trade, and their land. These were all given over into the ownership of the kolkhozes. At the same time war was declared against the kulaks, slightly wealthier peasants who made use of seasonal hired labour. They were persecuted or even murdered out of hand. Next the term 'kulak' was extended to include all wealthier peasants and all who did not want to hand over their horse or their cow, who were not too keen on taking their one sack of grain to the communal barn. They were forcibly 'dekulakized' and also exiled to Siberia and the North. No preparations were made for the formation of the kolkhozes. The confiscated cattle were often left unfed, and grain would rot away in a collective farm's barn that as like as not had a hole in the roof. There was absolutely no incentive to work. Half the cattle and a large part of the grain was destroyed. The volume of agricultural production was halved. The government was forced to introduce rationing, the shops emptied of food, and the black market flourished. A famine started which, together with the war against the peasants, carried away millions of lives.

When all this became clear Stalin was forced to slow down and even reverse his course. In his article 'Dizzy with Success', he attacked the local authorities over what he called excess zeal in collectivization. The villages were granted a reprieve, things became a little easier, production started growing, and rationing was at last abolished; but agriculture remained in a depressed state. The villages were finally ruined by the war. The menfolk joined the army, and the entire burden of carrying on agricultural production fell on the women's shoulders. The peasants were enslaved by the administrative system. They could not leave their collective farms, much less settle in the city. They could do none of these things because they did not have internal passports. To move to the city and work there, a peasant had first to receive administrative permission and then an internal passport.

Stalin virtually restored the food tax by introducing the system of state procurement. A sizeable proportion of the peasants' produce was taken away by the state in return for a symbolic payment that did not even cover costs. Furthermore all means of production, such as tractors, combine harvesters and other agricultural machinery, ceased to belong to the collective farms. These were transferred to the state mechanical-tractor stations (MTS), which had various privileges the collective farms did not have. The people employed there were highly paid machine operators, and the village was obliged to give them the best houses and so on because they did the mechanized work on the land and at harvest time. Collective farms paid the state for the labour provided by the MTS. Naturally the rate was not fair: the collective farms paid more than the value of what they actually received. What was left of the produce after the state procurement had been met was also sold to the state, for slightly more money – but the rate was still unfair. As a result of this system the collective farms had very little produce and even less money. The peasants worked under duress: they could not refuse to work, because then their personal allotment was taken away from them and it was this tiny scrap of land that to a great extent fed the family. Agricultural work was depersonalized and was even calculated in so-called 'duty-days'. At the end of the year the peasants were paid for the number of 'duty-days' they had done in accordance with the harvest and the means at the collective farm's disposal. Usually they were paid in kind. For instance a peasant would be given 300 grams of grain, a little hay and a few kopecks per 'duty-day'. By and large the peasants could be said to live in a primitive subsistence economy. Almost every household kept a cow, hens and pigs, which to a certain extent kept them in food. The peasants would take part of the produce from their personal allotment to the kolkhoz market in town several times a year and would use the money thus earned to buy sugar, clothes, household utensils etc.

As it happened, in 1953–4 I visited several villages in the middle region of Russia, relatively close to Moscow. This was because in 1953 I married Zoya Kupriyanova, then a student at the Moscow State Institute of Economics, whose parents were from Zhokhovo in the Vladimir region, about 150 km from Moscow. She maintained close links with her family and friends there, and I also visited her parents' village and several of the villages around there. There were no services in the village. There was not even a shop; to buy anything one had to go to the neighbouring village, where the shop was open twice a week. But there was not much to be had even when the shop was open: vodka, sugar and a few consumer goods. The households were entirely self-sufficient. Most families even made their own bread. Meat, dairy products, eggs, potatoes, vegetables, mushrooms – all that was produced by each family. There was practically no trade in the village. It had no road; only a path led there. It was situated on the bank of a river, in a high place, but in the spring, when the river flooded, one could get to it only on a horse or a tractor. In some years the peasants would be paid nothing for their 'duty-days'. I can still hear them complaining that they had a new chairman of the collective farm every year, all of them drunkards. Once the peasants insisted that a woman should be appointed chairman, but soon even she started drinking. Possibly the situation was different in other places, but almost half the villages at that time had no electricity, even though there was a power line nearby.

From time to time my wife's parents would get visits by peasant women from the collective farms who had come to town to sell various things on the market. People who brought their produce in large bags on their backs were in those days called bagmen: they sold their produce on the market and went back to the village, having bought sugar and other things. Of course, they had no money for hotels or taxis despite their heavy bags. The money they made was pathetic – not more than 20–30 roubles in old money (2–3 roubles since the reform).

The future of the country depended on its agriculture, especially as two-thirds of the country's population lived in the villages. Their lives depended on the development of agriculture; but then so did the lives of the urban dwellers.

At the September 1953 Plenum of the Central Committee of the CPSU, Khrushchev spoke at length about the appalling state of agriculture. The most important part of his speech was a series of suggestions for the economic reorganization of the countryside. These suggestions seemed absolutely incredible for those days. Events speed up in times of reform: Stalin had died in March, and by September a whole series of new and well-documented proposals had been prepared with the aim of rapidly developing agriculture.

First and foremost, the September Plenum abolished the state procurement of agricultural products, and we have not had any kind of food tax since then. It was also decided to raise prices on agricultural products and introduce fair prices for goods traded between town and country. At the same time, taxes were reduced and peasants were encouraged to cultivate their private allotments. Various resolutions designed to help the villages were passed. The September Plenum was the beginning of a new start in our agriculture: it was integrated into the country's trade and financial system, and the collective farm peasants' pay became monetary rather than in kind. We had arrived at a more advanced form of payment for the peasants' labour. The September Plenum also greatly increased the collective farm peasants' income. Previously it had been a fraction of industrial workers' pay; it was the September Plenum that began the move towards equalizing the two. The collective farms acquired greater economic independence, and new, more energetic and more knowledgeable people took over their leadership. Under Khrushchev a new call was sounded and thousands of leading communists responded to it:

134

go to the more backward collective farms and develop them. Advances were made in agronomy, especially the wider use of crop rotation and a greater emphasis on preserving the soil's natural fertility. Agricultural productivity, which had stayed at the same low level in the years before the war, with virtually no growth at all, increased in the immediate post-Stalin period. Before 1953, the grain harvest in the Soviet Union had amounted usually to 7–8 centners per hectare; by 1958–9 it rose to 12–13 centners. At the same time the 2-kg barrier on dairy cattle productivity was also broken.

In 1954 an important decision was taken about the cultivation of virgin and fallow lands. The aim was to develop agriculture and solve the problem of grain shortages not by increased productivity but by bringing new lands into the equation. This combination of extensive and intensive development helped to increase the volume of agricultural production between 1954 and 1959 by 7.4 per cent per annum. This was the period of the fastest growth in agricultural production in our country, and it was achieved by the use of economic methods of management and by enlarging the market for agricultural produce. These same economic methods of management were then partially adopted by some branches of industry producing consumer goods and by the trade network; but that was as far as anybody went. On the whole the administrative system remained in place and eventually triumphed once more.

The steps that led to the curtailment of the economic reform followed each other slowly. The first actually appeared to be a progressive move – the abolition of the MTS and the transfer of their agricultural machinery to the collective and state farms. The move should have united the peasants with the means of production, and a new, more effective productive force should have resulted. But Khrushchev, in his usual impatient and cavalier fashion, put this correct and far-reaching idea into practice by administrative methods, in other words, by pressure from above. The collective farms were given no time to prepare for it. Suddenly their savings were taken away to pay for the tractors and combine harvesters, and they were left with no development funds. The whole question of maintenance, the supply of spare parts and fuel had not been thought through. The collective farms' budgets now had to stretch to include hundreds of thousands of mechanics, who became part of the farms. The state, it is true, gave money towards their wages, which they had guaranteed. Nevertheless the whole process had not been organized properly and agricultural machinery was not utilized more efficiently; quite the contrary, maintenance was abandoned and the production surge slowed. On top of that, the state, under pressure from the Ministry of Finance, raised prices for fuel and spare parts.

Soon after this Khrushchev came up with a new idea: a sliding scale for the purchase price of farm produce. In the years when the harvest was good and the cost of production low, purchase prices would be lowered accordingly, and in bad years, with high costs, prices would be raised. So in 1958, when the harvest was good, the purchase price was lowered; but it was not raised again in the subsequent years when harvests were bad. In other words, administrative pressure once again made the relationship between town and country unfair. Once again there was a careless redeployment of resources away from the villages and the economic base for the growth of agriculture was undermined. Diktat methods began to predominate again. Clearly Khrushchev and his entourage were dizzied by their successes in agriculture in the years between 1953 and 1959. They started setting completely unrealistic aims. The seven-year plan for the development of the national economy intended agriculture to grow 1.7 times. A more realistic development was the inclusion of agricultural tasks in the CPSU's new programme adopted at the 21st Party Congress in 1961.

At this time there was much talk about the need to catch up with and overtake the United States and other developed countries in per capita production of meat and milk. The republics and regions were given a new task: they were instructed to double their agricultural output and given practically no time in which to do so. Everyone exaggerated their figures or lied outright, and a great many arbitrary decisions were taken. The result was that agricultural growth became three or four times slower. In fact this vital branch of our economy approached stagnation. And as usual the main blow was directed at household allotments: these were abused as private property, and were blamed for the fall in production because the peasants allegedly spent too much time on them. There were difficulties with fodder for the peasants' own cattle, the limits on the number of cattle one could own became harsher, the size of the allotment was reduced, and so on. In other words, economic forms of management were finished. After

Khrushchev's 'voluntary' resignation was accepted, another agrarian policy document was rushed in front of the March 1965 Plenum of the Central Committee of the CPSU. Once again state purchase prices were raised, and the size of the state purchase was decided for the following five years. All produce in excess of the plan was to be bought by the state for one and a half times the base price. Once again great attention was paid to the help the state could give the villages. Previously unheard-of sums of money were provided for land reclamation, greater production of fertilizers and the development of agricultural technology. The new planning system was to give the collective and state farms a great deal of independence. Once again private allotments were encouraged. In other words the emphasis was once again placed on economic incentives.

This time, however, unlike in the days of Khrushchev's reforms, the leadership went further. Under the direction of the Chairman of the Council of Ministers, Alexei Kosygin, a set of reforms was developed for the industrial sector. These were presented at the September 1965 Plenum. The Kosygin Reform, as it is frequently called in the West, sharply reduced the number of fixed items in an enterprise's plan, thus allowing greater independence on the spot. In 1967 a reform of wholesale prices also increased economic incentives. Realized production and profit were now accepted as the most important indices of an enterprise's activity. Enterprises were allowed to establish their own bonus funds from their profits on the basis of a set of rules. The size of these funds was left to the enterprises. The idea of the reform was eventually to substitute wholesale trading for the centralized distribution of equipment and material. However, this goal was not reached.

I should also mention that before the introduction of these economic reforms the sovnarkhozes, the regional economic departments set up by Khrushchev in 1957, were abolished, leaving us once again with ministries for different sectors. Khrushchev's many different planning agencies, created by him after the abolition of Gosplan, were also scrapped and a central planning agency was reconstituted. At the same time the State Committee for Supplies, the Committee for Science and Technology and several other central departments were reorganized. As they had never been truly independent, these agencies could not supervise enterprises in detail and were therefore occupied with the larger problems of economic development in their respective sectors. The results of this reorganization coupled with the greater independence of the enterprises were reasonably good. Productivity in industry rose considerably, by 32 per cent in the years 1966–70, whereas growth had been only 25 per cent in the preceding period. The amount contributed by industry to central funds also went up in this period, though it had been going down before that. Material resources were better used, that is to say, enterprises cut back on their outrageous stockpiling of supplies and kept more equipment in service.

But more important than these improvements in efficiency and quality was the fact that this was the first time that economic methods of management were widely used in industry and agriculture. There was even an attempt to move the construction and transport industries over to similar economic methods. A plan was in fact worked out for the building industry and even introduced, but it was a half-hearted and incomplete attempt which produced no results. The idea was that the construction industry would be paid for completed works according to contracted prices, whereas under the previous system builders were paid for the amount built with an allowance for their expenses. This idea was distorted to make it possible to pay for completion of certain units within construction jobs. These units were in turn broken down into smaller ones, and we were back where we started. The economic reform of the building industry was not successful. A flurry of activity took place in the transport industry as well. But although the one experiment in adopting economic methods, by Mosavtotrans, produced very effective results, the system was not introduced widely in the country's transport industry.

The system of management adopted during the economic reform did not last long. By the late sixties or early seventies the old administrative methods had mostly returned. One could point to many separate reasons for this. In industry it was because average incomes under the new economic methods rose very rapidly and in many branches overtook productivity. This led to problems in the market. At that point we could have adopted a new approach to this problem, as was done in Hungary in similar circumstances: we could have introduced an economic regulator to prevent excessive growth of incomes. Everything could have been normalized quite swiftly. But we stayed with the old methods and forcibly introduced a new plan heading which set tasks to increase labour productivity as against average wages. Next we experienced difficulties with lowering production costs, and so another centralized plan heading was introduced. By this time the ministries had established a strict control over their enterprises, and Gosplan and the ministries regained total control over production. Enterprises were now powerless against the might of Gosplan and the ministries. The trouble was that the new economic conditions had been introduced, not in the shape of a new law, but as a government instruction. Similar instructions, issued later, corrected and changed many points in the course of the reform. In the Decree on Socialist Enterprises, which was ratified by the Council of Ministers and which set out the rights and duties of the enterprises, article after article was countermanded and changed. There was no body in the country to defend the enterprises. The interdepartmental commission created in order to improve the system of management was situated very low in the pecking order and consisted of deputy heads of departments from various ministries who all pulled in different directions. In effect this commission, headed by the deputy chairman of Gosplan, finally finished off the reform.

As regards the reform within industry, it should be noted that the party organs might have accepted the need for it in theory but were not in fact included in the process and were thus unable to step in as the defenders of the enterprises' economic rights. On the contrary, they too used diktat methods and frequently usurped the place of the economic organizations. By the early seventies the authorities slipped into a kind of administrative hysteria which affected both industry and agriculture. Once again plans were proposed to extend the area of arable lands and the number of cattle. People used to say at the time that 'cows are what count to the regional party committees'. In other words even if a cow produced no milk, the collective and state farms had to keep it. They most certainly could not slaughter it or sell it, for they answered to the authorities, and the only thing which mattered was the head-count.

On the eve of perestroika – the state of the economy in the period of stagnation

The result of the return to administrative methods of management was that the country's social and economic development slowed down and showed signs of disarray. The reader might at this point ask me, as a number of people have: what was your position as a Soviet economist at this time, and what was the position of your colleagues? I must say that the criticism of Stalin's cult of personality and the relative democratization of society that characterized the early years of Khrushchev's rule had a beneficial effect on the development of economics as a science. Reference books with statistical data were now published, and new institutes of economics were formed. One of these was particularly important – Gosplan's Institute of Economic Research. This institute brought together all the best younger economists in our country at that time. Its founder and director for many years was Anatoly Yefimov, who later became a well-known academician. He managed to direct his staff towards the study of real economic problems and towards research into economic development using mathematical models. It was the first institution to carry out any research into the balance between various sectors of the economy, work which began as early as the late fifties. It was also the first economics institute to make wide use of a large computer. Under the direction of Vasili Nemchinov and Leonid Kantorovich, mathematical economics became important, and soon a new subsection of the Academy of Sciences was formed – the Laboratory for Mathematical Economic Methods. Conservative economists, led by the then Vice-President of the Academy of Sciences, Konstantin Ostrovityanov, put up a ferocious fight against this new trend, forbidding the publication of the relevant books and placing obstacles in the way of seminars and conferences.

I became involved in the study of economic mathematics around 1956, attending seminars on the subject and studying mathematics. There were two reasons for this. First of all I was working in the joint economic section of the Committee on Labour and Wages. I was trying to combine economic mathematical models of earnings, income and expenses of the population and began using an electronic calculating machine. At the same time I started giving evening classes at the department of political economy in

140

the Natural Sciences Faculty of Moscow University. I was asked to lecture on political economics in the mathematics department. At these evening lectures I became friendly with mathematicians, many of them about my age or just a little older, who inspired my interest in mathematics and helped me to study it. My interests in mathematical economics soon went beyond questions of wages and living standards. I began to study the balance between various branches of the economy and wrote a book on the subject. Next I wrote a book on the optimization of various problems, especially in agricultural production, and the deployment of resources. A very important incentive was an offer to lecture in the geography department of Moscow University. I was asked to teach a special course on the use of mathematical methods in economic geography, which gave me an additional reason seriously to study the whole subject.

About that time a furious battle was raging around the publication of Leonid Kantorovich's book *Economic Calculations for the Better Use of Resources*. I was drawn into the battle, the main protagonists of which were Kantorovich, Nemchinov and Ostrovityanov.

I have been very fortunate in that for almost a quarter of a century I have worked beside the outstanding scientist, even genius, Leonid Kantorovich. He is not simply my teacher in many separate aspects of our subject; he is also a close older friend. I first met him in the late fifties, when he was trying to have his book published. An extraordinary person with astonishing mathematical abilities, he left school at fourteen. At the age of fifteen he was accepted by the mathematics department of Leningrad University, and from the very beginning took part in research work there. By the age of seventeen or eighteen he had become a fully-fledged researcher, writing original papers that were published not only in the Soviet Union but in leading foreign journals. His work was on a new direction in a recently developed branch of mathematics connected with functional analysis, primarily in space normalization. But Kantorovich worked simultaneously on several branches of modern mathematics. He graduated well before the allotted time and stayed on as a researcher. At the age of twenty-one he was granted a doctorate by the Academy of Sciences solely on the basis of his outstanding contribution to mathematics, without having to produce a dissertation. I have already mentioned that I have been a member of the Academy for the last twenty years, and I cannot recall anything like this happening in all that time. In our country, unlike elsewhere, doctorates for outstanding achievement are conferred only in the most exceptional cases. Kantorovich was such a case. Soon after that he became a professor. Apart from teaching, he was engaged in research in the Leningrad section of the Institute of Mathematics. A man of wide interests, he once told me that in the late thirties he became interested in economics and so began looking into the problems of economic development. He came across an example concerning cleaning machinery used in Leningrad in the production of plywood. One can see now that this was a classical problem of linear programming which could not be solved by the usual mathematical methods. Kantorovich decided to solve it and succeeded with the aid of a completely new method he discovered. He called this method of solving optimization problems with linear limitations the 'multiplier'.

I have already said that Kantorovich was a genius. This fact showed itself in his discovery, a new branch of mathematics connected with the solution of optimal problems. What is particularly astonishing is that he applied a general method even to those frequent problems of optimization that could be solved using a specially developed simplified method. Thus from the very first Kantorovich proved the theorem of duality which is at the base of all optimization theories. What is even more astonishing is that he immediately understood what he had done and in 1939 wrote a paper, published by Leningrad University, on the connection between mathematical methods and organizational models. This was a short but fascinating work that anticipated the main directions in which linear programming and its practical applications would develop. He also formulated a whole class of optimization problems in economics: problems in transportation, in the deployment and loading of equipment, in the division and positioning of arable land, in materials preparation, and many others. At a stroke, he had solved the problem that had tormented leading scientists in America and other countries for about ten years.

However, Kantorovich's works were not understood by his contemporaries. He published a whole series of important articles and gave talks at the Academy of Sciences, many of which were translated into various languages. But his ideas were not fully understood and accepted, and it was therefore not until after the war that the study of optimization problems and linear program-

142

ming began in earnest in the West. From 1944–5 research groups set up during the war by the US Army and Navy began to formulate and solve military organizational and production problems, such as those concerning transport. Individual optimization methods were created in order to solve these. As the problems became more complicated, the appropriate methods evolved. And finally, some time in the mid-fifties, all these problems were summated, and more general methods of solving problems, based on proven theorems, above all the theorem of duality, were invented. Fifteen years after Kantorovich's discovery the whole idea was rediscovered in the space of a few months, first in the USA, then in other countries.

Kantorovich understood how important mathematical economics methods of optimization were for a socialist economy and burned with desire to place these methods at the state's disposal. He wrote notes to all sorts of people and knocked on all sorts of doors. But to no avail. The most likely explanation is that he was not understood. He began writing his popular book under the title of *Economic Calculations for the Better Use of Resources*. The war interrupted this, as Kantorovich was occupied with solving problems of naval warfare and strategy. After the war, the best people in physics and mathematics took part in work on atomic problems. All this distracted Kantorovich from his study of mathematical economics. But he never quite abandoned those problems. In Leningrad he, together with his many students, developed methods for solving transport problems, trying to apply these methods to concrete situations. His students worked on practical applications of the methods in Leningrad factories and on some farms. He organized and taught courses at Leningrad University for anyone who wished to learn these methods. Many of our leading economists who were young men at the time went through Kantorovich's school. But he did not succeed in publishing his book. It went from one leading economist to another, and opinions were, by and large, negative. The truth is that at that time attempts to use mathematical methods in economics were viewed as attempts to distort and nullify the qualitative meaning of economic categories, or, in other words, to substitute quantity for quality. And as many of the bourgeois economists used mathematical forms for illustrative purposes, our conservative political economists began to identify mathematical methods with bourgeois theorizing. This applied even more to the possible use of the

143

concept of maximum quantity. The greatest intolerance on the part of our political economists was reserved for the bourgeois school of maximum usefulness. And the fact that in Kantorovich's theory of optimization the optimal valuation is the maximum quantity immediately put into their minds the old concept formulated by the Austrian school of 'maximum usefulness'. I have been able to read some of these opinions. They were dangerous – dangerous to their subject. He was accused of spreading bourgeois propaganda, of trying to overturn Marxism and so on. One could be arrested for such things in Stalin's day.

My supervisor, Shamil Turetsky, under whom I wrote my master's thesis at the Moscow State Institute of Economics (I was an external student there from 1955 to 1958), had been the head of the prices department of Gosplan and had worked with the ex-chairman of Gosplan, N. Voznesensky, who was arrested in 1949 as one of the last victims of Stalinism. Turetsky told me that Voznesensky once asked him in and gave him Kantorovich's manuscript to read. This was still in Stalin's day. Turetsky read the manuscript and did not like it. I think he quite simply did not understand fully the usefulness to economics of optimal valuations. Kantorovich's style was very simple, but the book could not be simple: to grasp its meaning, a traditional economist had to read it very carefully, with pencil at the ready. It was also important not to approach it with any preconceptions. Turetsky was a very busy man and most probably he simply skimmed through the book without pondering it in depth. He expressed an opinion which was not very flattering, adding that he saw no need to publish the book. Voznesensky then asked Turetsky whether he thought the author ought to be arrested. Turetsky said no, as in his opinion the author was not anti-Soviet but genuinely misguided.

These were the conditions in which Kantorovich worked and fought for the publication of his book under Stalin. But the attempt to hide his light failed. In the mid-fifties, news of work by American scientists on the problems of linear programming filtered through to the USSR. There were discussions in seminars, and some people recalled the work of L. Kantorovich in this field. His work was reviewed and it became impossible not to acknowledge what this branch of mathematics owed him, though a number of enemies remained stubborn. At this point Nemchinov joined the fight, as he had decided to publish Kantorovich's manuscript no matter what. In the end Ostrovityanov, the Vice-President of the Academy, agreed, but made it a condition that Nemchinov should write a disclamatory preface to it. Nemchinov agreed and explained his decision to his friends: 'This book is of such importance that it must be published at any cost. People will read my silly preface and say that old Nemchinov was a fool. Let them. The important thing is that the book comes out.' The first edition was published in 1959 with the required preface by Nemchinov, who then continued to work with Kantorovich right up to his death in 1965. Furthermore, he arranged for Kantorovich to be elected as a corresponding member of the economic section of the Academy. Kantorovich's speciality was a completely new one, introduced by Nemchinov: mathematical methods in economic research.

I more than liked Vasili Nemchinov, I admired him as a true scientist and hard worker. He was an outstanding statistician and economist from that famous Russian school, the zemstvo statistics office, whose subject was primarily agriculture. Lenin thought very highly of this school of economists. It was on the basis of their calculations that he wrote his outstanding work, *The Development of Capitalism in Russia*, in which he analysed in great detail vast amounts of statistical material. Nemchinov can rightly be called the last of that fine band of economists and statisticians. Starting in 1920 he wrote a number of works and carried out an even greater number of statistical studies into the development of agriculture in our country. Although he worked in the field of economic statistics, he nevertheless used all the important achievements in mathematical statistics reached by, among others, the Russian scientists Chuprov, Lyapuhov, then Kolmogorov and so on. Nemchinov tried to use the methods of mathematical statistics in the study of agriculture. These methods became particularly important when used in processes of plant selection based on the teachings of Mendel and Weismann. Nemchinov actively supported these ideas.

Gradually genuinely scientific schools in our country were displaced by the pseudo-science of Lysenko after he became President of the Agricultural Academy. Nemchinov at the time was rector of the Timiryazev Academy of Agricultural Studies, the top educational establishment for the study of agriculture in our country. It was a staunch supporter of scientific genetics and stood up against Lysenko's ideas. In 1948 Lysenko utilized Stalin's cult of personality for his own purposes; he organized the notorious session of the Agricultural Academy and destroyed the study of biology. Stalin, of course, supported Lysenko. Nemchinov was one of the few people who spoke up against Lysenko at the session. For this he was expelled from the Timiryazev Academy and was for a time without any work at all.

One sad task that fell to my lot was to be a member of the commission that organized Nemchinov's funeral after his death in 1964. Together with friends, I wrote his obituary, which was subsequently signed by party and government leaders. That is why I was able to see his file, with all the various references given for him throughout his career, and complete with accusatory letters written when he defended the study of genetics.

He was a man of great courage: he risked his life to defend his opinions. Many scientists who defended true scientific biology ended their lives in gaol. Foremost among these was the world-famous biologist Academician Nikolai Vavilov.

Yet towards the end of his life Nemchinov once again joined the fight. This time he fought for mathematical economics – to great effect. Using the optimal approach he developed a theory of prices and wrote a book about it. He then widened his research and worked on the economic balancing of sectors. He set up the first laboratory for the study of economic mathematical methods within the Academy of Sciences and became its first head. He also organized the first department of mathematical economics in Moscow University and set up the first scientific council to award degrees in mathematical economics for work done in this field. It was before this council, chaired by Nemchinov, that I defended my own doctoral dissertation on the system of optimal mathematical economic models for long-term planning. The main opponent was Academician L. V. Kantorovich.

In 1960 Nemchinov organized the first Soviet conference on mathematical economics, at which supporters of mathematical economic methods banded with mathematicians and other representatives of the natural sciences to put up a fight against the old school of economics. The struggle went on. For three years public meetings discussed whether the work of Kantorovich, Nemchinov and Novozhilov deserved the Lenin Prize. There was no doubt at all in anybody's mind about Nemchinov's contribution to economics. Conservative economists suggested that he alone should be put up for the prize. He would most certainly have got it, but he refused to accept it unless Kantorovich and Novozhilov were put up with him. Twice he missed the prize because of this, as the opponents of mathematical economic methods used the pages of the party press to qualify Kantorovich's and Novozhilov's research as bourgeois, wrong, irrelevant to any practical problem and so on. Truth triumphed in the end, however. Other newspapers and journals (*Izvestiya*, for example) made space available, and I and a number of my colleagues managed to publish an article defending the candidates for the Lenin Prize and showing their real contribution to science. I myself, together with some of the other authors, spoke at a number of public meetings, and we tried to prove that these people's work was vital for economic research and practice. Finally, in 1964, the achievements of Leonid Kantorovich, Vasili Nemchinov and Victor Novozhilov were fully recognized, and they were awarded our country's highest prize – the Lenin Prize. Some time later, in 1973, Kantorovich received the Nobel Prize for Economics.

My relationship with Kantorovich, both professional and personal, was particularly close. When in 1961 I left Moscow and went to work in Academgorodok near Novosibirsk, I found that Kantorovich had already organized a department of mathematical economics in the Institute of Mathematics. My own job in Siberia was to organize a laboratory for research in mathematical economics. We had met previously in Moscow a few times, and in Siberia Kantorovich greeted me like a long-lost brother. He helped me to settle in my new home, which was not so easy, as Academgorodok was still being built and there were no shops, no offices and no transport to and from the city to the airport. It was particularly difficult to get anywhere in winter, because of the cold and the winds. There were virtually no telephones. But we all lived as one big family and were totally involved in our work. Kantorovich and I immediately organized a seminar for the two Institutes – Economics and Mathematics. Much of the subsequent work of the Novosibirsk economist mathematicians and mathematician economists resulted from these seminars.

Kantorovich was a man of many interests. He knew about the theatre and was instrumental in attracting theatrical groups from Moscow and Leningrad to Academgorodok. He was also a generous man, for ever presenting his colleagues with the new ideas he was full of. He had his own special view of economics, and a good deal of what he talked about twenty or thirty years ago is only just beginning to penetrate into our economic life. For instance he studied the need to introduce payments for resources, with

147

these payments being the ultimate test of efficiency in an optimal plan. Nowadays we all accept the need for payments for resources.

And now I want to talk about the Leningrad professor of economics and statistics Victor Novozhilov. By the time I met him in Nemchinov's flat he was quite old. Novozhilov was a man of the Russian intelligentsia in the best sense of that word. He had a broad cultural outlook, knew several languages, and was well versed in contemporary world literature on economics and econometrics. At the same time he was an original thinker who since the end of the thirties had consistently developed ideas about the commensurability of expenditure and its results in a socialist society where the national economic peak of efficiency comes above any separate local peak. He introduced into economic discussions the concepts of differential expenditures, of reverse connected expenditure, and of the efficiency norm, to which last concept he added his own new meaning, as he had a most profound understanding of it.

Towards the end of the forties several economic journals and conferences started up discussion about the efficiency of capital investments. Novozhilov for the first time made public his ideas of an optimized and holistic approach to the commensurability of expenditure and result. According to these ideas, the question of the effectiveness of capital investments is only part of a larger problem. Novozhilov was immediately accused of being a non-Marxist, a cosmopolitan, of borrowing his ideas from bourgeois scientists and of all sorts of other nonsense. He suffered for this: he was deprived of his professorship and for a long time could get only hourly-paid work.

Undoubtedly Novozhilov can take his place among the world's leading economists. In my opinion, his book *The Commensurability of Expenditure and Its Results in the Socialist Economy* is a classic that was not fully appreciated in Novozhilov's lifetime. Nemchinov, Kantorovich and I, after my election to the Academy, made enormous efforts to elect Novozhilov at least to the corresponding membership of that body – unsuccessfully. When Novozhilov died, Kantorovich said at his graveside: 'The fact that Novozhilov did not become a member of the Academy does not harm him. Novozhilov remains a great economist. But it has harmed our Academy not to have him in its ranks.'

Of course it would be wrong to suggest that developments in economics consisted entirely of mathematical economic studies.

But it became the symbol of progressive research at the time, as we gradually overcame dogmatism in science in the post-Stalin years. We could now have real discussions and arguments. One particularly fierce debate developed between those who supported the development of the market and the production of consumer goods and the so-called anti-consumerists, who thought that such production and the market would undermine the country's centralized and planned development. These debates led to others about the nature of prices under socialism, and these, in turn, were linked to such questions as how to make the most effective use of resources, including the most effective use of capital investment. It was in these conditions that we recognized the need to apply efficiency norms to capital investment. The formula $C + ER$ was established for the study of economics, where C is production cost, E the capital investment efficiency norm, and R the capital investment. There was now an active group advocating a change to single level pricing calculated according to the above formula. These prices could be computed, and from then on discussions could be conducted on the basis of concrete numerical evidence rather than in the abstract.

It was at this time, towards the end of the fifties and at the beginning of the sixties, that our ideas about economic methods of management were developed. The works of Kantorovich and Novozhilov provided the theoretical base for a system of prices and valuation of resources that would ensure independence for the enterprises for which this was a common goal. Incidentally the two men, who are both from Leningrad, had long been friends and had enriched each other's works. However, each arrived in his own way at his proof for the optimal functioning of the socialist economy. In real life, management was completely different, being still based on the administrative system; so at the same time as Kantorovich's and Novozhilov's theoretical work was being done, applied economics also developed attempting to create a new system of benchmarks for enterprises and to change the economic conditions for them. One of the economists who fought for economic reform in industry, and opened the way for it with his ideas, was Yevsey Liberman, a professor of economics from Kharkov. I knew Liberman well, was on friendly terms with him, and tried to publish articles by him and his pupils in the journal *EKO* while I was its editor-in-chief. Unfortunately Liberman's part in the theoretical preparations for the role of economics in our life was underestimated by other economists and by officialdom. When he died, only *EKO* published any special material about him and stressed his achievements.

On the eve of the economic reform, *Pravda* decided to hold a discussion about the perfectibility of the economic mechanism. The very first long article, with far-reaching proposals about profits and profitability as the main indices for evaluating the work of enterprises, was by Professor Ye. Liberman. He also emphasized the need to develop the socialist market. It was this article that made him well-known.

In many ways the economic reform proceeded along the path suggested by the scientists – but, of course, there are all kinds of scientists. The Praesidium of the Academy of Sciences organized a commission for the discussion of problems arising out of the economic reform. This discussion was to produce preparatory material for the forthcoming September Plenum of the Central Committee, which then took the decision to begin reform in industry. I was included in this commission – the 'Commission of the 18' – as I had just been elected a corresponding member in the field of economics. At that time the number of academicians and corresponding members concerned with economics was about a third of what it is now. At the head of the commission was the new vice-president: Academician Pyotr Fedoseyev, who had succeeded Ostrovityanov on his death. One of the members of the commission was Kantorovich, and it also included, apart from economists, power engineering specialists, chemists and others. On the whole the commission was a conservative one: the old guard who worried that 'something might come of it all' held a majority in it. I remember there were fierce arguments in the vice-president's office, during which Kantorovich, Mikhail Strikovich, an academician and specialist in power engineering, and I and a few others insisted that a price reform was essential. The commission did not agree with this, and its suggestions on the subject were considerably less radical than the ones adopted by the Plenum, which in the end decided on the reform of prices which, as we know, took effect in 1967.

In those years our prime minister, Alexei Kosygin, was surrounded by many talented economists and highly erudite scientists – among them Korobov, the deputy chairman of Gosplan, and Malyshev, the prime minister's assistant. They were genuine supporters of economic reform, and it was largely thanks to their

150

efforts and to their plans (Korobov, for instance, headed the working commission that prepared the reform) that decisions were taken and in most cases implemented. But there was no real support for the economic reform in party and government circles. The decision was taken, true enough, and was put into practice, but spokes were put repeatedly into the wheels of change.

In those years I met Kosygin several times, and my impression was that he did not fully understand how important the economic reform was or how prices and the market would affect the growth of economic methods of management. Of course he was a brilliant economist. His memory was phenomenal; he was extremely hard-working; and in many ways he was a man of his word. He was generally respected in our country because he stood out among the usual run of our leaders, who were complete fools with a worm's view of the world and a poor understanding of their jobs.

Kosygin, above all, was businesslike. But he too was a product of his era – a supporter of centralized measures. I remember that after a trip to, I think, Vietnam in 1965, he stopped over in Novosibirsk and paid a visit to Academgorodok. He expressed a desire to talk to Kantorovich and me. We had a very interesting meeting, but as soon as Kantorovich touched on the importance of a price system in the formation of new economic conditions, Kosygin interrupted him: 'What have prices to do with it? What are you talking about?' The astonishing thing is that these words were spoken by the man who led the economic reform, who developed and implemented it. I think Kosygin was not too upset when the economic methods of management were abolished. In many ways it was he who also restored the administrative system.

Much later, in the mid-seventies, I was reporting to the Praesidium of the Council of Ministers about the national economy's possible dynamics and about economic growth factors implied in the 10th Five-year Plan (1976–80). Kosygin was present. It was one of officialdom's sudden bursts of interest in scientific ideas. At the meeting, various scientists reported on the problems of the Five-year Plan, each concentrating on his speciality. It was my privilege to head the commission that examined the summated figures for the Five-year Plan. So there I was on the rostrum, trying to explain that it was not the aims of the Five-year Plan that were important but the ways and means that would help fulfil those aims. I then developed my ideas about a new economic reform, the need for economic flexibility, for investment policies, the redeployment of funds into engineering construction, and so on. Kosygin interrupted me somewhat rudely, and when I tried to cite examples from the 8th Five-year Plan (1966–70), during which we managed to increase economic growth and improve quality quite considerably by means of various reforms, he disagreed with me, maintaining that the subsequent years were not bad either, that it was incorrect to ascribe so much to economic reform, and so on.

I have to say that Kosygin, who when he was on the rostrum gave the impression of being intelligent and modest, though a little dry, conducted meetings of the Council of Ministers in an exceptionally rude fashion. He would interrupt almost every speaker, contradicted them unpleasantly, saying things like: 'What do you know about this anyway?' or 'Why do you raise this subject if you don't understand anything about it?' and telling off speakers in quite unmeasured tones. He obviously derived satisfaction from putting scientists down by showing up their ignorance of some matter or other. I was present at a number of meetings where I witnessed and even experienced this behaviour. On the whole it seemed to me that Kosygin's attitude to me was quite good and that he generally listened to what I had to say. But at that particular meeting he interrupted me constantly. And instead of speaking for twenty minutes, as I should have done, I was on the rostrum for over an hour, while he and his assistants hurled abuse at me. The whole thing ended in an uproar. As I was trying to prove that the tempo of our development would continue to fall in the 10th Five-year Plan if we did not do something, I produced the computer printout of the various possible results of our growth in the next five or ten years. These results had been formulated with the aid of a multi-sectoral economic model. I talked about these results and referred to the use of economic mathematical modelling in forecasting the development of the country. Kosygin snapped at me: 'And what on earth do you understand about models?' Until that moment I had listened patiently to all the rude comments that had been addressed to me. I had been told that I did not understand anything about metallurgy or engineering, that I was wrong to insist on the need for the redeployment of funds into engineering, that one cannot compare the proportion of capital investment in engineering with the proportion of capital investment in the industrial branches for which the machinery is intended, and so

152

on. I had listened to all that, but now I could no longer control myself and said very clearly and loudly that if there was anyone in that room who knew about economic mathematical models, that person was I. 'As for you,' I said to Kosygin, 'you really don't understand the first thing about it.' I was immediately sent back to my office; my report remained unfinished, and a whole crowd of various officials whose names one can never remember like the ex-finance minister, the ex-chairman of the Central Statistics Department and various assistants to the chairman of the Council of Ministers, started muttering that these scientists were really getting too big for their boots, and what did they know anyway about models or anything else.

This episode was characteristic of our leaders' attitude to scientific ideas and researchers in the period of stagnation. But my impression was that Kosygin was not an ill-intentioned man at all and that those comments seemingly aimed at destroying people's dignity were not really intended to do so. Nor did he particularly wish to show up a scientist's ignorance. He made the comments out of habit, according to the tradition he knew. Obviously he learnt this approach from his own bosses, who were all part of the Stalinist generation. They habitually used foul language at official meetings, where proceedings always began with the words: 'Women, if there are any of you present, please block your ears.' After this introduction came the foul language. There usually were some women shorthand-typists present. I witnessed some of this in action in the first years of my work on the Committee of Labour and Wages, where my boss was the old Stalinist Lazar Kaganovich. He was in favour at the time (1955), still a member of the Politburo, and never bothered about his language. He used to shout at people and sometimes even hit his assistants. He liked to slam his telephone down on his desk and shatter it. He did not raise his voice to inexperienced youngsters, but he liked to shout at his subordinates in my presence, thus making me into an accessory. At the Committee's party meetings, his speeches were greeted by thunderous applause which broke out as he spoke because he knew how to affect his audience emotionally. He was also rather witty. He had had only four years of schooling and liked to repeat the words: 'We did not graduate from any university.' Kosygin was a very different sort of man temperamentally and intellectually, but he grew up in that environment and had clearly picked up many bad habits.

Within a few days of the meeting where I was, metaphorically speaking, whipped, news of it went round Moscow – with the most unlikely additional details. On the one hand people spoke of my courage in daring to contradict, on the other of my complete inability to answer the most elementary questions on economics. In other words everyone felt free to invent new versions. Shortly after that, Kosygin summoned me and asked me to head the group preparing his report to the forthcoming Party Congress on the 10th Five-year Plan. I refused, because I was living and working in Siberia at the time and as head of the commission I would have to spend several months in Moscow, which would be difficult for me. But I agreed to become a member. I cannot say that my contribution was particularly large, but I took part in the preparation of materials for the 25th Party Congress, which took place in 1976.

Shortly before Kosygin's death he telephoned me in Siberia. I was summoned to the government telephone, which was in the study of the president of the Siberian section of the Academy of Sciences, on the second floor of the Praesidium building. My own office was on the third floor. Kosygin asked me to write him a frank account explaining why since 1979 our economy had suddenly started to function so badly. There had indeed been a sharp decline. In 40 per cent of industrial enterprises, according to the published figures, there was an absolute decrease in productivity. Agriculture had been in recession too since 1978; there had been no growth in the amount transported on the railways, and this was holding back the entire economy. There had been a sinister aggravation of shortages, and the situation on the consumer market had worsened sharply. I told Kosygin that of course I could analyse the situation, but I could not frankly posit all the questions, even to him. To which he said to me: 'What are you afraid of? They can't exile you any further than Siberia anyway.' I replied that the reason why I did not want to touch this theme was not that I was afraid but that as an economist I was not competent to do so; it was a question that should be addressed to those in charge of our economy and its development. I named a few ministers who in my view were complete fools and incompetents, who had destroyed the sector they were responsible for, reducing it, so to speak, to rubble. He interrupted me rather sharply and said that I was right; this was not my subject and it would be best if I did not write about it. I wrote a note in response to his question, and although I typed very few copies of it and sent them only to Kosygin and Baibakov, the chairman of Gosplan, nevertheless somehow our official circles found out about it.

My opening sentence made certain people particularly angry. I said that our economy was in a catastrophic state, and clearly the data in our statistical publications made things sound much better than they really were. I was once again dubbed a slanderer and was not allowed to go abroad. Until 1985 I managed to visit only Bulgaria and Hungary – and then only for short periods. And although I went through the due processes several times I was refused exit visas. I was stuck with another name that I now recall with great pleasure: 'the disgraced academician'. But I must say my relationship with my colleagues in the Academy and its Siberian section had not changed. I went on working with my colleagues and carrying out interesting research just as before.

I must return to the question about our economists. Where were they when the economic reform was being undone at the end of the sixties? Well, we were not idly sitting around. Our older colleague in the Department of Economics, Alexei Rumyantsev, became the vice-president of the Academy of Sciences, but unfortunately the intrigues of his enemies forced him to retire from that position after one term. Then after a five-year interval we were once again ruled by the omnivorous Academician Pyotr Fedoseyev. He was a philosopher and social scientist in the worst sense of both those terms. When the first attempts to revive the administrative methods became evident, a group of economists, mostly directors of the leading institutes, was working under Rumyantsev's leadership at a government dacha just outside Moscow on certain tasks set by the government. We decided to write a collective letter to the Politburo and to the General Secretary, Comrade Brezhnev, expressing our view that the economic reforms ought to be expanded. We added that it was becoming obvious that growth rates would decline if nothing new was done, that wide-ranging economic measures were needed, and so on. Incidentally we once more referred to calculations made with the help of dynamic intersectoral models. Our mistake was that we had the letter typed at the dacha: some helpful assistant saw to it that a copy was on Kosygin's desk the very next day.

Kosygin's attitude was extremely negative. We were called slanderers; it was once again pointed out that we did not understand anything, and so on. It makes one sad to think of those times. Naturally, after such a reaction to a serious comment, backed by proofs and calculations, we lost for a time all desire to produce statements of that kind. But even so economists tried individually, though not together as a group, to do something to improve the situation, to put the country on to a new path of economic development.

In those years, that is, the late sixties and early seventies, I at least had some faith in the leadership, despite occurrences of this sort. I still thought that the leaders would understand the situation and take some radical measures. I was strengthened in that belief by Brezhnev's end-of-year speeches at the plenums that met to decide the annual plan. In these he talked of the need for major changes in management, the need to take measures to speed up scientific and technological progress. It was even planned to have a plenum devoted specifically to these problems, and a number of us were asked to prepare materials for it. Our proposals considered expanding the economic reforms of the mid-sixties, emphasized the importance of trusts in industry, and developed ideas about the urgent need to redeploy funds into engineering and to change investment policies. We also expressed the opinion, backing it with solid arguments, that science and production should be integrated, and that higher education needed to be changed and developed; and we posited a number of other important economic questions. But the more we worked on the materials for the plenum, the less our higher authorities were interested in it. Various ideas expressed in these materials were lifted and used for speeches, but in the end our work was stopped, as the plenum did not in fact take place.

At that point it became obvious to many people that no radical decisions would be taken. In subsequent years commissions were formed, various concepts were developed, there was talk of a new economic reform, of new systems of management and of new ways to economic development; but one could clearly see that it would all come to nothing. I considered that I and the institute I directed, the Institute of Economics and Industrial Production of the Siberian Section of the Academy of Sciences, were duty-bound to take part in this work. In the Academy the work was directed by Academician N. Fedorenko, who throughout this period was secretary of the Economics Section of the Academy of Sciences. One commission followed another. New measures for improving management were worked out. This went on for several years, at the end of which, as was to be expected, the mountain gave birth to a molehill: the well-known decree of 1979 about improving the management system. This was a half-hearted and entirely unrealistic effort, because it represented an attempt to establish economic methods to fulfil administratively set tasks.

The huge managerial apparatus was working very hard at the time, as it had to issue scores of instructions and special decrees, without which the intended improvement in the management system could not be carried out. When all these instructions and decrees were put together they made up a thick volume, but no real work was done and the economy went from bad to worse. At the same time the work of genuine economists was rejected. They had advocated more radical reforms and a transition to economic methods. An insulting new label was attached to them – they were called market socialists and were virtually accused of undermining the great achievement of socialist society, planned development.

There was verbal support for proposals to speed up scientific and technological progress and to galvanize the economy in order to increase efficiency and quality; but no deeds followed the words. It is quite extraordinary to recall that the 9th Five-year Plan was called the welfare plan, though it was during that period that there was a sudden sharp decrease in our social development. The 10th Five-year Plan was called the efficiency and quality plan, although the lion's share of resources went to develop the production of fuel and raw materials. For the first time the growth of capital investment in engineering was lower than the general growth of capital investment in industry as a whole. It was during the 10th Five-year Plan that the growth of labour productivity in industry was halved, despite an enormous growth in production costs which made our goods less competitive on the world market. Nevertheless the work carried out by the economists did not go to waste. It was a foundation for the future. We all became more hopeful when Yury Andropov became General Secretary of the Central Committee of the CPSU. At the November 1982 Plenum he severely criticized our economic development, talked much of the need to tighten labour discipline, to liquidate disorder and slackness, which had indeed reached terrifying proportions. Merely the introduction of some order into our economic life had an immediate effect, and the speed of social and economic growth increased. But obviously what was needed was profound and radical measures. This was clear to Andropov himself, and a few

157

months before his death he set himself the task of developing a complete programme for the reform of the management system. Once again there were commissions, but work started then was gradually wound up under Chernenko.

It was not until March 1985, when Gorbachev became General Secretary and perestroika was declared to be the aim, that any serious work was done in practice. As Gorbachev has said more than once, perestroika did not appear out of nowhere. I believe that even the theoretical aspect had already been prepared, at least partially, by the collective efforts of a whole group of economists who worked on the problems of economic reform in the mid-sixties. In the years of stagnation they remained supporters of a transition to economic methods of management, and they continued to work out plans for the formation of a new economic and administrative system.

Lessons to be drawn from history

One further aspect of the new economic reforms in our country is worthy of consideration. Our reforms have all involved the democratization of society, including economic life, and increased involvement in work and social matters. To some extent this has to do with the fact that all major changes of direction are preceded by periods of stagnation and imbalance which need to be overcome. Most people understand and support such changes, especially as political moves in periods of economic reform are invariably accompanied by increased material incentives. These arouse popular involvement and interest. Naturally the periods discussed differ as to the extent of the changes made and the level of democratization introduced. When our society went over from War Communism to the NEP, this widening of economic freedom and the general transition to peacetime existence were accompanied by increased democracy and glasnost (openness). This was particularly apparent in the first few years of the NEP, while Lenin was still alive, because he thought the strengthening of the democratic base was of paramount importance. When we later went over to Stalin's administrative methods, this democratic foundation was fairly swiftly done away with. The new methods of management were more suited to the barracks, based as they were on commands.

Khrushchev's reforms after Stalin's death were ineluctably linked to a general democratization and social development that was in turn connected with the rejection of the personality cult. Greater enthusiasm and more initiative, together with the expansion of economic research, helped to speed up social development. But, as I have already said, Khrushchev himself changed, so that by the end of the fifties or certainly by the early sixties glasnost was severely restricted and the old administrative, 'diktat', barrack-room methods were revived and strengthened.

As far as democracy is concerned, the economic reforms of the mid-sixties produced less change than any others. There were some positive developments – subjectivism and artbitrariness in management were removed, the endless round of reorganizations was stopped, and some stability was introduced into people's lives. At the same time the press and other media remained under fairly strict control. No measures were taken to involve the workers at large in management or to develop any kind of openness in society. The fact that it was so easy to wind up the economic reform and reintroduce administrative methods of management in industry and agriculture is to a great extent due to the lack of democracy at the time. Stability gradually became stagnation, until our society required complete restructuring to renew it and drag it, now near crisis-point, out of its mire.

The history of economics shows that man is always the moving force because of his drive to realize his wishes, while the speed, extent, depth and span of any reform depends on the involvement of the individuals implementing it.

Our reforms have all had a great deal in common, and their proponents and opponents have always had similarities. Our reforms have all started from the top, at the initiative of a leader. This is a trait of our socialist society. Lenin decreed the change from food tax to food distribution, the transition to economic methods of management, and the development of the market. It was on Khrushchev's initiative that the reform in agriculture was begun. After Stalin's death and the officially initiated renunciation of the personality cult, we had officially inspired economic reforms in agriculture and industry. Our present reforms may justly be ascribed to Mikhail Gorbachev and other political leaders. But all these ideas can be realized only if the political leader expresses his society's subjective demands, if what he is suggesting is timely and is in fact the wish of the working masses. At the same time, reforms can only be successful if the working masses are involved in them.

Thus it is that the moving force in economic reform is the highest leadership of the country, supported by the more advanced section of the working population, by the intelligentsia, the working class and the peasantry. The chief enemy of any reform is bureaucratism, a term now synonymous with the administrative system of management. This is quite understandable, since our economic reforms have all aimed to undermine the power of the bureaucracy by depriving it of its life-blood, the right to dictate decisions. Bureaucratism is personified by those members of the apparatus at all levels to whom individual power and privileges are more important than the development of society as a whole. This rather large group of party, government and economic organizers have found allies for their defiance of perestroika in the old-fashioned economic directors, in the conservatively inclined intelligentsia, and in those members of the working class who did well out of the old, deformed society and are not happy with the higher demands placed on them by the new administrative system.

I must therefore repeat that in order to generate widespread support for our economic reforms we must involve the people in implementing them. The people must be the co-authors of and co-contributors to the reform. If this is not the case, then the bureaucratic apparatus triumphs again, and the political leaders and reformers lose.

Having examined some common aspects of the economic reforms, we must now ask why the previous reforms, all of which successfully gave our economy a useful push and produced obvious results, were always overturned after a period of between five and eight years. Each burst of development generated by the reform was inevitably followed by a period of distortion, increasing imbalance, and of negative economic growth tendencies.

The first time an economic reform was overturned was when Stalin broke with the Leninist principles of socialist construction and abolished the NEP. He used demagoguery in maintaining that he was faithfully following Lenin's path, quoting Lenin out of context to justify himself. This was nothing but demagoguery and lies. In reality the political system changed totally under

Stalin. The power of the Soviets was abolished, the apparatus became Stalin's servile tool, and harsh administrative, barrack-room methods were introduced in the management of the economy and other aspects of people's lives.

Was this development inevitable, and was it rooted in socialism itself? This question is posed more and more frequently by students at the moment. I share the view of the majority in thinking that Stalin's dictatorship and the tragic consequences of the personality cult were not inevitable. There were other ways: Lenin pointed them out. Socialism could have been built democratically. At the same time, the fact that this is how our history developed shows that there were certain historical preconditions for the personality cult. It was one eventuality waiting for its chance. The most important chance that made such a development possible was the low level of democracy in the first years of Soviet power. To a great extent this was connected with the low educational level of the population and its historical alienation from political power. The Communist Party, particularly that section of it which had been educated on Leninist principles, was very small and was unable to counter the concept, alien to true socialism, of the cult of the leader.

The growth of the personality cult was gradual, but it eventually vanquished the various opposition groupings within the Party. Stalin first allied himself with one group to smash another, then turned the same weapon against his former allies. Having divided the Party and surrounded himself with a powerful punitive and propaganda apparatus, he finally seized power. Once he had that, he took advantage of certain trends, in particular the need for industrialization and peasant co-operatives, to destroy the relationship between goods and money and to replace it with direct distribution. He thus introduced 'diktat' planning and instituted a totally administrative system of management.

Things went differently when Khrushchev's reforms were killed off. We must not forget that he was personally inconsistent, dizzy with success and boastful, traits that finally led to arbitrariness. But here, too, the deeper reason lies in a lack of understanding of more democratic forms of government. One man, Khrushchev, held enormous power in his hands: he was the Secretary-General of the Central Committee of the CPSU and also the Chairman of the Council of Ministers. He did in fact make a few modest attempts to introduce democracy into government. For the first time some limits were placed on the length of time any official could hold his post. This limit was two terms, though in exceptional cases people could be elected for a third term. This was not real democracy, however, just a pretence. Therefore, although glasnost began to flourish after the rejection of the personality cult, it was very swiftly muzzled. But this is not the full explanation. The return to administrative methods in the late fifties and early sixties, putting an end to the economic reforms introduced at the September 1953 Plenum, was to a great extent due to the incompleteness and inconsistency of Khrushchev's reforms.

First of all, only agriculture was reformed. Industry, construction, transport and other branches of the economy were left under administrative control.

Secondly, even in agriculture the central item was regulated by the administration: the amount of agricultural produce to be purchased by the state was decided centrally, as were the prices to be paid for it. The price to be paid for any surplus produce sold to the state was also fixed at the centre. For all that the decisions of the September Plenum had appeared to be revolutionary when compared with the preceding period, there had been no definite, irreversible change to an economic system of management. After the events of the 1956 counter-revolution which destroyed the Hungarian economy, our comrades in that country introduced a new order in agriculture, fully and consistently using economic methods of management. All forms of state planning 'diktat' were abolished. In other words all state control over the purchase of agricultural produce was abolished. The agricultural enterprises could decide for themselves what to sow and what to grow. Their decisions were taken on the basis of a system of prices and contracts with industrial, food processing and other agricultural enterprises. That is why, although thirty years have elapsed, Hungarian agriculture has not experienced a decline. Despite the fact that several times less capital is invested in agriculture in Hungary than in the USSR, Hungary's agriculture continues to develop and is one of the most efficient in Europe, producing 1.3 tons of grains and more than 150 kilograms of meat per head of population. A sizeable proportion of that produce is exported to the capitalist countries of Europe and to the Soviet Union.

Finally, the third reason for the premature failure of Khrushchev's reforms is that the economic reform was not viewed as part of a general social reconstruction but was seen as something alien being forced on the country.

So the backsliding to administrative methods under Khrushchev was largely caused by the insufficient depth and radicality of the reforms in the transition from administrative to economic methods, their incompleteness, the lack of co-ordination between economic and social reforms, and the retention of administrative methods in the management of the economy and society at large.

The economic reforms initiated in industry and agriculture in the mid-sixties were killed for similar reasons. Today, however, we are doing things that were never done before, for example introducing economic methods of management into industry as well as agriculture. It is true that agriculture and industry do not present a united front any more in our country, as the relations between them have been complicated by administrative decrees to such an extent that no real market has been established between the two branches. I should re-emphasize that the reform was incomplete, since on the one hand it did not extend to construction, transport and other branches, while on the other it did not really affect the central economic departments, the ministries, or the supply system; it involved very little change in the wages system; nothing was introduced into international economic relations; and, most importantly, the old investment and the old scientific and technological policies were to a great extent retained. Meanwhile the economy was growing and demanding ever greater inputs. Most of the profits earned by our enterprises were used for this centrally controlled and rapidly growing state expenditure.

Other lessons can be learnt from the errors of Khrushchev's reforms. The economic reforms in agriculture in the fifties were put into action against a background of social transformation connected with the renunciation of the personality cult and with greater civic awareness on the part of the country's citizens. In the mid-sixties social changes were minimal. Stability turning into stagnation is one way of describing the life of our society in that period. Economic reforms were completely dissociated from social ones, since there were no social reforms. No serious attempts were made to develop democracy in either our economic or our public life. In those years the concept of self-government was viewed as an importunate demand which had nothing to do with the development of socialism. The reforms of the mid-sixties were even more half-hearted than Khrushchev's and not just in agriculture.

Again the idea of a centralized purchasing plan to be implemented by directives remained in place. In industry there was a decrease in the number of defined tasks, but the main headings – the volume of production to be realized, the main items to be produced, the size of the wages fund, the amounts of profits and of capital investment, the rationing of resources, and the scientific and technological tasks to be done – all these were firmly set from above. It was therefore not difficult to stray from the path of economic methods back to the more familiar one of administrative 'diktat'. I have already explained how it happened: first one requirement was introduced by 'diktat', then another, then a third, until finally the long-term economic changes which had been intended were abandoned, and the centralized guardianship by the ministries of every procedural detail was regained. And there you have it – a resurrected administrative system. And while Khrushchev had to seriously reorganize one economic branch after another to return to the old methods, Brezhnev did not need to do anything of the kind. Under him, there was a gentle but fairly rapid descent into a system where economic methods could only function in conjunction with administrative ones and thence to a full 'diktat' administrative system. The whole process took just a few years.

Important lessons can be drawn from all of the above, and we drew them at the time perestroika was introduced. Those who are following the development of our perestroika have probably noticed that at almost every plenum, Gorbachev's speeches return to the lessons of the past, particularly to the years of stagnation and what caused them. I have often heard people ask why we go on digging the same patch. Why do we go on about the past? I think that to achieve the aims of perestroika we must overcome the tendencies of the past; we must destroy the braking mechanism and strengthen the accelerator. But to do so we must understand the past, we must understand how the braking process arises, what it consists of, what it really is. We must understand how those negative tendencies ever came into being, so that we can overcome them. I was therefore not particularly surprised when Gorbachev approached me and others before the April 1985 Plenum, and also before the June 1985 meeting of the Central Committee on the subject of technological and scientific development, and especially before the 27th Party Congress, for a detailed analysis of the demise of the NEP, describing how the braking process in the administrative system had arisen, what its characteristics were, why the previous economic reforms had failed, what lessons we could draw from our historical experience, and so on and so forth.

But gradually even I began to think that we talked too much about the past. In fact I began to think that it was wrong to blame everything on our predecessors: we were not that much better ourselves. In particular when the January 1987 Plenum was in preparation I gave voice to some objections. I thought there was little point in treading over the same ground after the 27th Congress, where everything had seemingly been said about past mistakes and every lesson studied carefully. I thought it was time to finish with the past.

Fortunately I was ignored. The analysis of the past at the January Plenum was more profound than any before. It clarified the main causes of our past mistakes and drew the main lesson from them; and it showed that previous analyses had not been sharp enough. It was at this Plenum that we clearly understood that the main, the most profound, reason for the deformation of socialist society, for the failure of economic reforms and other progressive initiatives, lay in a lack of democracy, in the way decisions were taken behind closed doors, and in the absence of any kind of control over the activity of the country's leaders. And the following all-important conclusion was drawn: that it is the full development of democracy within society and within the economy that will be the motivating force of perestroika and will make it irreversible.

This is the main lesson to be learnt from our past misfortunes. Having learnt this lesson I think that we shall have to return to the past again and again. We cannot say that we have fully understood all the internal tendencies that created the braking mechanism in our development and led to the disjunction of the production sector and its needs. When we analyse why perestroika is so slow and why it has encountered so many difficulties, we always mention as the most important reasons the fact that we underestimated the forces of inertia and resistance and also that we underestimated the extent of our economic deformation, the extent of the imbalances, and the extent to which we had fallen behind in our development. This important conclusion was drawn at the 19th Party Conference and may be summarized as follows: we did not fully understand how deep a hole we were in or how

165

steep the sides we had to scramble up were. This is the most important reason for the slowness of our progress and for the fact that our achievements are far more modest than they would have been had we fully understood what sort of obstacles we would meet and have to overcome. The measures we took initially were not far-reaching enough, because we did not have a clear idea of all the obstacles and obstructions we would have to face.

Our economic history is not over; it is history in the making, as we select our path to the future with one eye on the past.

How does perestroika differ from the unsuccessful reforms?

To sum up all the above, we should note three main differences between the present radical reconstruction of our economic management and the economic reforms of the fifties and sixties. First, the present reconstruction of our society and, in particular, of the economy is an all-round, holistic process, whereas past reforms were partial and limited. Secondly, the reform of management is a radical one, as we intend to introduce a system of management based on economic methods to replace the old system of administrative 'diktat'. In the past, reforms were limited to half-measures, and the administrative system was retained in the most important parts of the economy. These reforms sought only the partial introduction of economic methods. Thirdly, the moving force behind the present reconstruction of our economy is the democratization of our society. Above all, we intend to introduce self-administration and to involve the workers in administration. The earlier reforms did not emphasize democratization, self-government or any kind of realistic involvement of workers in management. Let us therefore look in greater detail at each one of these points and analyse what we have been able to do in the early stages of perestroika to reform management and thus determine what problems still await solutions.

The first point concerns the fact that perestroika is an all-embracing and holistic process. It is not just that we have proclaimed an overall reconstruction, a renovation of the whole of our socialist society and the revolutionary restructuring of all its

166

aspects. The most important thing is that we should follow the same route in our practical implementation of perestroika. There have already been great changes in the sphere of ideology, glasnost and truthfulness. At the 19th Party Conference the political system was reformed, and at the July 1988 Plenum the resolutions of the Party Conference were implemented by the setting of practical tasks and time limits. There is also a plan to reform the legal system and the judiciary. In other words we intend to reform the entire political, ideological and legal structure of our society.

A total reform of the economy should go hand-in-hand with the above. It is not just a question of radically reforming management. We need simultaneously to change our actual economic strategy and economic policies. A new investment policy has been announced which will promote the reconstruction and technical re-equipment of all branches of industry. New measures have been adopted to speed up scientific and technological developments and to integrate science and production. A strong new social policy is being worked out; a new international economic policy has been proclaimed and is being put into practice. In other words we are trying to drag the economy out of the mire with the help of two ropes: a new bill of rights and a new economic mechanism and management system.

It is worth noting that the transition to a complete new system of management is also all-embracing. We are making radical changes in the position of the main productive link, the planning system, in price formation, finance, banking and payment for labour. We aim to introduce wholesale trade instead of the centralized supply of materials, technological equipment and so on. The reform is intended to penetrate every section of the national economy and to involve every management activity. This will be a truly total reform of management, unlike the best of the previous attempts, that of 1965. The present economic reform has already demonstrated by the actions taken that it differs from the others not only in its breadth but in its depth. In 1965 the planning system, the organizational structure of sectoral and regional management, and the financial and banking system, were not intended to change. Today we have every intention of uprooting the existing system in order to create a market for the means of production, to change over to a system of financing according to long-term rules, to create new banks, to strengthen the commercial side of their activity, and so on. The 1965 reform involved state

167

enterprises and collective farms. Now, on the other hand, we are witnessing a development of pluralism in our attitudes to property. In every sphere of activity co-operatives and personal enterprises are springing up. This is new. There is also another radical difference between our reforms and previous ones: collective forms of labour organization and of incentives are developing rapidly. Most importantly, there has been a sizeable increase in collective lease-holding, the highest form of the renting relationship.

In the past, our reforms have involved a dabbling with prices. We are now planning a total price reform which will affect all prices for one simple reason – we intend to reform the very system of price formation and to allow free and contractual pricing. None of this existed before. The economic reforms of the past did not even touch international economic relations. Now we intend to allow enterprises and organizations to participate in the socialist international market. Some enterprises and conglomerates will even be allowed out on to the world market. More joint enterprises are being formed on Soviet territory, and we have declared our intention of making the rouble convertible. There are other differences between the present reform and past ones, but I think that what I have said is sufficient to show that these reforms are radically different and more comprehensive.

The situation at the moment is that only about half of the national economy has changed over to the new economic conditions. We have not yet carried out the price reform or adopted a system of wholesale trading. Banks have not yet gone over to a complete system of cost accounting and self-financing. The restructuring of sectoral management has not been completed, and the radical reconstruction of territorial management has not even begun. So we are about halfway to the total reform of all the branches of our economy. The crucial changes will take place in the next year or two. 1989 is intended as the year for the start of the price reform, for the large-scale transition to wholesale trading, for the banks to change over to a system of complete cost accounting and self-financing, for the widespread introduction of leaseholding, and for the reform of the political and judicial systems. By 1990 these changes will be mostly completed. We shall therefore enter the nineties with a basically different economic mechanism and management.

At the same time we shall not be able at this stage to renovate in any significant way the technological base of our society or to achieve a radical reconstruction of our economy and make our industrial output competitive. We are at the very beginning of a move towards solving our social problems and during this period we shall not be able to improve people's lives radically. Nor shall we be able to achieve a complete financial balance, to saturate the market with goods, or to end shortages and queues. We need time. Therefore if we intend to have perestroika in the widest sense of that word, we have to admit that it will not be completed in the 12th Five-year Plan. We shall have to work even harder on some of its aspects in the next five-year plan. This proves what we have said all along: perestroika is not a short-term campaign but a lengthy process of revolutionary reconstruction that will involve our entire society, starting with its productive base and finishing with the highest sphere – our culture, morals and ethics.

The other characteristic of the present reconstruction of the economy and its management, as I have already mentioned, is the series of radical measures aimed at introducing a new economic mechanism based on economic methods to replace the old administrative method of management by 'diktat'. During the reform of 1965 we retained the plan headings consisting of annual instructions from the top. Even after the reform, this was the way in which certain indices, such as the volume of realized production, the wages fund, profit levels, the actual goods to be produced, limits on the main types of resources, funding for them, and so on, were established. The decree for the present reform completely ends directional planning. No tasks will be set from above for any of the headings mentioned. One of the most important aspects of the administrative system of management is the centralized system whereby materials and technological equipment are supplied. This was retained in previous reforms, whereas we have made it our aim to abolish the system and replace it with a multi-channelled wholesale trade in capital goods. In due course, limits and funds should disappear, and their place will be taken by a free market in capital goods.

The centralized distribution system was not our only problem. In the past we had to live with a tightly defined system of centrally set prices. At present we are working on a reform of price formation which aims to limit the number of centrally established prices and to increase the proportion of contractual and free prices in the capital goods market as well as in the market for consumer goods and services.

The changes planned for the financial credit system will be far more profound. In the past this sector was left to function in a centralized way. We are now considering going over to a financial market. Financing will, by and large, remain regulated. This will undermine the fiscal character of our financial policy, and it will have to learn how to produce financial incentives. The greatest changes will take place in banking. New banks are being created, while the old ones are changing over to a system of cost accounting and self-financing. They will begin to be commercially active. A new market is being created and is developing, though at present only in a very limited way: this is the market in commercial paper. We already have some shares and bonds, and more will be issued. We intend to introduce cheques and credit cards, and so to do away with differentiated types of rouble. Gradually the rouble will come to correspond to its true value and will even become convertible. One of the basic principles of the new economic and managerial system will be the widespread use of leaseholding arrangements. This will transform the worker in a socialist enterprise from a wage-earner into a co-master or co-manager of the leased means of production and will provide a new motivating mechanism and new possibilities for involvement.

It is difficult to overestimate the vital importance of our plan to create a pluralist attitude to property. There is a powerful movement, which is encouraged by the state, for the creation of co-operatives, for the stimulation of personal enterprise on a self-employed basis, for the development of individual domestic holdings, for the individual construction of housing and for private gardening and allotment cultivation.

The main characteristic of the administrative managerial system is the petty supervision and detailed control of subordinate enterprises and organizations by the departments above them. This supervision and control applies not only to the final results but to every intermediate step, all defined by a large number of instructions and decrees. We will end this detailed control and supervision. Since in the new system the state will not be responsible for an enterprise's accounts, there is no need for the state to interfere with those accounts. Equally, an enterprise will no longer be responsible for the state's debts. Control will be achieved through the rouble and the final results of an enterprise's activity.

These genuinely radical measures, in contrast to the half-measures of the previous reforms, should change our economic system root and branch. The first things the economic system will deliver will be an end to shortages, the abolition of the dictatorship of the producer, and a move towards demand-led production which will satisfy social needs. We shall have to ensure that the markets exist, that they are saturated with goods, that there is competition, and that the consumer has a choice. If all this happens, the market will fulfil its main function in fixing the social cost of labour by reflecting this in a product's price and will regulate production.

There will be other qualitative changes. We shall move from an extensive economy to an intensive one; in other words, our economy will no longer develop at the expense of increased use of resources. It will become profitable for workers to find and use reserves and to speed up social-economic development. We will then continue to develop through increased efficiency and improved quality of output. We must create an economic system that will be receptive to new scientific and technological ideas and will be able to use these ideas rapidly and flexibly in new products and technologies.

This rejuvenated economy will turn its face to the people. The whole point of economic management is management through and by the people's economic interests. Under this kind of management, enterprises, working collectives and individual workers will require new economic conditions that make it possible to work profitably, while at the same time what is profitable for them will be profitable for the whole of society. In other words we must construct a system in which the interests of society, of the working collectives and of the individual workers will all be on the same plane. Of course, it is unlikely that these interests will coincide completely, but they will coincide in basic, vital matters. Individual welfare is the guarantor of social welfare. By enriching society, a person enriches and ennobles himself. Thus economic development is also a social act. Production economics becomes social economics, economics for people and their welfare.

All this is still only an intention as yet, but that does not mean that it consists of idle ideas and abstract dreams with no roots in reality. The intention permeates the document we have already adopted which formulates the ethical bases for the new economic and managerial systems. We have without doubt begun the transition from the administrative to the economic system of management. But we are still at the beginning. For the moment the administrative system is still more powerful and still influences our enterprises and society at large. This influence is exerted not only through the old economic forms – the old price system, the centralized supply system, the various limits dictated from above and so on – but also through some of the new forms. The administrative system has temporarily invaded the newly created economic system of management.

In the plan for 1988, state purchase orders were fixed according to the rules of the old administrative system as a directional plan dictated from above. The right to fix state purchase orders was handed over to the ministries, and they used this as a powerful weapon in reasserting their administrative 'diktat'. This mistake has been fully understood, and as of 1989, the ministries have been denied the right to decide state purchase orders. The share of production taken up by these orders will in any case decrease from 90–100 per cent in 1988 to about 60 per cent in 1989. In the processing industry the share will be less than half. The next step, a further decrease in state orders to something like 20 or 30 per cent of production, will be taken after the price reform and change-over to wholesale trading in the following five-year plan for the years 1991 to 1995.

Norms for the following were very largely centrally set by the administration: the wages fund, the amount of deductions from profits, the rate of allocation of residual profits into incentive funds for enterprises that had gone over to the new economic methods. The setting of these norms was also handed over to the ministries and departments. By and large they set individual norms for each enterprise and were guided in this process by the directives and tasks of the five-year plan established under the old system. This shortcoming has also been recognized and will be overcome in the new five-year plan, in which such norms will be unitary for the whole country and will be established by the highest authorities, either for the whole economy or for separate branches of it. There are other ties that make enterprises dependent on their 'own' ministries that have yet to be abolished. The ministries still exercise detailed supervision and control, although their administrative powers have been checked somewhat. But they will lose this kind of power completely only when wholesale trade becomes established, when they will not be able to use such strong levers as the setting of norms and funds. Then the enterprise will, quite independently of the ministry, form its own productive funds, buy

172

the necessary materials for its work, and create direct links with other enterprises.

Although one of the first lessons to be learnt from the past is that half-measures and half-hearted interventions will not achieve anything and that until the administrative system is abolished completely it will remain an obstacle in the path of reform, and although we have concluded that what we need is not half-measures but radical steps to introduce economic means in place of administrative ones, we still left room for half-heartedness in our Law on Enterprises and other basic laws; indeed this immediately affected the development of the reform. We have a saying, however, which goes like this: 'The great man is not the one who makes no mistakes, but the one who learns from them.' Fortunately we have understood our mistakes and have taken certain steps to correct them and, I hope, to prevent them from recurring in the future.

Last but not least, I must mention economic democracy, self-government, the participation of workers in the management. This is perhaps the most important aspect of the whole process, and in this area we have implemented certain radical measures the like of which have not been seen before. We have decided that the working collective will hold a vital position in the new system. It will have the right to make the final decision on the enterprise's plan and on the distribution of the incentive fund, to elect the director and other managers, and to form a council that will represent it in the enterprise's day-to-day activities. This progress will take place against a background of general democratization, increased self-government, and more power being handed over to the Soviets.

Democratization as the main moving force of perestroika

We view democratization as the main moving force behind perestroika and the chief guarantee of its irreversibility. But we did not come to this conclusion immediately. Glasnost and other democratic attributes were first developed immediately after the April 1985 Plenum of the Central Committee, but the full importance of democracy for the development of perestroika did not become apparent to us for another two years. It was proclaimed loudly and clearly at the January 1987 Plenum, which had actually been called to discuss personnel policies. Nevertheless, the most important point raised at the Plenum by Mikhail Gorbachev was the question of democracy. At the time many people thought it had been raised for purely propaganda purposes, because no steps were taken to further democracy after the Plenum. But what it did do was to awaken thoughts of this in many people and to push the media to a discussion of this allegedly complicated question. There followed an attempt to do away with the 'black spots in history', and this widening of glasnost prepared the ground for realistic measures aimed at the widening of democracy.

At the June 1987 Plenum an important step was taken towards democratization in management. This was the transition to self-government about which I have already written briefly. The Law on Enterprises ratified this important new idea. But a year and a half passed before the democratic ideas were turned into concrete policies. This happened when the 19th All-Union Conference of the CPSU, which took place at the end of June 1988, passed resolutions about reforming the political and legal systems, the struggle against bureaucratism, and the development of glasnost. Everything was said and done with a view to democratizing the Party and society as a whole. The most important tenets of this vital aspect of perestroika are contained in the general resolution prepared at the end of the conference by a commission under Mikhail Gorbachev: *On the Democratization of Soviet Society and the Reform of the Political System.*

Why do we need widespread democratization? Why is it that perestroika cannot become irreversible unless it is supported by democracy? Why is it the moving force of perestroika? Previous reforms failed precisely because they did not include the people, because they could be stopped or banned by a small group, or even by one person, as in the case of Stalin (or Khrushchev in the later part of his rule). Brezhnev could have done the same, but by the time he achieved unlimited power he was very ill and the country was in fact governed in his name by his entourage.

It is only through democratization that the workers can be included in the process of perestroika because only democracy can give all power to the people. People will care about something that depends on what they do. They will work harder if they know

174

that by doing so they can influence a course of action. To achieve this, we must involve the masses in management, ensure that they participate in discussions about possible developments, about the deployment of funds, or about which measures should be carried out first and which second. For the very word democracy comes from 'demos', which means the people; so democracy means literally the rule of the people.

Writings on this subject, particularly in the West, often use the word 'liberalization'. That is not a bad word, and the process of liberalization is not a bad process. But still its meaning is different. Liberalization means allowing things; it means power being granted from above. The higher authorities can allow freedom in a particular sphere, that is, they can liberalize that sphere. Then again they can limit that freedom. The people do not participate in liberalization, though some parts of the population may benefit from the process. Democratization is a qualitatively different process. Through it the people acquire power, and that is something not doled out by decrees from above. And we, the supporters of perestroika, wish to deepen and widen the process. We stand for genuine democratization. The more conservative forces in our society, to be found above all in the ruling apparatus, often on a very high level, are in fact opposed to many aspects of perestroika but have to take into account the need for glasnost. They want to reduce the process to one of mere liberalization, that is, they want to dole out freedom in doses decided behind closed doors by themselves, and, if need be, to take it away in the same manner. As we know, this has already been tried, especially in connection with glasnost in the press.

Nina Andreyeva's article in *Sovietskaya Rossiya*, which openly attacked excessive glasnost and the new habit of telling the truth about the tragedies of the past, was widely seen as the manifesto of these conservative, anti-perestroika forces. Fortunately our party and state leaders responded crushingly to this attempt to undermine perestroika and to unite its opponents, all those who dislike glasnost and truth, all those who fear true democracy. We need a radical reform of our society and Party to ensure political and judicial democracy. The main tenets of such a reform were formulated at the 19th Party Conference.

I participated in the conference, having been invited to attend all its sessions as a guest. Many people in our country, and especially friends and journalists abroad, have asked me: why is it that you, who have done so much to further economic reform in the Soviet Union, were not elected to be a delegate at the conference? Let me answer that question once again. Every person has his role in life and his allotted place. I have never been a politician and have never participated in large political forums. I have never been a delegate to any district, city or regional council, let alone the Supreme Soviet. I have never been a delegate to any Party congress and certainly have never been a member of the higher Party authorities. There are good reasons for this. I have devoted my life to scientific research, and by this work I have achieved a high position in science, if that has a meaning in science. Scientists hold elections too, and they are considerably harder to win than the ones for the Party organs. After all, there is competition, and voting is secret. To become a corresponding member of the Academy of Sciences one has to win at least two-thirds of the votes, that is, two-thirds of the members first of one's own department (in my case the Department of Economics), then of the entire Academy. To be elected secretary of my department, that is, head of the Department of Economics, I had to submit to a secret ballot first at the general meeting of the department, then at the general meeting of the whole Academy. The same general meeting elected me on to the praesidium of the Academy. I am, therefore, one of the few academicians who are members of the Academy's praesidium and of its body.

What is the proportion of academicians to the population of this country? On average there is one for every one million people, and the number of the members of the praesidium is one-tenth of that. So what would be the point of me, a man who is not a politician, who has chosen to be a scientist, becoming a delegate to a Party conference or congress? I am working for perestroika in any case, and if important economic questions are ever discussed, as they were at the June 1987 Plenum and often are at meetings of the Council of Ministers, or other forums, I invariably take part in the discussion. Furthermore, I take part not only in the open debates but also in the preliminaries – the preparation of the materials needed for the discussion of important economic problems and for the decisions to be taken. Of course I do not do the latter all on my own but as one of a group.

Democratization is not simply a process whereby workers become involved in management, become part of perestroika, thus increasing their working and social activity. What is very important is that in conditions of real, free-ranging democracy, secret and unilateral decisions which often do not take into account the interests of society as a whole, the interests of the people, will become an impossibility. Under glasnost – democracy – all important decisions are taken openly before the whole of society. Society takes part in the discussions, evaluations and elaboration of each of these decisions, and this ensures that they are better-founded and more in keeping with the needs of the people. Furthermore, collective work on a decision creates an atmosphere that is favourable to its implementation, because it is during discussions that people come to understand its importance and urgency, and discover the best way of implementing it. Sometimes practical steps are taken even before a decision is actually formalized. This ensures that a good decision is put into practice with maximum ease. The relatively short experience we have had of glasnost and democracy – only a few years, after all – has shown quite clearly that this process is immensely important to the development of the country. I shall quote one example that I happen to know from first-hand experience.

There is an interesting story connected with the proposed taxation of the newly created co-operatives and their members. As everyone knows, we have, in the course of perestroika, encouraged the development of co-operatives in every sphere of our economy. An emergency decree was agreed on allowing the creation of such co-operatives without undue delay. In a very short time, just a few months, about 10,000 co-operatives were set up on the basis of this emergency decree. At the same time we began to prepare a new Law on Co-operatives. The preparations were thorough and open. Members of the co-operatives, scientists and the public at large were involved in the work. It was then thrown open to a general discussion, which became very lively across the country. About 80,000 suggestions and amendments were proposed. The draft was then written up by a competent commission, discussed at a congress of collective farm members, and finally presented at a session of the Supreme Soviet by the Chairman of the Council of Ministers, Nikolai Ryzhkov, who spoke at length on the subject and presented careful arguments. Everything was open and above board, and the law was ratified. But behind closed doors a small number of people, led by the Minister of Finance, held discussions of their own and worked out a system for taxing the co-operatives and their members. No member of a co-operative, no scientist, no representative of the public was allowed anywhere near this discussion. In fact none of them knew that a mine was being laid underneath the mighty building of the co-operative movement. Within the government, the tax proposal was also discussed by a select group of people and was immediately passed – without any real discussion, as it turned out later – by the Praesidium of the Supreme Soviet, which published the new decree. Even before the discussions about the co-operatives had been completed it became clear that a gigantic blow had been struck against them. The tax to be imposed was not simply progressive; it rose to 90 per cent of a highly paid co-operative worker's income. The tax was in fact prohibitive and immediately created an enormous barrier against the development of co-operatives. This decree stayed in force for three months. A number of co-operatives had to close down because of this destructive tax system, and others had to curtail the volume of their production. The decree held back many potential members of co-operatives.

When the decree was published there followed a storm of protests from the co-operatives, from scientists and from the public at large. Public opinion was so negative that the deputies of the Supreme Soviet discussed the whole problem at their commission sitting, the prelude to a full session. It was then discussed at the general session of the Supreme Soviet, and the decree was not ratified. As it had previously been passed by the Praesidium of the Supreme Soviet, this created a totally new precedent in our political life. But even after this, the decree remained in force for some time, simply out of inertia. It was finally annulled by the government and the Praesidium of the Supreme Soviet under the pressure of the well-founded criticisms expressed by public opinion. But once again it was the Minister of Finance, Boris Gostyev, who was asked to prepare a new plan for taxing the co-operatives. He did so with members of other organizations and presented it to the Council of Ministers. The Council then held a special meeting to which members of co-operatives, scientists and various other specialists were invited. The whole question was discussed in detail for eight months, and this second proposal was rejected too. The next request for a proposal was accompanied by a direct instruction to formulate it in such a way as to encourage the development of co-operatives.

I spoke up, together with others, against the plan to tax the co-operatives. When the Economics Section of the Academy of Sciences discussed the projected Law on Co-operatives, it called a large meeting together with the Institute of Law and Justice and invited a number of other specialists. We unanimously criticized and rejected the new tax on co-operatives and their members. After the discussion, we wrote a letter to the Supreme Soviet requesting it not to ratify the decree. Some of us spoke at the commissions of the Supreme Soviet devoted to this problem. Members of the department are now taking part in the commission preparing a new plan for taxing the co-operatives, and I hope that this one will be acceptable. Development in the co-operative sector has speeded up after this show of support from the government and public opinion. By the middle of 1988 about 40,000 co-operatives had been organized. They have formed their own associations and unions and are playing an ever-increasing role in economic development.

This is not the only example I could cite. There have been cases where glasnost helped to solve ecological problems, as for instance on Lake Baikal and Lake Ladoga. In other cases glasnost has helped to preserve ancient monuments which were about to be demolished by over-zealous officials. It was glasnost that allowed us to understand fully the mistakes made by Gosplan, the Ministry of Finance and Gossnab in the setting of state purchase orders and economic norms in the plan for 1988. The mistakes, on the other hand, had been made possible by the fact that discussions about these matters were carried out in secret behind closed doors. Arguments presented by economists were not taken into account. The whole problem was not discussed in print; the opinion of managers of enterprises was not canvassed.

This sort of approach was criticized by the Central Committee and the government, and when the results of the transition to new economic conditions were analysed, the work of those particular departments was deemed to be unsatisfactory. The membership and above all the leadership of the Commission on Management were changed: Nikolai Talyzin was replaced as chairman by Yury Maslyukov. Immediate measures were taken to change the way in which state purchase orders were set. I took part in two discussions on the subject conducted by the Council of Ministers – openly, and with the participation of specialists. Managers of enterprises were also invited to these discussions. They too spoke at the meetings. After detailed debate an emergency regulation on state orders was adopted for two years. This has recently been published in the *Ekonomicheskaya Gazeta*. Glasnost and democracy once again allowed us to make a more balanced and sounder decision which will advance the economic reform of management.

WILL THE SOVIET
ECONOMY OPEN UP?

*The new political thinking and Soviet
international economic relations*

Our economy is in many ways a closed economy, in that external economic ties play a lesser role here than in many other countries. The USSR's share of the world market is at least five times lower than our share of world industrial production. And our activities on the world market are very largely in exports of fuel and raw materials and imports of machinery, equipment, food and metal products. We have only a negligible amount of scientific and technological and financial ties with the outside world and engage in very few joint ventures. Furthermore, the rouble is not convertible.

Before perestroika the country's internal economy was separated from the world economy by a thick wall, because all international economic activities had to go through an intermediary, the Ministry of Foreign Trade. Our ministries, conglomerates and enterprises had no direct outlet either to the socialist or to the capitalist market. If an enterprise produced something that went for export, it was paid according to the internal price structure, ignoring the product's value on the world market. The hard currency thus earned went almost entirely into central funds. So it was not of any benefit to an enterprise to produce anything for export, to become involved in international economic activities; it was simply an additional burden, one which was, moreover, strictly controlled. If an enterprise failed to produce export goods it had been instructed to produce, its manager and workers would be deprived of their bonuses.

The fact that our economy was closed made us self-sufficient by necessity. We did not make effective use of the international division of labour. This separation between our internal and our external economy has severely affected many aspects of our economic development. First of all it is detrimental to the quality of our output, since we do not have to compete with other countries. Since a good deal of our output is not for export, and many of the branches of our economy do not produce for export at all, we have distanced ourselves from international standards. We do not know what the real demands of an exacting consumer are, and we have not followed developments in those spheres of activity. The absence of any kind of co-operation leads inevitably to technical backwardness and poor quality.

Self-sufficiency is particularly harmful in a time of rapid scientific and technological development, when demands concerning quality change rapidly and new products and technologies appear all the time. When a producer has to consider only his internal market (particularly when there are shortages), he feels he has a monopoly. He can go on producing the same obsolete item year after year and never bother to think about improving its quality or the technology behind it. Because of this we have fallen badly behind in the last fifteen or twenty years, even in those areas where in terms of quantity our production has been on the same level as world production, for example the manufacture of passenger aircraft. An inability to enter the world market creates a hothouse atmosphere for enterprises and organizations. They are not forced to change their product, improve quality or adopt new technology. The workers of those enterprises, their managers, designers, engineers and others, do not sell their output abroad, do not work together with foreign firms, and do not, therefore, participate in the world experience of production. They continue to stew in their own juice. Ultimately, they generally fall behind.

But there is another side to the question. Trade between countries is the economic basis for co-operation between the peoples of those countries. If we work together with other countries in the economic sphere, we make it possible to co-operate in other spheres, in politics, in the fight for disarmament, for security and peace.

This alienation, this closed economy to a certain extent corresponded to the old outlook that divided the world into different political systems which had to be in confrontation, a world of enemies struggling against each other. The old thinking was based on the premise that every problem had to be approached from the position of class. From the class point of view, the West's businessmen were exploiters. This being so, we had to avoid dealing with them except when there was no alternative. And so we used international trade only for special one-off purposes or to help in speeding up our development or improve efficiency. We used trade, quite frankly, to mend the holes in our national economy, to deal with certain imbalances, to overcome our backwardness in particular spheres, and so on. If we had trouble with agriculture, then we imported food; if our own pipe-making industry could not produce enough pipes, we imported them on a massive scale; if our chemical technology and chemical engineering were falling behind, we would buy whole chemical plants from the West, complete with technology.

Perestroika has led to a new political view. New approaches have been developed and new policies formulated in all spheres, including that of external economic relations. But the foreign economic policy we have promulgated in the last three years is a sort of synthesis of our external and our internal economic policies. Our new political thinking has changed our attitude to the world. We now understand more clearly that the world is one whole and every part of it is interrelated with every other. We have seen the importance of approaching problems of co-operation, and indeed all other world problems, such as those of war and peace, not from a class position but from a general human position. When we look at an external political problem now, we do not try to look unilaterally to our own interests, we do not simply try to get what we want and never mind everyone else. Now we try to understand the other side's point of view. We try to find some common ground, some mutuality of interests, because we now think that if we act in this way our co-operation will be mutually beneficial and therefore stable and long-lasting.

Having adopted this approach, we have begun to look at our

183

own country as an indivisible part of the whole world of nations and our economy as a part of the world economy. We have analysed the situation and come to the conclusion that our level of foreign trade, our position in the world market, does not correspond to the economic, scientific and technological potential of our country. From this we have drawn the inevitable conclusion that we must become more involved in the international division of labour, in the system of world economic relations. In other words we must make our country more open in the economic field. But not only in that: our new outlook demands that we become more open in the spheres of information, culture, science and technology.

At the 19th Party Conference, which introduced a new stage in the implementation of perestroika, special emphasis was placed on the need to utilize the advantages of the international division of labour. It was further emphasized that we must increase trade with other countries on terms of mutual profitability and must set our sights on a complex system of international co-operation in science, technology and production.

Such radical changes in our foreign economic policies will lead to great changes in our internal ones as well. Once enterprises and conglomerates have been given a great deal of independence, once they have gone over to cost accounting, self-financing and self-management, the whole question of foreign economic links will arise in a completely different form.

Foreign economic relations will now involve enterprises, conglomerates, and also ministries which deal with special branches of the economy. The monopoly enjoyed by the Ministry of Foreign Trade has been liquidated and the ministry itself reorganized. At first most ministries and departments, as well as more than 100 enterprises and conglomerates, were given the right to engage in foreign trade directly. Then, in early December 1988, the Council of Ministers looked at the country's experiences so far and passed a resolution entitled *The Further Development of Foreign Economic Activities by State, Co-operatives and Other Social Enterprises, Conglomerates and Organizations*. This decreed that all enterprises, co-operatives and organizations which produced competitive goods or provided competitive services could engage in foreign trade directly for both export and import. This constitutes a radical change in the economic mechanism. Enterprises and conglomerates are going over to a system of cost accounting in hard currency,

184

and they are expected to cover their currency expenses from the hard currency they earn, by selling their products or services. Previously almost all their hard currency was taken away from the enterprises. Now a considerable proportion remains in their hands, to be used freely for their own purposes. This provides immediate incentives for the enterprises to earn more hard currency and to become involved in foreign economic activities. Furthermore the above-mentioned December decree on this subject allows the enterprises and conglomerates to spend their convertible roubles, the currency of other Comecon countries, and up to 10 per cent of their other funds, including convertible currency, on acquiring consumer goods, medicines and medical technology, on improving material and technological conditions at the workplace and outside it, and so on. All such expenditure must be decided on by the workforce.

We have set new guidelines for the development of our economy, its various branches and enterprises. Our task is radically to improve the quality of our output and its competitiveness. For that we must cross new technological boundaries, ones that are the same the world over. We aim some time in the future to achieve top levels of labour productivity and other indices of efficiency. These new guidelines require active co-operation with foreign partners, because it is only on the world market that we can prove the competitiveness and quality of our goods.

Extensive scientific and technological co-operation with foreign firms will allow us to understand better the levels of technical development we must achieve. Therefore our new economic strategy demands greater economic co-operation with other countries.

The new strategy for foreign economic relations

All the above shows that the most important decision resulting from our new ideas about foreign trade was the decision to increase rapidly all foreign economic activities. In fact, they must develop more rapidly even than our internal economy. We intend to double the general volume of production within the Soviet Union in the fifteen years from 1986 to 2000. At the same time we intend to increase the volume of foreign trade by 2.2–2.4 times. Exports

185

must grow even faster, by something like 2.5–2.7 times, to get rid of the foreign debt we already have. The Soviet Union's share in world trade will then rise from the present 4 per cent to 6 per cent in the year 2000. Our internal economy will then become part of the international division of labour, and exports will make up 9 per cent of the national economy, as opposed to the present 6 per cent. At the same time our economic development will be affected by imports. Even now up to 20 per cent of the growth in the number of cars and equipment and up to 15 per cent of the growth in retail consumer goods is due to imports.

It seems to me that prioritizing the development of foreign economic relations over internal economic development to the extent described above represents the barest minimum. The figures were decided on at a time when foreign trade was virtually at a standstill because of the drop in the price of oil and other raw materials. Nor could we take into account the influence certain aspects of perestroika should have on this development, as any effects were not yet noticeable. We had only just started implementing the various measures, and in any case they were not really sufficiently radical, comprehensive or consistent. I shall talk about that later on. So, in my opinion, we ought to make greater efforts to develop foreign economic relations faster than home production. Only then will the Soviet Union become a great trading power as well as a great industrial power.

Let us look at the effect the reconstruction of the USSR's foreign economic relations has had on external trade. I have already mentioned that the Ministry of Foreign Trade lost its monopoly. The newly formed Ministry of Foreign Economic Relations was to a great extent freed from any operative commercial function. In the past the ministry had eighty foreign trade organizations. This number has been reduced to twenty-five. These are involved in trade in oil and other kinds of fuel, food and other goods that could be of importance to the state as a whole. All other foreign economic matters are now the province of the relevant ministries. For example, Avtoexport now comes under the Ministry of Automobile Production, Tratorexport under the Ministry of Agricultural Machinery, Stankoexport under the Ministry of Machine Tools, Soyuzkhimprom under the Ministry of the Chemical Industry, and so on. In 1986, a new permanent authority was created under the Council of Ministers, the State Commission for Foreign Economic Relations. In addition the importance of the USSR

Chamber of Industry and Commerce has grown. In accordance with our policies of democratization, this body is becoming the representative of our country's business circles. Alongside the Chamber, new associations are being formed, such as business associations with other countries, a council of directors of joint enterprises, and so on. The Chamber has the right to propose plans for legislation, maintain contacts with associations of entrepreneurs, provide consultancies, organize exhibitions, issue licences, and so on.

As I have already pointed out, a fair number of our ministries and departments, all the republican Councils of Ministers, and also the cities of Moscow and Leningrad have been given the right to engage in foreign trade directly alongside the larger conglomerates, enterprises and some co-operatives and their associations. Permissions are given by the State Commission for Foreign Economic Relations, which decides how competitive a product is and examines the activities and experience of the organization making the application. The number of organizations and enterprises becoming involved in foreign trade has grown year by year. Since we started in 1987, all these ministries, republics, conglomerates and enterprises have accounted for 20 per cent of the country's foreign trade and for more than 40 per cent of exported machinery and equipment. Although these organizations had very little experience, they nevertheless managed to overcome the recession in our foreign trade turnover.

It must also be pointed out that the status of those enterprises and conglomerates that have entered the external market through intermediaries has changed. In the past all external relations, too, were based on the administrative method. Now they are based on contracts and each enterprise has the right to choose with whom it will deal and on what conditions. As for economic connections with partners from socialist countries, there no intermediary is required; each enterprise can establish its own connections. These conditions also apply to cross-border and littoral trade, of particular importance to the Baltic states, Western Byelorussia and the regions of the Far East. The turnover here in 1987 exceeded 200 million roubles.

Our newly reorganized foreign economic activities and new economic mechanism have allowed us to overcome the dire consequences of the drop in the price of oil and other raw materials which were the mainstays of Soviet exports. It is enough to point out that because of this drop in prices the Soviet Union lost 20 billion dollars in her trade in the period 1985–8 with the capitalist countries alone. In 1986–7 there was an absolute reduction in Soviet foreign trade turnover, and in the past two years it has fallen by about 10 per cent in current prices, i.e. from about 142 billion roubles to 129 billion roubles. Since at the same time our trade turnover with other Comecon countries not only did not fall but actually rose a little, it is safe to say that there was an enormous reduction in our trade with the developed capitalist countries. In 1985 turnover was 38 billion roubles; in 1987 it was 28 billion roubles. Our trade with the developing countries also fell from 17.2 billion roubles to 14.5 billion roubles. It is worth noting that this reduction in value of foreign trade occurred because of the price factor; the actual volume of foreign trade increased. In 1988, foreign trade turnover in current prices increased by 2.1 per cent and rose to 132 billion roubles, but because the export price of oil fell, the value of our export trade also fell by 1.9 per cent to 67 billion roubles, although its physical volume had gone up by 4 per cent. Of course these results could have been considerably better if we had kept to our original decision to stimulate the work of enterprises actually producing for export.

As early as 1986, we decided that a sizeable proportion of the hard currency earned from the export of goods and services ought to be left in the hands of the enterprises, conglomerates and organizations which had generated them. How much should be left to them was set at different levels for different branches of our economy. In my opinion the residual share should be as high as possible, for as things stand the amount left to them at present is not sufficient to act as an incentive for increased export. In the motor car industry, for instance, only 30 per cent of the hard currency earned from export is left to the enterprise. This is clearly insufficient. To encourage the development of co-operatives it has been decided that they will be entitled to 100 per cent of the hard currency they earn. But the ministries and departments that stand above the enterprises use the contradictory nature of our various rules and regulations to cream off into central funds as much of the hard currency as they see fit, rather than a certain sum up to 10 per cent of what has been earned. This attitude is depriving some enterprises of the possibility of being self-financing in hard currency, and they have found themselves unable to import the equipment that would in turn enable them to expand their production for export.

This is, unfortunately, a common attitude in the way we operate our foreign economic activity. In the past enterprises lost their hard currency in order that some other current aim should be reached. This weakened the incentive to provide more for export. Today, however, this sort of attitude is inexcusable when our whole intention is to provide the entire economic mechanism with long-term, stable rules and regulations that cannot be disrupted by anybody.

This brings us to the central problem of our attitude to foreign trade as part of our socio-economic development. In the past we regarded foreign trade as something secondary, just a way of filling up any holes in the national economy. Now we have a new strategy for foreign economic relations and a completely new model for our activities and must therefore look at this trade as an important independent factor in increasing production efficiency and influencing social development. The old attitude meant that our foreign economic relations were limited to a simple exchange of goods. In Marx's words, 'cloth was exchanged for clothes'. We were not good at inventing new productive forms of economic co-operation. The new models we have selected are rightly called industrial-technological and competitive. Their influence on the socio-economic development of our country will increase in the future.

Our new view of foreign economic activities assumes that foreign trade will grow faster than the overall economy within the country. In my opinion we should adhere to this idea very strictly and not rely on the old residual method of fund allocation for foreign economic activity. I think that if, for instance, there is demand on the internal market for a ton of some product but at the same time there is a possibility of selling that ton of goods for export, we should follow our policy of giving precedence to foreign trade and release that product for export. This principle is based on the premise that at the moment a ton of produce sold abroad will bring our country greater benefits than if it were sold on the home market.

On what do I base this opinion? I base it on a wider approach to the importance of foreign trade than we have ever had before. There are two aspects to this. Firstly, we must admit that the development of foreign links is important because it increases the efficiency and quality of our production and helps the growth of our national economy. The products we sell will bring in hard currency that will enable us to buy other products which as a rule will be of more use to our economic development than the original product would have been. Moreover, every time we sell our products we strengthen our position in the market and make further selling easier, since we have created pathways down which we can send more goods abroad to the foreign consumer. We all know that it is easy to lose a market for a product and quite hard to break into a market, to overcome competition. Therefore we must treasure every success. Another effect of exports is as follows: since any product has to compete with similar ones on the world market, Soviet producers, managers, engineers, and designers can compare their own products with analogous foreign ones and draw useful conclusions that will lead to improvements in quality and a reduction in the cost of production. This is particularly important because foreign markets are quite seriously regulated in other ways: there are environmental, health and safety standards to be met, certification is required for various technological products and so on. In order to sell our goods we shall have to work hard; we must send people abroad, which will give them much useful experience. Moreover, their experience of international economic conditions and of marketing will also be of value in our own internal activities. In other words the effect of foreign economic links in our internal development will be profound and very complex.

Nor must we underestimate another aspect of the whole problem. Foreign trade strengthens co-operation between nations, eases mutual understanding, makes the solution of political and other problems easier, and creates an atmosphere of trust, security and peace. Trade is after all considered to be the harbinger of peace. Through wide-ranging trade links nations learn to enrich each other and to understand each other's economies and science and technology. Lively trade always leads to lively cultural and scientific connections. This is very important in this one world of ours. Of course the relationship between trade and international politics is two-way. A political move towards disarmament creates a favourable atmosphere for the development of international trade. We know that during the Cold War economic relations between the USA and the USSR suffered badly and virtually ceased to exist. The USA constantly operated embargoes and discriminatory policies against us. The USSR was included in the list of countries that provided little for the American market. As Mikhail Gorbachev remarked during one of his meetings with President Reagan, we had successfully proved to each other that we could manage without mutual economic relations. But why cut off our noses to spite our faces? Once the two sides began to negotiate on matters of foreign policy, they also managed to improve their economic relations and increase co-operation. Given the industrial might of the USA and the USSR, it would be possible to increase trade between the two countries five or ten times over. But this can happen only if no discriminatory or other barriers are put in the way of the normal development of foreign economic relations, if there is a favourable atmosphere, and if we have established a system of international security.

This system of international security will consist primarily of a respect for the legitimate rights and interests of all participants in the world economy and a recognition that they are each responsible for their own economic activities. More concretely the following principles can be defined: firstly, no country should seek to harm another's national economy; secondly, countries should hold peaceful negotiations over economic problems without resorting to force; thirdly, no country should undermine another's economy through economic blockades, embargoes, sanctions, and so on; fourthly, there should be an undertaking not to use international trading relations to exert pressure on the internal or external affairs of another country. Obviously economic security cannot be a one-sided affair. It must be jointly agreed and based on peaceful co-existence and co-operation.

In the last few years, that is to say, during perestroika, our country has been particularly scrupulous in fulfilling these demands of international economic security. We wish to establish mutually beneficial relations with all the countries of the world. We do not seek unilateral benefits, because we understand that only by making allowances for mutual interests and mutual benefits can we construct permanent and effective economic relations.

At the same time we are being subjected to discriminatory measures by other countries, in particular the USA and other members of NATO. In 1949, on American insistence, a co-ordinating committee for the control of exports to the socialist countries (COCOM) was created. It has issued a list of many thousands of products and about 750 items of technological equipment which may not be exported to the socialist countries, particularly the Soviet Union, because they might be used for military purposes.

The USA has also invoked other discriminatory measures, boycotts, embargoes, and sanctions directed mainly against the USSR and Poland in the late seventies and early eighties. In particular the United States tried to make it more difficult for us to build the gas pipeline from Urengoy (in North-western Siberia) to the western border of the Soviet Union. The USA unilaterally suspended the supply of vital pipelaying and other equipment. We were forced urgently to redeploy our forces and funds. Within about six months we began manufacturing our own 16,000- and 25,000-kilowatt gas-pumping turbines. We also started producing small quantities of our own pipelayers and other machines which until then we had purchased wholly from abroad. In the end, the pipeline was completed in record time and we managed to fulfil all our agreements with our western partners.

Of course, we are now in a period of warmer international relations; and while there is progress in negotiations on military and political matters no one should use crude economic intervention methods like boycotts and embargoes. But the USSR still does not have most-favoured-nation status with the USA, and the resulting high tariffs mean it is not profitable for us to sell to America many products we might otherwise export there. A number of other serious difficulties in international economic relations arise out of the activites of COCOM.

Nevertheless, trade turnover between the socialist countries, including the Soviet Union, and the developed capitalist countries is growing systematically. The Comecon countries increased that turnover from about 4 billion dollars in 1955 to 110 billion dollars in 1987, with the Soviet Union's share increasing from 2 to 45 billion dollars.

The concept of international economic security can only be viewed as part and parcel of a new international economic order with some principles echoed in the tenets of the international security system. I am talking here about the need to regulate world economic relations at the inter-governmental level and the democratization of the whole system of international economic relations by political means. This assumes that economic aggression will be abandoned and that each country's right to use its own resources as it sees fit will be respected.

At the same time the new international order requires a mechanism for redistributing world production in favour of the developing countries. This would mean establishing fair prices for raw materials, food and industrial products. It would also require a lowering of interest rates and a repudiation of the use of foreign debt as an excuse for interfering in a country's internal affairs. It would be easier to establish this new order if there were a definite move towards disarmament. At a conference in New York in August 1987 devoted to the whole subject of the interconnection between disarmament and development, the Soviet Union and the other socialist countries suggested that an international fund for disarmament and development be set up. The idea was to create a special mechanism to allow part of the money released by disarmament to be directed to the problems of the developing countries and also to global problems facing humanity as a whole. The possibilities are not unlimited, since military expenditure in the developed countries makes up 6 per cent of their GNP, about twenty times as much as is given in aid to the developing countries. To make this whole idea realistic, the USSR suggested that each state should prepare a national plan for converting the production of military technology into peaceful production.

In a speech to the United Nations in New York in December 1988 President Gorbachev announced a sizeable unilateral reduction of Soviet military forces in Europe and the withdrawal of part of the Soviet army from the European socialist countries. At the same time, he said there would be a reduction in military expenditure and the development of military industry would be curtailed.

It is therefore obvious that foreign economic relations are just one constituent of foreign relations. In particular there is an organic interrelationship between military, political, ideological and other relations. The Soviet Union's strategy has consisted of an effort to achieve security and stable world peace in all those spheres. One part of this strategy is to ensure that we are more active in developing economic relations with other countries. Furthermore, in order to participate more actively in the international division of labour we must make extensive changes in the structure and style of our foreign trade.

In 1987 60 per cent of the Soviet Union's exports consisted of fuel and raw materials; only 15.5 per cent was machinery and equipment, 3.4 per cent chemical products and 2.6 per cent consumer goods. Even in the seventies, and certainly in the sixties, the proportions were far more satisfactory: machinery made up more than 20 per cent of the total, considerably more than fuel and electric energy. Now we export three times more fuel and electric energy than machinery and equipment.

Of course, as the Soviet Union occupies one-sixth of the earth's surface it has enormous natural resources, many of which can be extracted very efficiently. Exporting them is therefore very profitable. Our country will go on exporting oil and gas and petrochemicals in large quantities. It will also continue to export wood and other raw materials, as well as prepared raw materials. But what will change will be the ever-growing share of processed goods from state and co-operative enterprises, above all machinery and electronic goods, which will be exported in addition to all the more traditional goods.

The Soviet Union will specialize increasingly in the export of industrial goods, particularly machinery, equipment and chemicals, and also of a large selection of services. Even in the export of raw materials we shall emphatically try to sell them in processed form. This applies especially to wood, where we aim to increase exports considerably. As for fuel, exports will remain large but stable in volume, while structurally they will change so that a greater proportion will consist of gas and coal rather than oil. We have elaborated a special long-term programme for developing our export base for the future. This is founded on the specialization and industrialization of our exports, and its aim is to ensure that this considerable structural change in exports will be achieved.

It should be noted that in world trade processed goods make up about 70 per cent of the turnover in goods, with machine tools making up about 30 per cent of that. In our country machine tools make up 28 per cent of the entire volume of production but only 14 per cent of exports.

There will be a considerable change in Soviet imports as well. At the moment these mostly consist of foodstuffs and raw materials for the production of food, particularly grain, meat and butter. In the last five-year plan, up to 24 per cent of our imports were of this group of products. Since then the import of foodstuffs has decreased a little, making up only 16.1 per cent of the whole in 1987. There is no real need for our enormous imports of metal products (particularly pipes), which in the last five-year plan made up 11 per cent of the total volume of imports, but went down to 8.1 per cent in 1987. We firmly intend to become self-sufficient in staple foodstuffs, particularly in fodder and dairy and meat products. In the next five-year plan, imports of foodstuffs should therefore go down considerably. We are also conducting a radical restructuring of our steel industry, and I believe that soon many of the metallurgical products we now import will be produced here.

By the year 2000 we intend to increase the proportion of manufactured goods in Soviet exports from 30 per cent to 65 per cent, and the proportion of machinery and equipment from 15 per cent to 40 per cent, while reducing the share taken up by raw materials and fuel to just 25 per cent. In imports, the proportion of machine tools will go up from 40 per cent to 55 per cent, as we shall be concentrating on machinery as an investment for the future and will want to import the technology we need to re-equip our engineering works.

The content and direction of our foreign economic relations will change considerably. At the moment a large part of our foreign trade consists of simply buying and selling goods, mostly on a fairly well-balanced basis. In future foreign trade will be multi-faceted, because it will be accomplished through convertible currency. Within the development of foreign trade relations, the proportion of goods produced by co-operatives will go up quite sharply. There will be a real development of non-traditional trade in order to generate wide-ranging productive links between our enterprises and organizations in different countries. The trade in services like engineering will develop even faster than the trade in goods. In such cases the countries supplying the technology (and here the Soviet Union will on some occasions import and on others export) will also install and commission the plant and maintain, overhaul and modernize it if necessary. Scientific and technological links will develop particularly fast.

Our country will also play a more active part on the financial markets. This will be made possible by the increase in financial links between our country and others.

All of this put together will quite noticeably raise the effectiveness of our country's foreign economic links with other countries. According to our estimates, about one-tenth of the general increment in the national income will in future come from foreign trade. Furthermore, in the period up to the year 2000 greater efficiency in foreign trade should save us 130–40 billion roubles

195

in capital investment and release about 15 million workers.

We shall develop links with all countries and in all spheres. But of course the development of economic links with the socialist countries, particularly the Comecon ones, has a special significance for us. The socialist countries' role in the world is growing. At present they produce about one-third of the world's national income (the Comecon countries produce about a quarter). But the socialist countries' share of world trade is more modest, only about 12 per cent. The USSR leads here, because its share of the joint and national income from industrial production is two-thirds and 42 per cent of the goods turnover within Comecon. Of the USSR's own goods turnover, 43 per cent is with the Comecon countries. This is almost three times the volume of Soviet trade with the developed capitalist countries.

During the 12th Five-year Plan, 74 per cent of the Comecon countries' oil and petrochemicals, 99 per cent of their gas and 88 per cent of their electric energy were imported from the Soviet Union. In turn the Comecon countries sent 60 per cent of their exports to the Soviet Union.

What can we expect in the future? According to current trends it would appear that international trade will grow faster than internal productivity. So more and more of the goods and services a country can provide will go on to the international market. This tendency can be observed worldwide. Since 1950 the volume of world trade has increased twice as fast as internal productivity in the capitalist world. The forecast is that in twenty years' time about one-third, or even more, of the world's production will be involved in international trade. This tendency will bear ever more strongly on the development of the socialist countries, particularly as the socialist countries have traditionally shown greater growth than other economies. Since 1970 gross national income has increased 5.3 times in the socialist countries, only 2.9 times in the developed capitalist countries, and 4.7 times in developing countries.

This period was not in fact a particularly favourable one for the economies of the socialist countries. Growth had slowed down quite noticeably, and some indices of economic efficiency, such as labour productivity, energy and metal production, and the return on capital investments, did not improve when compared with the capitalist countries. In future we may expect a certain acceleration of socio-economic development in the socialist world, and this will be connected with an increase in the average annual rate of economic development in the USSR from 3 per cent in the previous five-year plan to 5 per cent and more in the nineties. In China the economic growth rate is quite high. Since 1980 national income has grown annually by 9 per cent on average, while in industry it has grown by 12 per cent and in agriculture by 9 per cent. Other socialist countries have also initiated profound reforms, and we can expect that the result will be faster economic development there too.

At the moment the Comecon countries are united in their efforts to restructure their economic mechanisms and to integrate them. One of the important aims of this integration is to create a unified market for the Comecon countries and to encourage, naturally enough, productive, economic, scientific and technological co-operation on a well-regulated and democratic basis. The measures we have taken in our country to allow enterprises and organizations to establish direct links with organizations in the socialist countries on a contractual basis will greatly help the integration process. The connections thus formed will affect co-operation in production, scientific research, training of personnel and so on. The partners will discuss among themselves the nature of their agreements and decide, again among themselves, what goods to produce. Soviet enterprises and organizations are very interested in forming such links, because all the currency they earn will stay with them. Today, when the rouble is still not convertible even into the currencies of the socialist countries, when the Soviet Union does not as yet have wholesale trade, and when the old internal prices, so different from world and Comecon prices, are still in force, such direct links are still by necessity limited. But they are growing all the time. The price reform in the Soviet Union, the transition to wholesale trade and the introduction of the convertible rouble will all help to broaden relationships between enterprises in different countries. We have also passed a law that allows the creation within the Soviet Union of joint enterprises with partners from socialist and other countries. International conglomerates have also been created, whose joint activity is based on a co-ordinating programme. Other joint enterprises for carrying out research and development work have also been set up.

Like the other socialist countries the Soviet Union wants to encourage the development of economic relations with Europe's capitalist countries. The recently established official relations between Comecon and the EEC will, in our opinion, lead to increased trade between the two groupings. This is particularly important because 60 per cent of the whole turnover between East and West is in trade between the EEC and Comecon. The recent agreement has created favourable conditions for overcoming the economic split within Europe and for creating one European home.

The joint declaration signed by the two organizations also makes it possible for the EEC to make agreements with individual members of Comecon. As has already been mentioned, negotiations are under way at this very time with the USSR and also with Rumania, Czechoslovakia and Hungary. Better economic conditions based on agreements between the EEC and individual countries will not just improve international economic conditions but will also spur us all on to greater efforts to solve Europe's common problems connected with power engineering, transport, ecology and technical collaboration. Undoubtedly this will increase possibilities for mutual financial aid, promote the eventual organization of a joint currency market, and foster collaboration in science and technology and the training and retraining of personnel, in particular of managers.

There are great untapped possibilities for developing economic relations between the USSR and the USA. The progress made towards the solution of our military, political and regional problems has improved the general climate between the two countries. Recently there have been noticeable, even radical, changes in the thinking of the people of the two countries and their attitudes to each other. This process was greatly helped by the development of glasnost in the Soviet Union, by the Telebridges organized between cities (for instance between Washington and Moscow), and by increased travel in both directions by people from wider sections of the population.

My opinion on these matters does not come simply from the press; I have witnessed the process myself. I was fortunate enough to be one of the consultants at Mikhail Gorbachev's talks with President Reagan in December 1987, and helped in the preparation for Gorbachev's meetings with representatives of America's business and intellectual circles and also took part in the actual meetings. I was much impressed by the interest expressed by the American public in perestroika, in close co-operation between the two countries, and in the personality of our leader, Mikhail Gorbachev. But on that occasion I only managed to visit Washington and New York, as a considerable proportion of time was taken up by meetings, breakfasts, dinners, press conferences and business meetings – everything that went with the actual meetings. But later on, in February–March 1988, I went on a longer trip to the United States. Then – apart from New York and Washington – I visited Chicago, Minneapolis, Los Angeles and San Francisco. In each of these cities I met many people and spoke to large audiences of entrepreneurs, journalists and politicians at scientific conferences, in universities, and so on. I visited a number of families and saw again a number of my old friends, as this was not by any means my first trip to the United States. I made fairly frequent trips there in the years between 1974 and 1978, and when I compare them with my recent visits the difference appears to me to be striking. More recently I have felt that there is an enormous, genuine interest in what is going on in our country, and a desire to acquire more information, particularly on the subject of economic changes. A typical question was: what can we do to help perestroika? What can we do to make perestroika irreversible? In my talks in the US Senate, the State Department, and the Department of Trade, certain constraints were observed, but in my meetings with businessmen in Chicago, Minneapolis and Los Angeles there was a great deal of friendliness, warmth and openness. Therefore I believe that the ideological conditions are right for improving economic, scientific, technical and other links between our countries. I am told that in the last few years 180 funds have been created with the express purpose of improving relations with different sections of Soviet society. My trip too was organized through one of these funds, by the Essalen Institute in California.

A month after my return several hundred American business-men came to the Soviet Union for a conference which had been organized by the Association for Soviet-American Trade Co-operation (AMSTET). At the same time, various trade nego-tiations took place, and, naturally enough, I met many of the participants. They said that if sufficient organizational and other efforts were made, then the volume of our trade with the United States could increase in the foreseeable future by 5–10 times. They added that we could in a short time set up hundreds of joint Soviet-American enterprises in the Soviet Union. To achieve this – and I am a great believer in the need for it – we must create the requisite conditions.

An important step towards this goal was initiated by one of the USSR's long-term partners, Occidental Petroleum, headed by Armand Hammer, to whose residence in Los Angeles I was invited. We talked about the creation of a gigantic joint enterprise to be called Tengis-Polymer which would include, apart from Hammer's company, two Italian companies and one from Japan. This joint enterprise, which will cost something like 6 billion dollars, will produce per year 1 million tons of polyethylene and polypropylene, as well as 1 million tons of granulated sulphur, using raw materials from the Tengis oil and gas fields and hydrogen sulphide deposits in the Gilev region of Kazakhstan on the north-eastern shore of the Caspian Sea.

I am against gigantomania. In fact I have frequently criticized the fact that we get too involved in the construction of giant enterprises like the Kama Automobile Factory, which makes 150-ton lorries. I think we must develop small and medium-size enterprises in the Soviet Union, and even in our efforts to collaborate with foreign firms we ought to try and work not just with the largest firms or international companies but with middle-sized and small enterprises, many of which have very high technical potentials.

Nevertheless in a large country like the USSR there are always very large problems whose solution demands big investment. At times like these we need the large capital that is at the disposal of the leading capitalist countries and their banks and companies. The Tengis-Polymer joint enterprise is one of the ways in which the recently discovered offshore oil and gas deposits in the Caspian could be utilized. And there are more resources besides the Tengis one: the Astrakhan and Karachegan gas deposits are already being worked, and other discoveries are being made all the time. There is a unique concentration of chemical raw materials in the area. The USSR is after all very backward in the processing of modern chemical polymers, and we need large-scale collaboration in order to develop the riches of the Caspian region. In my opinion Tengis-Polymer is just a beginning.

There is an ambitious plan to develop hydrocarbon deposits, above all the uniquely large deposits of natural gas to be found on the Yamal peninsula. But this is the Arctic, and one of the harshest parts of it. The Arctic is a desert where soil acidity is very high, temperatures very low, winds fierce, and there is absolutely no productive or social infrastructure. Everything must be started from scratch, thousands of kilometres away from any inhabited place. We shall therefore need completely new technological solutions and new approaches to the work. Of course we have already had similar experience in the development of the world's largest gas deposits in Urengoi, which is on the Arctic Circle, and we are close to completing the development of the Yamburg deposits on the shore of the Ob, 200 kilometres north of the Arctic Circle, where conditions are extremely hard. But the Yamal is far more difficult. We could organize extensive collaboration, especially as we can approach the shores of Yamal peninsula all the year round with Soviet atomic ice-breakers. The gas, or at least some of it, could be processed on the spot into ammonia or methane and then taken in tankers to the countries acquiring it.

Let us now look at an absolutely vital new state programme for speeding up the development of the Soviet Far East. We intend to invest 238 billion roubles over the next fifteen years in order to raise production there by 2.5–3 times and to create a machine-tool industry. In this work too we could involve large-scale joint enterprises whose aim would be to develop the area's natural resources (coal, hydrocarbon, non-ferrous metals, chemical raw materials, and unique forestry resources) and to improve the productive and social infrastructure (agriculture and the building industry) in order to help develop the processing industry on the spot. A joint enterprise would also undertake the development of related service industries and many other matters.

The United States, whose West Coast, with its enormous economic potential, is particularly well placed to become involved in the development of the Soviet Far East, might be interested in joint ventures there. Other possibilities for large-scale collaboration exist: for instance, Japanese companies might be interested, and Japan has, as we know, amassed an enormous amount of capital. Of the twenty-five largest banks in the world, the top seventeen are Japanese, and Japan's annual trade surplus is in the region of 100 billion dollars. I believe we could find effective ways of collaborating on a large scale with Japan. At the moment economic relations between the two countries are at a very low level, which is not unconnected with the fact that political relations are also very cool.

At the invitation of the Japanese Ministry of Foreign Affairs, I visited that fascinating country, looked at a number of its leading enterprises and talked to Japanese businessmen. Many of the latter displayed considerable interest in the possibility of developing relations between our two countries. The Japanese public was keenly interested in the problems of perestroika. As soon as that process began, a Japanese publishing house commissioned a book from me and insisted that it should be produced at lightning speed; in other words, it was to consist of already published articles and interviews. This was published immediately in Japan, and later another of my books was issued there, a work specially intended for the western reader in which I discussed the problems of the economic restructuring of the USSR. I believe the present lull in relations between our countries is only a temporary phenomenon; any minute the dam will burst and there will be, I hope, an immediate growth in our trade.

Another important aspect of the Soviet Union's economic policy is the number of agreements we have with developing countries. More than 14 per cent of our exports go to them, and more than 8 per cent of our imports come from them. Furthermore the Soviet Union gives technical aid to developing countries of the socialist persuasion by helping with a large number of building projects. In 1987 thirty-two such projects in Mongolia were completed with Soviet help.

As a socialist country that defends the poor and deprived, we have always paid a great deal of attention to the plight of the developing countries. When the socialist revolution took place in Russia, our country too was underdeveloped, with a poor and semi-literate population. The problem of underdeveloped countries is one of the central socio-economic problems of our planet. One billion people in these countries live below the poverty line, 780 million suffer from malnutrition, 850 million are illiterate, 1.5 billion have no access to medical assistance and 1 billion live in intolerable accommodation.

To overcome their backwardness, to make that jump into modern civilization, the developing countries must have a higher than average growth rate. This was happening until very recently. From the early fifties to the early eighties, the developing countries raised their share of the GNP of the non-socialist world from 16.4 per cent to 20.1 per cent. Their share of world exports had also grown considerably in that period, reaching 31 per cent in 1980.

But despite this fast economic growth, the difference in indices of production and consumption per head of population compared with the developed capitalist countries remains the same, at about 11.6 times. A considerable difference has persisted in the level of labour productivity: in industry it is 5.8 times lower, in agriculture 17.8 times lower. All these indices are affected by the huge population growth in the developing countries, which for many of them constitutes a serious problem. In some of the developing countries up to one-third of the people cannot work because of the rapid population growth and so lead lives of abject poverty.

The data given above on rates of economic growth are for the thirty-year period up to the early eighties. Unfortunately it must be said that since that time there has been a noticeable slowing down in the economic and social development of the developing countries. These countries' share of world exports has also gone down, as has the volume of their imports. Trying to maintain their standard of living, many of the developing countries have reduced their savings, making it more difficult for them to think of future development. The main reason for the serious socio-economic difficulties experienced by the developing countries is the big increase in their foreign debt. By 1987 this had grown to 2.4 times its 1979 level and at the moment it stands around 1 trillion dollars. What are the consequences of such a high debt? First of all, repayments absorb one-third of these countries' incomes from their exports of goods and services. Normally the situation is deemed to be critical if repayments make up 20 per cent, or at most 25 per cent. Fifty-five per cent of the developing countries have been termed hopeless debtors. Since 1984 the inflow of capital into the developing countries has actually been less than their payments to the developed countries.

The effect of this enormous foreign debt has been particularly harmful in Latin American and African countries. The problem of foreign debt links the developing and developed countries, and we must all search together for ways of democratizing the socio-economic development of the Third World. To achieve this we might limit the annual repayments exacted from the underdeveloped countries to a certain proportion of their budget; and in some cases where income is particularly low, as in sub-Saharan Africa, the debt could be written off altogether. We ought also to get rid of protectionist duties on goods and to create favourable trading conditions for the debtor countries.

I have already spoken of the need to introduce a new international economic order and a mechanism for the fair redistribution of world produce in favour of the underdeveloped countries. It must be pointed out that the developing countries spend quite unnecessarily high amounts for military purposes. In the mid-eighties their expenditure was almost 15 per cent of the whole world's military expenditure, amounting to 125 billion dollars. Annual purchases of armaments account for 14 billion dollars. In order to solve the problems of the Third World, we need a common policy, agreed under United Nations auspices.

At the United Nations the Soviet Head of State Mikhail Gorbachev announced our suggestions for the solution of the debt problem in the developing countries and showed that our country was ready to take an active part in every effort to solve this crucial problem.

Three months before this notable speech, UN Secretary-General Peres de Cuellar invited fifteen or twenty 'outstanding people', as he put it, to New York to discuss the problem of debt in developing countries. Quite unexpectedly I found myself on that list, the only person from my country. Not only am I not 'outstanding'; I cannot claim to be an expert on this complicated socio-economic and political problem. At the same time I was flattered to receive a personal invitation, and for two months I prepared myself intensively for the meeting. I studied the materials, met representatives of UNCTAD and of the debtor countries: Brazilians, Africans and Yugoslavs. The meeting was very interesting for me, because the participants included experts on the subject who demonstrated quite clearly that the problem was a global one and that there was a need for political leadership from the United Nations if the problem was ever going to be solved. They also explained a possible mechanism for such a process. I too made various contributions, among them a suggestion that we needed to work out a special programme for credit security which would in future make it impossible for countries to be drawn into excessive debt and would allow banks and other creditors to avoid a situation where they were unable to recover their loans in the normal way. The central economic idea I put forward was that there ought to be a connection between the amount a country should be expected to pay back annually and that country's development indices. This connection should be made in such a way as to ensure that there should not be any excessive demands for repayment, which would produce stagnation of the developing country's economy and would not be good either for the debtors or for the creditors, since the latter would be deprived of the economic base that allows debtors to pay off their debts and to import goods and develop their markets.

As can be seen, the Soviet Union's external economic policy is multi-faceted. Our aim is to collaborate with all the countries of the world and to strengthen and invigorate our links with all states and nations.

Joint enterprises with foreign firms

One important new development in the USSR's foreign economic activities is the creation of joint enterprises. As far back as the twenties, plans to set up joint firms using foreign capital on Soviet territory were mooted, but in fact, for ideological reasons, very little foreign capital was actually invested. A radical change in such thinking followed the April 1985 Plenum which announced the new economic strategy. By 1 January 1989, 191 joint enterprises had been registered on Soviet territory, with both Soviet and foreign organizations and firms participating in all of them.

Under what conditions can joint enterprises be set up in the Soviet Union? The state guarantees the security of the foreign partner's property and the right to transfer profits in the currency of the country in question in accordance with the foreign capital invested. Foreign firms which set up a joint enterprise have the right to participate directly in the management of that enterprise. Joint enterprises get priority in any building work they need: they operate freely outside the scope of the state plan or of any purchase orders; and they are free to carry on the import-export side of their activity in their own way. All the above conditions generally apply to joint enterprises operating anywhere. We also have some special rules devolving from the specifics of our country, which is a socialist country. Until recently the law insisted that 51 per cent of the capital should be Soviet, and as a consequence it was the Soviet side that controlled the position of the chairman and general manager of the enterprise. Furthermore, owing to the non-convertibility of the rouble, the enterprises must exercise cost accounting in hard currency, that is to say, any expenditure in non-Soviet currency had to be covered by income in that currency.

The state can take a tax of up to 30 per cent from the profits earned by a joint enterprise, but this is reduced in the first years of the enterprise's activity. Agreements have been reached with a number of foreign companies setting lower rates of 10 per cent and 20 per cent. The joint enterprise's earnings abroad in foreign currency are taxed at 20 per cent. This makes it profitable for the enterprise to use its earnings for growth or re-equipment and opens up another possibility for the use of currency: the purchase of Soviet goods for sale abroad. Joint enterprises are free to use and organize labour as they see fit, but they must conform to Soviet labour laws. That still leaves a lot of freedom for setting rates of pay and organizing the workforce. The state takes it upon itself to pay benefits to workers in joint enterprises, just as it does with other workers. In the case of disagreements and the closing down of joint enterprises, all decisions will be subject to international regulations.

Why set up joint enterprises in our country? First of all, they are of great importance in our stated aim of broadening our foreign economic relations and international collaboration. Through the joint enterprises we want to attract advanced technology and managerial experience. Furthermore, joint enterprises should eliminate the need for a number of imports and develop our export base, since part of the output of the joint enterprises will have to be sold abroad to cover their foreign currency expenses. It is also important to remember that these enterprises will attract additional financial and material resources for the development of social production. We look upon these enterprises as something mutually beneficial. What, in our opinion, will attract foreign firms to create joint enterprises on Soviet territory, rather than elsewhere? First of all, there is the matter of the large Soviet market and the possibility therefore of large-scale production for that market. Of course there is a certain limitation here. In order to provide a return on the foreign capital invested in the enterprise and to ensure that the foreign partner makes a profit in his own currency, part of the output of the enterprise, quite often a considerable part, will need to be sold abroad.

The possibility of large-scale production in the Soviet Union will allow companies to utilize the most advanced production technology and thereby reduce costs. These costs will be further reduced by the relative cheapness of labour in the Soviet Union due to the fact that a sizeable proportion of welfare benefits are paid by the state out of its own budget. The relative cheapness in the Soviet Union, of land and buildings, and of water and other natural resources, will also be an important factor. In many places the infrastructure is already in existence. The sciences are highly developed in the USSR, and in many fields it will be profitable to set up enterprises whose production utilizes those strengths.

All these factors act together. Many foreign firms have looked for, and indeed found, some sphere of activity and production where it would be particularly profitable to have a joint enterprise on Soviet territory. Let me quote one example, a joint enterprise with the Italian FATA group. The reason why I choose this particular example is that I have had contacts with the firm and was their consultant on a number of questions. FATA has collaborated with the USSR for a long time, having supplied the foundry and other finishing equipment for a number of projects. It already has a representative in Moscow. Together with the Soviet Foreign Trade organization Prommash (an enterprise that builds machinery for the food industry), FATA built a number of joint enterprises in Volsk in the Mari Autonomous Republic, which is on the middle reaches of the Volga in European Russia. Volsk was chosen because a factory was being built there and one of the completed sections seemed entirely suitable for a joint enterprise. It was decided to start production of refrigerator cabinets of various kinds. The possible volume of production was given as half a billion dollars a year. So large a scale of production made it possible to use automation. The factory intended to use only 2,000 workers, so the level of labour productivity was going to be almost twice as high as in the engineering factories of America. When we take low production costs and other favourable factors into account, the total cost of the cabinets was going to be considerably lower than in countries with smaller volumes of production. There is a demand for refrigerator cabinets all over the world, and so some of the production would be sold for convertible currency, while most of it would be sold in the Soviet Union. This joint enterprise is regarded by FATA as just a beginning, and the company are already discussing the possibility of extending production and making refrigerated containers. The more one eats, the hungrier one gets, and FATA is beginning to put forward far-reaching schemes for the creation of a whole system for the storage, transportation, processing and packaging of food that would be operated by a whole group of foreign companies, with the whole process co-ordinated by FATA itself.

Even a small joint enterprise is a kind of a window into our country for a number of foreign firms. If a firm finds out about our economic mechanisms through the setting-up of a small joint enterprise, it might decide to conclude larger agreements with the appropriate Soviet organizations and to develop mutually beneficial connections. Here is another characteristic example. Foreign firms that manufacture personal computers and write programs do not have good communications with the USSR. Most of these companies have no representatives in our country, and they do not know much about us. But the western market for personal computers is saturated, and competition there is cut-throat. On the other hand the Soviet market for personal computers, which in time could absorb millions and tens of millions of them, is at the moment there for the taking. Also these machines are constantly updated by improving the design of the computers and their microprocessors (such as Motorola and Intel), which are growing more and more complicated. New systems may also be designed to use even faster CPUs and transputers. These will require special programs, which must be written in a very short time. This means that as many programmers as possible must be involved. In the Soviet Union we have as many programmers as the United States – around 300,000 of them. So the production of programs in the USSR is guaranteed and might cost considerably less than it would in the West. At the same time the computer company would acquire an outlet on the Soviet market. The existence of a particular joint enterprise would promote the sale of that particular brand of personal computer in the Soviet Union, and it might become possible to manufacture or assemble the computers locally. It will also be necessary to translate potentially useful programs into Russian and to create new ones specially for use in the USSR. I am not even talking about any other benefits that might arise from such links. We must take into account that mathematical studies have traditionally been strong in the Soviet Union, and many of the innovatory ideas of modern mathematics, connected, for example, with optimization, were first worked on in our country. This was not an accident, because, as we have seen, it was a Soviet scientist, Leonid Kantorovich, who, though a professional mathematician, won the Nobel Prize for Economics precisely for his development of the theory of optimization.

In what particular sectors do we consider the creation of joint enterprises particularly valuable? I have often heard representatives of western companies saying in meetings that they lack precise information about the particular branches and projects for which we want an influx of foreign capital. But in June 1988 we worked out and transmitted to the West a list of more than 320 projects which are open to foreign investment for the years 1988–91. Some of these projects have a specific and clear purpose: they are connected with the solution of our food problem. In particular we are interested in projects for the processing of agricultural produce, for speeding up the development and re-equipment of light industry and other consumer and service industries. A large amount of capital is invested in all these branches. I should also mention the needs of the medical industry and the health service, which are being accorded the highest priority in our economic development; and another branch of the economy that has priority is the technical re-equipment of our engineering industry. This includes the production of domestic tools, electronics and computer equipment.

In the course of perestroika we have sharply increased the amount invested in engineering. In 1981–5 capital investment in engineering went up by 24 per cent but in the period 1986–90 it will go up by 80 per cent. Moreover the proportion invested in re-equipment and technical reconstruction, which used to be only one-third, will now go up to about half. The co-efficient of renewal of machine tools will go up by 3, 4, 5 times in various branches. Consequently the nature of our output will change too. In 1985 engineering returned only 3.1 per cent profit. In 1987 this went up to 9 per cent, and by 1990 the co-efficient will rise to 13 per cent. Obviously international collaboration in the shape of joint enterprises could be highly effective in the technical re-equipment of thousands of our engineering firms.

We have also in the course of perestroika adopted an intensive programme for the 'chemicalization' of the national economy. The Soviet Union leads the world in the production of a series of chemical raw materials, including artificial fertilizers, but in other branches of chemical production we have fallen far behind, both in terms of production and of know-how. That is why the creation of the large Tengis-Polymer joint enterprise, about which I have already written, is so important. It will produce 1 million tons of polymers per year.

Another important direction in which joint enterprises could develop is the utilization of natural resources. The USSR, a huge country with a territory of over 22 million square kilometres, is simply stuffed full of natural resources. We are, after all, the only country in the world that can satisfy all its own needs in fuel and raw materials and still export the balance. But such enormous riches and the ease with which they can be extracted have caused a somewhat profligate attitude, a kind of carelessness towards nature. We are now converting to a policy of economy and care about ecology and our environment. This requires a different approach and the complex use of raw materials. We must also think in terms of wasteless technology. This applies to the processing of wood, to the extraction, enrichment and processing of minerals, particularly of non-ferrous metals. Western countries have already started on this path of resource-saving, wasteless technology, utilization of by-products and recycled materials, and we can learn a great deal from their experience. But the whole process could also be very profitable for our western partners as well, either in the form of compensation deals that could provide for services to be paid for in part by produce or in the usual form allowed for by joint enterprises.

In my trips to the West I have often discussed this matter of Soviet practice in the formation of joint enterprises. I remember a particularly interesting debate near the beautiful Lake Como in Northern Italy. The discussion took place in a famous villa on the lake's shore, the Villa d'Este, which reminded me of a royal palace. A famous expert on joint enterprises, Professor Ulmar from Genoa, read an important paper on Soviet practices in the organization of joint enterprises, and my task was to reply to his paper and answer questions from 200 or so participants, many of whom had experience of organizing business links with the USSR. Having delivered the paper, the professor gave me a list of 99 questions posed by businessmen and students of Soviet affairs. I was not surprised, either by those or any other questions, because not long before I had held a series of discussions on the same subject with American businessmen and specialists during my two-week visit to the United States. Sarah Kelly, a law professor from Minneapolis and an expert on Soviet joint enterprises, led the discussion very ably and directed the question session. Both in Italy and in the United States, I said jokingly that I could not understand why they asked me such questions when there were leading experts present in the same room who could answer them much better. The response to that in both places was loud laughter. The participants in the discussion wanted answers from the horse's mouth.

So what are the most difficult and the most obvious questions that arise on the subject of joint enterprises in the Soviet Union? Before I deal with these questions and the answers to them, I should point out that this is our first attempt at organizing joint enterprises and therefore we have neither the appropriate experience nor the requisite legislation. Moreover we have no tradition of preparing formal, especially legal, documents. In our country documents are prepared by the apparat, i.e. by officials, many of whom think themselves the cleverest people in the world. Today one of them might prepare a document on joint enterprises, knowing nothing about them and without studying international experience; tomorrow the same person may be preparing a document on joint enterprises abroad, basing his opinions on his own experience. And so it goes on. Unfortunately we do not involve lawyers enough in this work, despite the fact that we do have qualified lawyers in our country, many of whom know about foreign rules and regulations. Of course we do not have enough of them, but we do have them. Lawyers do get involved in most cases when documents are drawn up, but the lawyer's voice is just one of many and is not always taken into account. In general, the legal side of matters, the whole field of precise formulation, has never been one of our strengths. Under Stalin, our laws had a propagandist rather than a real meaning, and they were broken and ignored in the crudest possible fashion. This sort of nihilist attitude to judicial matters and accepted norms is deeply ingrained in our people, particularly our officials, who consider their own word to be law and do not trouble themselves unduly with formulation.

We are changing these attitudes in the course of perestroika and are beginning to pay greater attention to the whole subject of law. At the 19th Party Conference we put forward a plan to turn the Soviet State into a legal state in which the law would indeed be supreme, to develop a respect for law in the population, to encourage respect for our rights and duties as enshrined in the Constitution, and to guarantee the people protection against abuses. This whole movement for legality, for increasing the importance of lawyers, is greatly influenced by the fact that our leader, Mikhail Gorbachev, is himself a lawyer, a graduate of the most important school for Soviet lawyers, the Faculty of Law of Moscow University. Nevertheless nihilistic attitudes to the law and to lawyers live on.

Here is an example, which happened quite recently. When the government Commission on Management was formed, twenty people – managers of central economic departments and several economists – were asked to participate. Not one lawyer was invited. How can one discuss the legal aspects of the restructuring of management and the economic mechanism if there is no lawyer to define the process? That is why our funadamental laws and decrees often include imprecise articles capable of several meanings and not fully thought through. And that is why we are always chopping and changing them. Unfortunately this applies to our laws on joint enterprises, which do cover important and substantial matters but also contain unfinished matters, contradictions and confusions that in turn create more problems. However, as these problems appear, we do try to solve them.

In a recent decree issued by the Council of Ministers in December 1988, *Further Developments in Foreign Economic Relations*, the conditions for the creation of joint enterprises on Soviet territory were liberalized. Until this decree one of the conditions, as we have seen, had been that 15 per cent of the capital would remain in Soviet hands and that the higher management consequently had to consist of Soviet citizens. But after 1989 the share of capital in Soviet and foreign hands will not be regulated and may be decided on by individual agreement. The chairman and the general manager may be citizens of a foreign country. Furthermore the principal lines of activity for each enterprise are decided by consensus.

The system for hiring and firing workers, the methods and rates of pay and material incentives have all been simplified. Goods brought into the Soviet Union by joint enterprises for the further development of their own production will have minimal duties exacted, and accommodation and other services for foreign workers will be paid for in roubles. Special allowances are being made in the matter of taxes on the profits of companies involved in the Far Eastern economic region.

If a joint enterprise produces popular consumer goods, medicines or products that require a great deal of research and are of major importance to the national economy, the Ministry of Finance has the right either to exempt from tax the profits due to the foreign participants for that part of the output taken abroad or to reduce the tax on them.

We are also looking at the possibility of creating zones where conditions for joint enterprises will be particularly favourable. Such zones exist in China, and have on the whole been successful. We have examined the possibility of creating such zones in the Far East. In my opinion we do not have to limit ourselves to the organization of special zones but could allow especially favourable conditions in any particularly important branches of the economy. I would nominate as such a specialist sphere the production of consumer goods and the organization of services which vitally affect the balancing of our consumer market by mass-producing goods for which there is a particularly high demand.

I persist in putting forward ideas about specialized economic zones and fields because not many joint enterprises are being formed at the moment. As I have already said, 191 joint enterprises have been registered on Soviet territory. If we consider that there are in our country hundreds of thousands of enterprises and organizations, 46 thousand of them in industry alone, the figure of 191 is not particularly inspiring, and these enterprises' possible share of production cannot but be paltry.

It should be noted that in other socialist countries where conditions for the creation of joint enterprises are more favourable, there are considerably more of them. The first of these countries to start creating joint enterprises was Yugoslavia in 1968, followed by Rumania in 1971, Hungary in 1972, Poland in 1976, China in 1979 and, finally, the USSR in 1987. Hungary for instance already has more than a hundred joint ventures, while Poland has around 700, the western investors there being mostly of Polish descent. In Yugoslavia there are around 200 such enterprises. But the most obvious example to study is China, where there are more than 5 thousand enterprises with a total capital of 20 billion dollars. I think we shall need hundreds, maybe even thousands, of joint enterprises in the future, and to achieve this we must create conditions which will first encourage people to start them and then enable them to grow.

Other difficulties arise out of the fact that the rouble is not convertible. Our country does not possess free currency reserves that could be used for the free exchange of profits earned in roubles into foreign currency. That is why we introduced the notion of cost accounting in foreign currency, and this limits the activity of foreign firms quite considerably. Under this rule it is necessary for part of the production, possibly a sizeable part, to be sold in the West and for joint enterprises to have some income in foreign currency to pay for their expenses in that currency. The income earned in foreign currency has to cover the capital invested by the western partners in that currency, the western partners' share of the profit, and the funds to be exported for the purchase of foreign supplies. Western companies, however, see the main aim of creating joint enterprises as the sale of products on the Soviet market. Many of them do not want to export any output to the West, because this would mean competing with themselves.

This question cannot really be decided until the rouble has become convertible. A great step forward in that direction will be taken when the rouble is made convertible within our country, as this will provide a better balance in purchasing power in the Soviet Union. However, we did not wait for that to happen but introduced another measure to make conditions easier for potential western partners. If the hard currency income of a joint enterprise is insufficient to transmit their profits abroad, they are allowed to use their residual profits for the purchase of Soviet goods. Furthermore the partners' share capital can be evaluated in any currency they choose.

There is one more, we think temporary, difficulty, which is connected with the way supplies are provided in our country. One of the legacies of the old administrative system of management is the centralized distribution system under which joint enterprises get their supplies from the appropriate ministries and departments. There are often difficulties attached to this – one has to put in a request at a certain time, and so on. Consequently agreements for the organization of a joint enterprise are made between three, not two, partners: the Soviet and the western partners and a third party – the supplier (that is to say, the ministry). All this makes the creation and running of joint enterprises difficult. But from 1989 wholesale trade will become more important, and by 1990 it will be the main channel for the supply of material resources. This will apply both to Soviet and to joint enterprises.

As we can see, conditions for the formation of joint enterprises are improving all the time, and our western partners should have fewer problems. Of course, quite a lot needs to be done to create a favourable socio-economic and psychological climate for the creation of joint enterprises. Those western firms whose representatives I have met are always complaining about bureaucracy and red tape in the Soviet Union. Negotiations sometimes take many months, or it may turn out that the Soviet representatives are not fully empowered to make agreements. The final decision is then put off, and negotiators change and everything begins again. They have also noted certain failings in correspondence from Soviet organizations like Gosagroprom. And some of the problems which come up are most peculiar. When I was in Italy, I was approached by the manager of an old and most prestigious restaurant who had been negotiating with a Soviet cinema centre that was moving into a new building and wanted to open an Italian restaurant as a joint enterprise. His rather bemused question was about a law of ours which prevented him from importing the famous Italian cheeses without which he could not produce Italian dishes. The reason given for this was laughable: it was claimed that cheeses have bacteria in them that could infect our cattle. All the countries of the world import Italian cheeses, and only we have such a problem.

Naturally this particular problem was rapidly solved. But it is a small yet telling example of the strength of bureaucratism and the administrative approach in our country. After all, we have no experience in the setting up of joint enterprises. Most of the people involved in the process have not had to do anything like this before, and a number of them are afraid that it might 'get out of hand'. These difficulties will be overcome as we develop and extend our activities.

I have noticed that firms working in the Soviet Union for the first time, who do not yet know the ropes, have a harder time of it. Companies which have been collaborating with our country for some time and have representatives here can solve problems such as these quickly and easily. We have, however, made enormous advances in the last three years in the liberalization of our foreign economic system and in the transition from centralized to economic methods. A large number of problems have yet to be solved, starting with the ease with which visas are issued or how firms are served by the Soviet arbiter, right up to living conditions for the western specialists – all of this on top of any problems that arise out of the work of joint enterprises themselves.

It is not enough to examine only joint enterprises on Soviet territory. The internationalization of production and capital leads inevitably to the need to create joint enterprises and trusts in other countries as well. The USSR has some, not very large, experience in this matter. Soviet investment abroad applies mostly to the infrastructure servicing our country's foreign economic links. Storehouses, bases, service networks and transport companies have been created, and there are several banks abroad funded by Soviet capital. Altogether there are at present about 120 firms abroad in which some Soviet money is invested. For instance there are a number of companies with some Soviet capital connected with Soyuzkhimexport, the foreign trade organization which comes under the Ministry of the Chemical Industry. These are SOGO in France, SOBREN in West Germany, SOKTIMESS in Italy, SOBER in Sweden and INTERPROM in Austria. When I was in Sweden I met the management of SOBER and once again ascertained that there was total objectivity in the foreign approach to joint enterprises. Working in capitalist countries, Soviet representatives of the joint firms learn the scientific, technological and economic achievements of western firms in their field and successfully promote Soviet goods abroad.

Our task is to increase the number of joint enterprises involving Soviet investment abroad. Nor should we think only in terms of trading enterprises; we must consider manufacturing ventures as well, since we will not be able to develop our foreign economic links effectively without them. This applies particularly to engineering goods, which often need servicing and even modifications to adapt them to western standards. For instance the considerable exports of passenger cars from the Volga motor factory, which in 1987 exported about 170,000 Lada cars, would not have been possible without a whole network of joint enterprises to finish the cars and promote sales. This does not simply facilitate the export of Soviet products and raise their prestige; it also has profound effects, above all on the quality of the goods, because the manufacturer is informed of the higher expectations of western consumers.

Recently it has been proposed that we should collaborate with companies from the developed countries in joint enterprises in the developed countries and in Third World developing countries. These suggestions are particularly topical for the countries of western Europe, since from 1992 they will be functioning within a single market and it will be easier for them to trade within that market than to bring in goods from outside it.

The internationalization of production and capital has led in other countries to the formation of large multinational companies occupying key positions in many economic spheres and developing faster than other companies. The socialist countries have not yet adopted this particular form of internationalized production. But the creation of joint enterprises, particularly multi-faceted joint enterprises, on the territory of socialist countries is a definite step in that direction. And we can in time expect the multinationals to open branches in the developed socialist countries.

In conclusion let me emphasize once more that there are truly great possibilities here for the development of joint enterprises and organizations involving Soviet and foreign partners.

Will the rouble become convertible?

Will the rouble become convertible, and if so, when? This is one of the most frequent questions I have had to answer in many discussions at home and abroad.

I remember an interesting conversation I had this winter with the President of the Republic of Finland, Mayist Konvist. I went to Finland because of my book, in effect a dialogue with the noted Finnish politician, member of parliament, and journalist and television reporter Syuponnen. President Konvist is a well-known specialist in finance and banking who at one time headed the Finnish State Bank. It was no easy task for me to talk to him, because his questions about the restructuring of the Soviet Gosbank and the convertibility of the rouble were highly professional, and in return, of course, he expected me to give highly professional answers.

As an economist who has avoided narrow specialization, I have naturally studied the problems of finance and credit. Now that we are trying to lay the scientific foundations of the new economic system I frequently have to work with financiers and bankers. I understand very well that the transition to an economic system of management will not be complete until the rouble is a fully-fledged currency, because economic management is in effect management through money, through a financial, banking system. I have tried to put our research into financial and credit problems into actual use both as head of the Economics Department of the Academy of

Sciences and as head of the government Commission on Management.

This is particularly important because the administrative system of management that has held power in our country for the entire lifetime of a whole generation, or for the last five or six decades, has always belittled and distorted the role of finance and banking in management. Banks were under the rule of the Ministry of Finance and were in effect channels for money given to them by the government under the so-called credit plan. This plan did not simply specify how much money was allocated year by year; the banks were also told how they were to use that amount, who they were to give credit to, on what terms, and so on. The decisive role in the preparation of the credit plan was played by the Ministry of Finance, which had a special department for the purpose. Gradually the whole financial and banking system became, so to speak, self-sufficient in the sense that no outsider was allowed into the 'kitchen'. Nor was any information published about the circulation of money in the country or about credit resources and their use. If any information did come out, it was always disjointed and unsystematic.

Of course economists were not allowed anywhere near those problems either. The Ministry of Finance had its own institute, NIIfinance, a small and quite good organization which was, unfortunately, completely bogged down in ministerial tasks. As for the only three banks that existed in the Soviet Union in the past, Gosbank, Promstroibank and Vneshtorgbank, they were not even allowed to have a research section, never mind a whole institute. As nobody from the USSR Academy of Sciences' institutes or from higher education establishments was allowed anywhere near those banks or their internal statistics, and as that statistical data was not given even to the Central Statistical Department, our banking activity could not have any well-researched or scientific basis. If an academic institute specializing in some aspect of economics tried, despite everything, to do research into its subject, the results were immediately rejected and the researchers accused of ignorance, distortion and so on. It was difficult to carry out any research in those conditions and even more difficult to educate the next generation of researchers or financiers.

And so those sections of the Institute of Economics of the Academy of Sciences and similar institutes which specialized in finance and banking gradually disappeared. The old researchers who knew their stuff gradually retired, and because of the lack of data and these negative attitudes no new generation was educated to deal with such problems. In this way whole branches of economics died out in our country.

And yet we used to have good traditions and good specialists. Let us remember the years of the New Economic Policy. Our country entered the NEP as a consequence of the First World War and the Civil War (1914–19) with a completely destroyed financial system and with galloping inflation. After the introduction of the NEP, we managed to restore order in the financial, credit and monetary system within a year or two, and by 1922 the rouble had returned to its pre-war level (a hefty 1.9 dollars). We issued gold coins which were quoted on the foreign currency markets in accordance with their gold content.

A great deal of serious research into finances and banking was conducted in the twenties. Lenin attached special importance to the problem of banking and its organization, the development of finances and money turnover under Soviet control. He wrote that the circulation of money was one of those things which, if not kept in order, meant the whole of the economy was not in order. He thought that banks should be the main economic establishments in the socialist society and that the most important level for regulation of the economy was the financial one.

Later on, late in the twenties, during the transition to the administrative method of management, the market curtailed, the rouble's gold content no longer bore any relation to its value, and gold coins were abolished. The declared exchange rate for the rouble throughout the thirties bore no relation to its actual purchasing power.

Stalin's approach to the whole question of exchange rates is best demonstrated by the following story. March 1950 saw the return to pre-war levels of production in our country, and the question of increasing the purchasing power of the rouble and strengthening its role was raised. Stalin ordered that the exchange rate be calculated. This was carried out in the Central Statistical Agency under Valierian Sobol, the head of the balance section of the Soviet economy. He carried out comparisons between the purchasing power of the rouble and the dollar when applied to consumer goods. Stalin wanted the rouble to be valued high, and those making the calculations knew this. They therefore used types of consumer goods and standards of comparison which were particularly favourable for us in their attempt to overvalue the rouble. This was the process they adopted: they would note various items, usually chosen because they were particularly favourable for us, then they would add another 15 per cent for the supposed better quality and greater longevity of our products. They would compare, for instance, the length of time American shoes and our hobnailed boots lasted and would then add a correcting factor because our boots lasted longer than American shoes. Stalin had given them one week for the whole of this task. Towards the end of that week, everyone who had any part in the exercise was working literally night and day.

The head of the Central Statistical Agency, Vladimir Starkovsky, incidentally the only more or less important personality in the country who was a Komi, was a talented man and had even been elected a corresponding member of the Academy of Sciences, a position he very largely used for the falsification of material to please Stalin. He was in charge of our statistics for almost thirty-five years from 1939 onwards, and in this time he managed to destroy most of the data and falsify the rest. For instance, Khrushchev in his published speeches says of the good harvest results for 1970 given by Starkovsky in the regular digest from the Central Statistical Agency: 'I think only Starkovsky could say this. No one else could think of that phrase. I know him very well: he is a man who can apparently make bullets out of shit.' This same Starkovsky in those days spent all his time in Mikoyan's office. Mikoyan was Stalin's assistant at the Council of Ministers. At the last minute Mikoyan went into Stalin's office and waited for the results there. Sobol, who had been in charge of the calculations, was in Starkovsky's office at the Central Statistical Agency, sitting by the government telephone. After a great deal of head-scratching to make the rouble worth as much as possible, it was decided that 1 rouble would be worth 14 dollars (in old money: in 1961 Khrushchev revalued the rouble at 1 for 10; so in new money this meant that 1 rouble was worth 1.4 dollars). At last the calculations were finished in the middle of the night and sent immediately to the Kremlin. Sobol and the others were greatly surprised when a little while later they read in the newspapers that the new exchange rate was 1 rouble for 4 dollars. This rate was established in March 1950. When they asked Starkovsky what it meant, he rather unwillingly told them that Stalin had looked at their calculations, frowned, picked up a blue pencil (apparently he very rarely used a pen, preferring pencils of different colours) and crossed out their figure, substituting '4'.

When the monetary reform of 1961 was carried out and the rouble was revalued, its gold content was also announced: 0.987412 grams of gold for one rouble. According to that calculation, a dollar was worth 90 kopecks – and this was the new rate set against the main exchange currency. We still to this day use the rate against the dollar to set the rate against other currencies, making certain adjustments for the fall in the rouble.

This brief story demonstrates that under an administrative system the exchange rate can only be a formality, not a true rate. In fact, under a system where each enterprise is given directions from above about what to produce, what resources it has been allocated, who it is to sell to and in what quantity, how much to spend and on what, the rouble cannot have a unitary purchasing power. In such conditions, money could not fulfil its basic and most important role: it could not measure cost or control circulation. It could not measure cost, because prices were set arbitrarily. There was an insurmountable barrier between world prices and internal Soviet prices. In effect we did not have the unitary price level.

Historically the price for fuel and raw materials was not calculated according to real costs and was therefore at least two or three times lower than world prices. Also the prices set for agricultural produce were very low, because it was profitable for the state to sustain these prices and for the money thus saved to be redeployed in heavy industry or for other general necessities. Retail prices for bread, meat and dairy products were based on these low purchase prices. The last time these were changed was in 1962, and therefore to this day they reflect the purchase prices set at that time. In 1965, after the March Plenum, the state purchase prices were raised and thus overtook retail prices, which are still artificially low. For instance the retail price for meat is about one-third any realistic estimate of what it costs to produce. That is why we have other prices for meat, not just the ones in the state shops. There are the prices in the co-operatives, where meat costs about twice as much as in the state shops, and there is the peasant market, where prices are about 2.5 or 3 times as much as in the shops. So we have three markets for meat and some dairy products. Naturally while we have such a price system there is no point in thinking about a properly valued rouble, let alone a convertible one. A properly valued rouble presupposes first of all that there is a well-founded system of price formation that demonstrably works on the market. We cannot yet demonstrate anything of the kind, as the consumer market is distorted and there are all sorts of shortages. We cannot even demonstrate what sort of price should be set for those goods which are in short supply. And although we do have the peasant and co-operative markets where prices are established more or less according to supply and demand, only a small proportion of our meat and especially dairy products gets to them.

The situation is even worse when it comes to capital goods – worse because there is no market at all and the arbitrarily established prices for oil, fuels and raw materials, just like the arbitrarily established prices for chemical products, metals, and so on, are not decisive prices in the sense that there is no possibility of choice. Each consumer has to take what he is given in the amount he is given, according to directions from above. He does not need to worry about money. The plan usually supplies each consumer with enough materials to enable him to recover his material costs.

Under the administrative system, a whole range of different roubles is available. The most valuable rouble, the rarest one, is the kind given to an enterprise to be converted into dollars or some other hard currency at the official rate. The next in importance is the cash rouble, which can be used to buy goods on the consumer market. Under the administrative system, the amount of such roubles to be doled out to enterprises is established from above and is strictly adhered to. As a rule overspending is not allowed. The best-liked part of this cash is the so-called casual pay fund. This can be used to hire specialists from outside under contract. It does not matter if their main pay is from another enterprise. The financial authorites watch this fund very carefully, and the slightest irregularity can be used as an excuse for cutting it back.

But the most important cash sum allocated is for wages. The entire control system has one aim and that is to prevent the non-cash, 'lighter' rouble from being used to augment the wage roubles. The administrative system wants a solid wall between the two. But however subtle the financial agencies get, there are always some holes through which the cash drains. And so the purchasing power, 80 per cent of which is generated from the wages fund and 20 per cent from pensions, welfare payments and stipends, is always greater than the supply of goods. It is therefore

222

very hard for people to use the roubles available to them effectively, since the choice of goods on the market is very small, there are enormous queues and so on.

There are also gradations and divisions within the framework of money that is not actually paid out in cash. It is hard to obtain capital for investment, particularly for tied building projects, that is, projects on which building organizations are ordered from above to work. Here is a typical scenario: a certain enterprise or organization has capital given to it from above and wants to invest it in a building. Such a building will generally cost less than the capital at the enterprise's or organization's disposal, making for a shortage of building projects. Since under the administrative system building work is not done at one's own expense, is paid for by the enterprise itself not out of its own earnings but out of money given to it from above (that is out of very easy money indeed), everyone wants to build something. Everyone wants to have capital allocations and everyone petitions for some. Having obtained this, the next step is to contract for the work to be done. The easier part is to acquire equipment, particularly if your demands are not too high and you are prepared to accept slightly inferior stuff. But equipment is allocated by warrant, and it is not so easy to get a warrant – one must apply in good time and fight for one's application before one can get one. With a warrant, however, it becomes possible to contact the producer of a certain machine or piece of equipment and acquire it at the state price. The same rigmarole applies to obtaining fuel, raw materials, supplies and spare parts.

It was harder under the administrative system to get money for accommodation or other social building projects, as the money for this was shared out on the so-called residual principle. In other words, money was given only after the demands of defence and industrial construction had been satisfied. Every enterprise had a large waiting list for accommodation. One did not have to pay to acquire a flat and the rents covered only about a quarter of the accommodation's maintenance expenses. The rest was covered by the state. Of course it is difficult to build sufficient accommodation on that kind of money. There was always less being built than was needed. In the years of stagnation, say in 1984, most enterprises gave accommodation only to engineers and to those workers who had applied for a flat something like eight or twelve years before. In any case, accommodation was available only if the

223

living conditions of the given family, examined by the social commission or by a commission nominated by the Soviet, were particularly difficult. In some organizations only those families were allowed to queue who had less than 6 square metres of living space for each member or those whose accommodation did not have any modern conveniences.

Let me quote a concrete example to show even more clearly how bad it is for our development not to have a properly valued rouble which could be used to buy anything at all. Let us imagine that a laboratory in an institute has developed a new piece of equipment which will considerably enhance the efficiency and quality of output of a whole branch of production. All that is needed is to complete the design, to check it and so on. There are organizations which would very much like to have the equipment. They are ready to pay money and to render any kind of assistance needed. But in our country, where the rouble does not have a real value, money cannot buy you anything. In order to proceed with its work on the equipment, the laboratory needs to hire more people. For that it does not need money in general but specifically cash for wages on the one hand and an increased limit on the number of workers it can hire on the other. Then the laboratory needs new accommodation. Since this cannot be had for money, some kind of decision is needed. In order actually to produce its first lot of equipment, the laboratory needs materials and equipment of its own. All this has to be ordered well ahead of time and is all shared out by a central authority. Some of the materials need to be bought from abroad and so on. But the roubles cannot help the institute. All sorts of resources are needed, each one of which is shared out separately, and each time obtaining them is fraught with difficulties such as the need to get approvals from other agencies and so on. If the rouble were properly valued, then everything could be bought. All one would need to do would be to value the equipment at a proper price and use the income to obtain accommodation, hire workers and buy all the necessary materials and equipment, including, if the rouble were convertible, anything that was needed from abroad. In this way scientific and technological achievements would be implemented far more quickly.

The development in our economic mechanism aims to ensure that the rouble will become properly valued by the end of this five-year plan. The centralized system of supply will to a great extent be

224

abolished, and we shall have in its stead wholesale trading in the means of production, making it possible to meet one's needs on the internal market. Enterprises and organizations will be able to hire accommodation for money. Some of their funds will be divertible into the wage fund, so that they can hire more workers. Only one problem will remain – how to make the rouble convertible. And, as we know, at the June 1987 Plenum a resolution was passed to make the rouble convertible first on the socialist market, then on the world market. The conditions for this development are being created in the course of the economic reform.

The first really important step is to make the rouble convertible on the internal market. By convertibility we mean the freedom to acquire all resources with the money – the use of money in its true meaning as the general equivalent and measure of cost and circulation. Secondly, during the total reform of prices and price formation due to be carried out in 1990, we intend to bring our prices closer to world market prices. At the same time all the prices in our country will be set at a single level. The reason why I continually speak of having the same prices in different branches of industry and areas is that at the moment we do not really have a single price system. The prices of various things have been revised in various years and are therefore incompatible. For instance, the retail prices for meat and dairy products were last revised in 1962, whereas the purchase price for the same products was revised subsequently in 1965 and 1982. The state retail prices for bread, meat and dairy products are set at less than cost, and the state subsidy on these products runs to more than 60 billion roubles annually. This sum is raised very largely from artificially high prices on manufactured goods.

Prices for fuel and raw materials are 2–2.5 times lower than world market prices. At the same time our prices for manufactured items, such as chemical and engineering products and, particularly, electronic goods, are higher than world prices. All these unreasonable differences in prices will to a great extent be smoothed out and done away with in the course of the price reform. At the same time there will be a change in the whole system of price formation. There will be far fewer centrally established prices and far more real and contractual ones. The movement of contractual and free prices will mean that world prices will be still more closely reflected in our internal ones. Centrally established prices will also be revised regularly, as price factors

225

on the world market and inside the country will change considerably. At the very least they will be revised with every five-year plan, or even more often in case of need.

As the new price system is brought in, we shall also start using the common system of setting duty tariffs, and this will go even further towards abolishing the differences between our prices and the rest of the world's.

Furthermore, to create favourable conditions for making our currency convertible we shall have to improve the entire system of foreign economic relations. We shall have to take a more active part in the international division of labour and to increase our country's share in world trade. We shall have to improve our balance of payments, raise the competitive quality of Soviet products and thus make our exports more effective and more reliant on manufactured goods and on the co-operatives. At the same time we must increase the effectiveness of our imports, reducing the proportion of food products, metal products and engineering equipment, and increasing the proportion of new technological systems and mass consumer goods in order to saturate that market.

One of the economic conditions that are absolutely essential if we want to make our currency convertible is that our country should participate more on the financial capital markets. In the past our participation has been one-sided – mostly we asked for credit and paid off our debts. In future our role on these markets must change. Our banks must also become creditors. Perhaps some time in the future bonds will be issued for foreign investors.

An important part of our move towards the convertibility of the rouble is the creation of joint enterprises in our own country and in others. The very existence of these enterprises will make the convertibility of the rouble more essential, for without it they will find it harder to work, and their effectiveness and flexibility both on the external and the internal markets will be sorely reduced. On the other hand the creation of joint enterprises and organizations in other countries will allow us to place Soviet capital abroad, and this will strengthen our financial position on the world market. At present, as we know, the Soviet Union owns shares in about 120 joint companies, including a number of banks such as the Moscow Narodny Bank in London, the Danube Bank in Vienna and the branch of the USSR Bank for Foreign Economic Relations in Zurich. These and others put Soviet capital to work abroad, and in future their activity too must become more effective. Soviet banks will also strive to organize consortia and associations of joint enterprises with foreign banks. The whole process will be made easier by the fact that new banks are being opened in the Soviet Union. Some of them are the new specialized banks, like Agroprombank and Promstroibank, which will eventually conduct their own foreign trade activities independently. There will also be new banks with shareholders, these being large specialist banks and other organizations. There will be a whole network of commercial banks, co-operative banks and so on. I believe many of them will eventually be allowed to conduct their own operations on the world financial markets.

There is one more condition for our change to a convertible currency: the inclusion of the USSR in various international economic organizations, particularly those connected with world trade, finances and the currency market.

The USSR takes an active part as one of the member-states in the economic organizations attached to the United Nations, above all the Economic and Social Council (ECOSOC), the Conference on Trade and Development (UNCTAD), the United Nations Development Programme (UNDP) and the United Nations Industrial Development Organization (UNIDO).

The USSR was one of the states which founded the programme for post-war international financial relations and took part in the conferences on the subject at Bretton Wood in 1944. Later, our country could not agree with the USA's attempt to make these organizations subservient to it and we therefore stopped participating in those activities, and eventually, along with the other socialist countries, we declined to join the General Agreement on Trade and Tariffs (GATT), the International Monetry Fund and the World Bank for Reconstruction and Development. The new conditions have led us to review our principal tasks and consider more radically involving our country in the international division of labour, and eventually making our currency convertible; we shall therefore now also reconsider our attitude to these organizations. Furthermore, the USSR cannot remain blind to the fact that these organizations were joined by Rumania (1970), Hungary (1982) and Poland (1986).

In August 1986 the USSR asked for permission to participate in negotiations with GATT in Uruguay. The idea was to take a constructive part in these negotiations and thus ease the process of the USSR joining GATT. But our request was rejected because of the negative attitude of the United States. Nevertheless we are continuing with our preparations to join GATT and are adjusting our foreign trade mechanisms to the rules of that general agreement. In particular, we have decided to renew and make more effective Soviet duty tariffs with the intention that they should influence the price of imported goods on our internal market. We intend to make the changes on the basis of the GATT rules. On 1 January 1991 the USSR will introduce the tariff description and coding system recommended by GATT for products in international circulation. At the same time we are developing non-duty instruments for the regulation of external trade relations, as is done in other countries. These would include licensing, quotas, standards, environmental and health requirements, rules for currency operations and so on. In the resolution on foreign economic activities passed by the Soviet Council of Ministers in December 1988, the appropriate ministries and departments were instructed to develop the concepts for a new tariff system and to adopt from 1 January 1989 a system of measures that would regulate the non-tariff aspects of our foreign economic relations. They are also required to speed up the presentation of duty statistics. This whole arsenal of GATT rules will be used in such a way as to ease the development of our foreign economic relations. Naturally this will happen only if other countries proceed along the same mutually beneficial path. At the same time, if certain countries take discriminatory measures against us, the tariff and non-tariff regulations can be used in response.

The agreement reached by the USSR with the EEC was a very important achievement. The USSR approaches such negotiations from its broad concept of 'one European home'. The proposal we have presented for an agreement with the EEC includes not only areas of foreign trade that involve maximum benefit and non-tariff agreements but also questions of industrial, technological, scientific and investment collaboration, exchanges of information, currency and financial operations, rules of competition, consultancy procedures, exhibitions, rules for business activities and so on. We have proposed that there should be a joint EEC–USSR commission to supervise the implementation of the agreement and to search for new ways of collaboration.

Another important problem that must be mentioned is the relationship between the USSR on the one hand and the International Monetary Fund and the World Bank on the other. I think we should try to start work in areas with good prospects, such as co-operation in research, meetings between experts on various problems of interest to both sides, and so on. The relationship could then grow closer and even lead to Soviet entry into these organizations.

The rouble can become convertible on the world market only if the Soviet Union and other socialist countries are no longer subjected to artificial discrimination and restrictions in their foreign economic activities, if there is economic security for all states. In connection with this the Soviet Union is actively developing a concept of safeguards in international economic security. This concept was presented by our country to the United Nations for examination. The Soviet proposal envisages the liberation of international economic relations from all that makes them difficult: the creation of a favourable climate in which every country can make the most out of participating in the international division of labour and reduce its risks to a minimum. The USSR supports the establishment of an international economic order that would seek to solve all the difficult problems confronting humanity at the moment. We envisage the establishment of such an order as something that will be achieved only through negotiations with the participation of all countries; we do not arrogate any special role for ourselves and believe that every country can make a useful contribution to the negotiations. Our basic position is that international economic security is an organic part of the whole system of international security, which encompasses the military, political and humanitarian spheres.

In connection with our intended transition to a convertible rouble, we have to face another important question – the evolution of the world currency system in which the rouble will one day have to take its place. As we know, post-war currency regulations were determined by the Bretton Woods agreement, which made the dollar the main currency with a fixed gold value attached to it. This agreement has now virtually disappeared; the world has gone over to the free pricing of gold and the stable gold standard has been abandoned. We now have a system of floating rates. Although the USA's share in the world market and the entire world economy has gone down, and will continue to do so, the dollar is nevertheless still considered the main currency in world calculations. Its role, however, is declining year by year.

Let us look at some statistical data. The USA's share in the

GNP of the developed countries has decreased from 53 per cent in 1960 to less than 40 per cent today, while the share of the Western European countries has gone up from 35 per cent to almost 40 per cent. This means that the EEC's GNP is virtually equal to America's. Meanwhile Japan's share has gone up from 5 per cent in 1960 to something like 17 per cent today, still 2.5–3 times less than those of the United States and Western Europe.

The USA's share of trade between the developed capitalist countries is more modest. Since 1960 its share of exports has gone down from 24 per cent to 15 per cent, whereas Western Europe's share has gone up from 56 per cent to 60 per cent, Japan's from 5 per cent to 15 per cent; in fact Japan recently overtook the United States in the volume of its foreign trade. At the same time the dollar has become weaker because of the growing American debt. Suffice it to say that in 1987 the US balance of payments was 156 billion dollars in the red, while Japan's was 86 billion dollars in the black, and West Germany's balance was also positive to the tune of 44 billion dollars. The dollar's role as the world reserve currency has become less important for yet another reason. In 1971–3 the United States refused to keep the price of gold at the level established in 1944, 35 dollars per ounce, and since then the dollar has not been very stable. In the decade from 1970 to 1980 it fell by one quarter, whereas from 1980 to March 1985 it rose sharply by more than one and a half times. This was followed by another sharp fall. At the moment the dollar is fluctuating around its 1980 value. In fact it would have fallen still further if the other developed capitalist countries had not artificially kept it high because the alternative would have made their own external economic relations more difficult.

At the same time, it would be wrong to underestimate the economic might of the United States. After all it does produce 40 per cent of the GNP of the developed capitalist countries. It also possesses more than half the scientific and technological potential of the developed capitalist countries. Behind the dollar stands the might of the country that produces it and its long history as the leading currency. And although the proportion of dollars held in official currency reserves continues to go down, they still remain the major holding. The dollar's share in official currency reserves has declined from 77 per cent in 1976 to 67 per cent in 1986, while the share of the German mark and the Japanese yen has gone up from 11 per cent to 22 per cent.

'I do not personally think that we shall ever return to a single world-wide base currency in the form of the dollar. In my opinion, we shall witness instead the gradual formation of regional currency zones within which trade will be far more intensive than with other zones or countries. Customs and other barriers to trade will be done away with in these zones and they will enjoy a freer flow of capital and movement of goods and labour. At the same time, each of these zones will to a certain extent protect itself from inflows of goods and capital from without. (In time, however, they may become more liberal about this.) Four such zones currently exist: (a) the American zone with the dollar as its main currency; (b) the European Community with the ECU or mark as its main currency; (c) the Council for Mutual Economic Assistance (Comecon) with the rouble as its main currency; and (d) South-East Asia with the yen as its main currency.

Let us look at the present state of world trade. Each of the regional associations listed above exports to and imports from Third World countries to the tune of 200–300 billion dollars. This is not counting internal circulation. Between all these currency zones a single approach to certain courses, to the definition of stability, and so on will grow up in time.

In what order will the transition to convertibility take place in the Soviet Union?

I believe the next step after the price reform and the establishment of correspondence between world and internal prices should be to introduce the notion of an internally convertible rouble which it will be possible to exchange freely for the currency of other countries. We might permit this for enterprises and organizations according to a realistic rate set in our country. Of course to achieve this we must seriously improve our foreign trade, we must have a favourable balance of payments, and we must have stable sources of hard currency. But I think all that can be achieved.

At the moment we have differential currency co-efficients (DCC). We do not want simply to substitute one co-efficient for several differentiated ones but rather to be able to exchange money freely according to that co-efficient. At the same time the rouble will become properly valued, will be used for the purchase of capital goods and so on. Thus enterprises and organizations in need of hard currency will be able to buy it in exchange for their roubles. The exchange rate will be set at such a level that supply and demand on the currency market will generally balance.

There could be two different approaches to such an internal currency market. We could either have a set exchange rate, fixed by the state, or we could have a floating exchange rate varying in accordance with supply and demand. In the latter case we would need to have a currency market. In order to make our economy function smoothly I believe the first method is more suitable, especially as our state has considerable currency reserves because the fuel and raw materials trade – the main source of currency for most socialist countries – is run by state trading agencies, and most of that hard currency goes into the state currency fund. The government will be able to use this fund to regulate and support supply and demand on the currency market according to the rate it has set. If economic conditions change drastically, the government will be able to alter the rate of exchange as necessary. This approach was tried in Hungary and was, in my opinion, quite effective.

The second alternative was adopted by, among others, Poland, which opted for currency auctions and a currency exchange.

In the December 1988 Decree of the Council of Ministers on the development of foreign relations there is a section on the transition from 1 January 1991 to new exchange rates in foreign economic dealings. Until this transition is achieved it is intended to have a 100 per cent surcharge on the rate of convertible currency against the rouble. So if, for example, according to the official rate 1 dollar is equivalent to 0.6 roubles, then after 1 January 1990 it will be equivalent to 1.2 roubles. There will be a consequent change in the rate of other freely convertible currency against the rouble.

In order to enhance the socialist incentives of enterprises, co-operatives and other organizations, it will be made easier for them to acquire hard currency resources and to buy and sell hard currency. They will be able to do all that at currency auctions organized by the Vneshekonombank of the USSR. I think such auctions will simply be a temporary measure until we can go over to a single exchange rate within the country, established by the government.

In principle it is possible to choose the second alternative and create currency markets. China has such a market for the exchange of the external yuan for the internal one. This gives the state and its departments some influence on the dynamics of the exchange rate and the currency market.

At the same time we shall proceed with the process of making the rouble convertible on the socialist international market. This will be the first step towards external convertibility.

The mechanism controlling the economic integration and activities of Comecon is in need of serious reconstruction. This is the opinion of the USSR and other socialist countries. Here too we shall need greater consistency in our price-setting systems and the interconvertibility of our national currencies. On that basis there will be a gradual shrinkage of the national market of the member countries of Comecon. This will lead gradually to the formation of free trade zones and possibly even to a single tariff within the socialist countries. So the convertibility of the rouble initially on the market of socialist countries is a realistic proposal.

All this will create the right conditions for the eventual transition to a fully convertible rouble on the world market. Of course we should like that to come about as soon as possible, but the process does not depend on the Soviet Union alone. Other countries, and other international economic organizations, will have to take part. In any case the internal convertibility of the rouble will affect the activities of the joint enterprises, and the convertibility of the rouble within the socialist countries will in many ways help to overcome the limitations we at present suffer from in our foreign trade. The fact is that our trade relations with other countries tend to be one-sided – they do not utilize all the multiple possibilities there are in trade. What we need is to cover our outlays in hard currency rather than just on the internal market. With the help of a single co-efficient of internal convertibility we can move from covering our outlays in hard currency to covering our outlays in general. This will get rid of the limitations that are at present placed on our enterprises and organizations and on the joint enterprises.

So even internal convertibility of the rouble will from the very beginning be a strong incentive for extending and deepening our foreign economic links.

It is hard to overestimate the importance to a country of making its currency convertible. The outstanding statesman of pre-revolutionary Russia, Count Witte, who was for many years prime minister and spent a great deal of his time studying financial problems, wrote in his memoirs: 'A state's prestige is not measured in the number of its soldiers or the firing range of its guns but in the stability of its currency.' Convertibility is the international acceptance of a national currency.

AFTERWORD
A STATISTICAL REVIEW:
THREE YEARS OF
ECONOMIC RECONSTRUCTION

The main aim of our economic reconstruction, of perestroika, is to solve social problems that had become urgent, to improve the welfare of the Soviet people, and to bring a new quality to the socialist way of life. Other countries have raced ahead in their standard of living, often spending beyond their means for a level of well-being that is higher than their productive potential. The situation in the USSR, on the other hand, is unique in that our standard of living is too low when compared with the country's mighty economic potential and the level of our scientific and technological development. The most characteristic aspects of our economy are totally distorted production costs and norms of industrial investment, huge losses and unutilized possibilities. That is why the main evaluation of our results must be carried out from the point of view of what has been achieved for society.

During the 12th Five-year Plan, we have somehow managed to

overcome the residual principle of money distribution for the social sphere and managed to give it priority. In the past, capital investment gave faster returns in industry than in the social sphere, but during perestroika there has been a redeployment of resources in favour of the social sphere. In 1986–7 capital investment in industry went up by 10 per cent, non-industrial investment by 18 per cent. This allowed us to overcome stagnation in the building of houses and in other construction work for social purposes. The number of houses built did not go up in the years between 1960 and 1984; in relation to the population it actually decreased by 30 per cent. It was only after the April 1985 Plenum that the volume of accommodation went up in absolute and relative terms. In 1987 about 15 per cent more new housing became available than in 1985. In 1988 about the same amount became available as in the preceding year. The quality of the accommodation improved somewhat, though the changes were not great. Similarly we have managed to overcome stagnation in the building of nurseries, kindergartens, schools, and health and cultural centres.

There has been a great increase in the proportion of the state budget directed specifically at the development of the social sphere. This is especially true in health and education, where salaries went up by 30–40 per cent. Together with other measures, this has led to some improvement in the quality of school education and medicine.

As we know, in the period 1960–84 our health statistics deteriorated. The mortality rate went up from 7.1 to 10.8 per thousand of population and average life expectancy went down from about 70 to 67.7. We have managed to overcome these negative trends. In 1987 the mortality rate went down to 9.9 per thousand and average life expectancy went up to about 70. This improvement in the health statistics is directly linked with the fall in the consumption of alcohol. The mortality rate for the working-age population went down by 20 per cent, and the accident mortality rate in the same age group went down by 37 per cent from the 1984 figures. It should be pointed out that this improvement took place only in 1985–6, when there was a reduction in the overall consumption of alcohol, both commercial products and moonshine. The decline in the illicit making of alcohol can be measured from the fact that consumption of sugar fell in those years by about 2 kg per head of population per year. We did, however, then make mistakes in our fight against alcoholism: prices were raised quite unjustifiably and deliberate shortages of wine and spirits were created. The production of moonshine went up again, as did sugar consumption, which leapt by about 5 kg per head per year. The mortality rate in 1987 went up again from 9.8 to 9.9 per thousand of population, while average life expectancy remained static.

Despite the undoubted success of our housing the social construction programme and the improvements in education and health, popular needs are not nearly as well catered for as they ought to be, and we still lag catastrophically far behind the developed countries. On average each person in 1987 had 15.2 square metres of living space. This is two or three times less than in the developed capitalist countries. Furthermore most of the accommodation in private hands (and this accounts for about 40 per cent) and one-tenth of state-owned accommodation has no running water, no drains and no central heating, let alone gas, hot running water, and telephones. Only 28 per cent of city families and 9 per cent of families in agricultural areas have their own telephone.

We have also fallen badly behind in health matters. Infant mortality in the USSR is over 25 per thousand live births, compared with 6–10 per thousand in the developed countries. While average life expectancy in the USSR has not yet reached 70 years, it is 74–78 years in the developed countries. So in this sphere we have made only a modest start in the three years of perestroika but this should turn into a radical break with the past.

When we look at the supply of goods and services, we can see that the results we have achieved are exceedingly modest. Use of material goods and services has gone up by 5.7 per cent in 1986, 3.3 per cent in 1987 and by 7 per cent in 1988. During the first two years of the 12th Five-year Plan, the volume of retail trade turnover (excluding alcohol) rose by 10.5 per cent; in 1988 it rose by 7.1 per cent. In the same periods, paid services went up by 19.2 per cent and by 17 per cent. According to Goskomstat (the state committee for statistics), real per capita income went up by 4.6 per cent in the first two years of the 12th Five-year Plan and by another 3.5 per cent in 1988.

When we evaluate all these statistics, given here in so-called fixed prices, we must remember that we have hidden inflation in the USSR, and it affects the consumer market. Current price statistics are based on a standard list of goods and do not take account of changes in the choice of goods. There is a constant process whereby cheaper goods 'melt away', only to be replaced by more expensive ones. It is estimated that this hidden inflation amounts to 3–4 per cent annually. If we adjust our calculations accordingly we see that real growth in the use of material goods and services was more like 2 per cent in 1986, slightly more in 1988. In 1987 the index stayed the same as in the previous year.

There has been a slight increase in the consumption of meat (2 per cent), milk (5 per cent), eggs (4 per cent) and vegetable oil (3 per cent). At the same time the consumption of fish went up and the consumption of fruit and vegetables went down from the 1986 figures. The slight fall in the consumption of bread was compensated for by an increase in the consumption of potatoes. In the first half of 1988, sales of meat and dairy products went up by 5 per cent, sales of vegetables by 6 per cent, while sales of fruit went down quite considerably.

Popular demand for meat, dairy products, fruit and vegetables is not particularly well satisfied by the state shops.

This inadequate improvement in the amount of food supplied to the population is connected with the development of agricultural production. In 1986 the volume of agricultural production went up; taking 1985 as 100, it reached 105 per cent. But in 1987 the level remained the same as in 1986, and in 1988 it went up by only 0.7 per cent. Food production went up by 5 per cent in 1986 and by another 4 per cent in 1987. In the first half of 1988, meat and dairy production rose by about 5 per cent.

When we evaluate how agricultural development is affecting the supply of food, we should remember that imports of grain, meat and dairy products were cut back in 1986–7.

Generally we are among the fifteen most developed countries in the world so far as food consumption is concerned, but when we look at housing, infant mortality rates, the development of the service industry, the supply of consumer durables and a number of other indices, we have to admit that we trail behind somewhere among the last of the top fifty countries. Yet despite our high position in the level of food supply, the organization of that supply is so bad that demand is to a great extent not satisfied. There are great differences in supply according to region; the choice is pitiful and the quality of some of the products is very low indeed. We have to conclude that in order to do away with imports of basic foodstuffs and to provide better-quality food, it is not enough to develop agricultural production and the food industry as fast as possible. We must try just as hard to improve the organization of the food supply. I am talking about restoring well-founded prices for food, improving quality, producing and selling a wide variety of produce. We must also think about a radical improvement in the eating habits of the population and in the transportation, storage and sale of food. There are scores of countries in the world with far smaller resources than we have which nevertheless manage to fill the shops in all their regions with a wide variety of food, somehow managing to use their resources more sensibly than we do.

Then there is the question of the supply of mass-produced consumer goods. Progress in this sphere has been totally unsatisfactory during the 12th Five-year Plan. In 1986–7 the volume of production of consumer goods went up by 7.8 per cent. The growth in light industrial production was only 3 per cent and in the clothing industry only 1 per cent. In 1988 the rate of increase in the production of consumer goods was 5.1 per cent and in light industry, which is included in that index, 4.3 per cent. When it comes to light industry, however, the main problem is not quantity but quality and choice. In sheer quantity we are one of the world's largest producers of shoes and cloth per head of population and have been achieving this for some time. But demand is not satisfied, because the quality and choice of what we produce bear no relation to the needs of the population. The same applies to a great extent to the more traditional manufactured consumer goods like television sets, refrigerators, washing machines, electrical goods and radios, where the same thing applies: there is enough quantity produced, but the quality and choice are not what the public wants.

In the last few years, there has been a huge increase in demand for completely new consumer durables such as video recorders, personal computers, air conditioners, and many other things. In this sphere we have fallen so far behind that we need very special efforts and a great deal of foreign capital to improve the situation. The same applies even more to passenger cars. According to Western European standards we ought to be producing something like 10 million cars a year, whereas we only manage to produce 1.3 million. In every developed country 10–15 per cent of the population's income is spent in one way or another on cars. Here we spend 1 per cent. In order to ensure a balance between purchasing power and material supply in future, we must rapidly develop our passenger car industry, again using foreign capital, and produce several kinds of widely available inexpensive cars.

As housing construction grows, so should the production of furniture. One cannot say that the process has been adequate either in quantity or quality. Even if we allow for a sizeable amount of imported furniture, we have to admit that sales of furniture went up in 1986–7 by only 10 per cent, whereas available accommodation increased by 15 per cent. In 1988 sales of furniture went up by 8 per cent.

Generally speaking we lag much further behind in the production of non-industrial mass-produced consumer goods than in the production of food. And we are even more backward in matters of quality and choice. The reasons for this backwardness lie in the inadequate development and technological backwardness of the enterprises which are supposed to produce these consumer goods. Until recently they were allocated completely inadequate amounts of capital and currency resources for their technical reconstruction and re-equipment. When the economic rules and regulations were established, an unnecessarily large part of the profit on mass-produced consumer goods was creamed off into the state budget, thus depriving the enterprises of an internal source of money for product, technological and social development. These shortcomings have now been acknowledged and we have decided on a series of measures to speed up the development of light industry and other branches of the economy geared to the production of consumer goods. It would be useful to supplement these central measures with increased economic incentives to produce more consumer goods and improve their quality.

Compared with the immediately preceding period there has been a surge in the growth rate in the sphere of paid services. But the general development of this sphere is relatively slow, and although growth is rapid, the absolute rise so far is not meeting demand. We shall have to keep up these high growth rates of 10, 15 or 20 per cent per year for the next few years in order to be able at last to offer a modern range of services.

As may be seen, we have not as yet generated a serious breakthrough in the mass-production of consumer goods. Demand for many items is not satisfied, and there are as many queues as ever there were. The gap between the purchasing power of the population and the material supplies intended to meet it is still there, as wide as before. In two years of the 12th Five-year Plan, the general wage fund has increased by 7 per cent, payments to collective farm workers by 9 per cent, and various other payments and benefits by 10.5 per cent. In the area of wages and payments, therefore, the five-year plan has been overfulfilled, whereas the mass-production of consumer goods and the volume of turnover in goods and services have not reached the planned indices. In other words the gap between the purchasing power of the population and the supplies to meet it is much higher than was predicted in the calculations for the 12th Five-year Plan. In 1988 the wage fund of the entire economy increased by 7 per cent, considerably more than had been envisaged in the plan.

The fall in the amount of wine and spirits purchased also affected the imbalance between the population's income and expenditure. In the first stage of the campaign against alcoholism (1985–6) the decline in purchases was connected with a real drop in consumption, and the loss of state revenues was more than compensated by the improved health of the population and other positive changes. But in the second stage, after another – in my opinion unnecessary – increase in prices and an administrative attempt to control the consumption of alcohol by force, the decline in purchases was more than made up for by an enormous increase in the production of home-distilled moonshine. As a consequence the state lost 8 billion roubles in turnover with no compensating factors. On the contrary, there was now a shortage of sugar, and popular discontent increased.

The changes in Soviet foreign trade also had a negative influence on the imbalance between supply of and demand for manufactured goods. Imports of manufactured goods for popular consumption, including cloth, decreased by more than 10 per cent, whereas exports of these goods from the Soviet Union actually went up. An extra burden was placed on retail trade turnover by the sudden abolition of Vneshposyltorg cheques, that is coupons which can be spent by Soviet citizens in special shops mainly supplied with luxury foreign goods. (These cheques are given to Soviet citizens who have legally earned foreign hard currency and brought it back home with them.)

Unable to spend the money it earns, the population has acquired enormous, absolutely unheard-of savings. In the previous five-year plan the average annual amount paid into the savings bank went up by less than 13 billion roubles. In 1986 the increase was 22 billion roubles, in 1987 24 billion roubles, in 1988 13 billion roubles. There has been a considerable increase in the amount of money kept at home. This too has lost the state an important source of finance. Unsatisfied demand has become a real problem, since people now have enough money in their pockets, or readily available from savings accounts, to buy up every item of high-quality goods as soon as it hits the shops. In these conditions the gap between purchasing power and material supplies to meet it has grown sharply. In my opinion the liquidation of this imbalance and the saturation of the market with various kinds of goods and services are the most important and the most pressing social problems for us to solve on the way to raising living standards.

It is not enough to discuss popular welfare only in terms of material consumption. It is very important that social needs should be satisfied and that there should be a choice in the material goods that consumers can acquire. Shortages deprive our consumers of that necessary choice, not to mention the fact that it wastes a lot of social energy through queuing, searching for the right goods, and so on. Not being able to find what they want, people buy something else, and their needs remain partially unsatisfied. In conditions where shortages are commonplace, there is a rise in the sensitivity barrier, and improvements are not seen as real improvements, since there are still shortages. That is why most Soviet families do not feel that there has been any improvement in their lives, although in absolute terms their lives have improved 2.5 times. They do not see the fruits of perestroika because there are still queues for housing, shortages of food and consumer goods, the service sector is underdeveloped, and so on. In this climate of dissatisfaction, slight improvements are not felt, whereas every tiny thing that makes people's lives even slightly worse seems particularly painful. People are unhappy about the sudden price rises caused by some of our reforms and the ever-increasing gap between prices in state shops and the peasant market. For example in June 1988 the prices on the market contrasted with state prices in the following ways: beef was 2.5 times more expensive, lamb 2.9 times, potatoes 3.6 times, vegetables 3.5 times, apples 2.5 times, and so on. As the controls on prices and other payments have been reduced, there has been a natural increase in the cost of, for instance, car ownership, subscriptions to magazines, and so on. People are particularly irritated by high prices in some of the co-operatives. The government appears to be taking no steps to solve these problems.

If we evaluate the results of social developments in the last three years as a whole, we must conclude that there have been certain positive shifts in the social spheres but no progress in satisfying the population's needs and demands. The gap between purchasing power and supply has actually increased. Most people do not feel any improvement in their lives. All this demands careful study and a series of effective measures to speed up social development.

There have also been some positive shifts in industrial economic development and in improving production efficiency.

The improvement in social productivity occurred first of all through a rise in labour productivity growth rates. The average yearly increment in labour productivity in industry was 4.5 per cent in 1986–8, as against 3.1 per cent in the 11th Five-year Plan; in the social productivity of agriculture the figures were 5.0 per cent and 1.5 per cent respectively, in the building industry 6.1 per cent and 2.6 per cent, and on the railways 6.1 per cent and 1.6 per cent. In all the various sectors, the target increases in labour productivity envisaged in the five-year plan have been overfulfilled. This means that for the first time the increment in social productivity has been due to a rise in labour productivity, a fact which holds for industry as well. That is why for the first time the whole increment in labour resources was directed during 1986–7 towards the service sector. All this ensured that the growth in labour productivity was faster than the growth of wages in that time, whereas during the 11th Five-year Plan average wages grew much faster than productivity in agriculture, in the construction industry and on the railways. There was some improvement in the figures for industry as well. This was the most important reason for the fall in production costs. In the two years of perestroika, production costs decreased in industry by 2.6 times and in the building trade by 4 times or even more.

In 1988 the rate of growth of labour productivity went up somewhat – by 4.7 per cent in the national economy, while average wages went up by 7 per cent.

There has been a positive shift in the use of the main productive funds. In comparison with the previous five-year plan, the rate of decrease in returns on this fund went down in industry 2.5 times and in agriculture twice. But despite this improvement in the dynamic of fund returns in 1986–7, they still decreased on average in industry by 1.3 per cent and in agriculture by 2 per cent. There is still much to be done in the use of our reserves in this matter. The full power of some of the enterprises has not been assimilated, the planned restructuring has not been fully achieved, and the construction of almost 30 per cent of the most important industrial buildings has not been completed.

There has been a slight increase in turnover in material resources. In the past the extent of unfinished construction and unused equipment kept going up, but in 1986–7 both went down somewhat. For the first time since the seventies, growth in the building industry has overtaken the growth in reserves, while in the past reserves had grown twice as fast.

The only efficiency index which has not moved positively is resource saving – the economizing of fuel, raw materials and so on. In 1986–7 only 57 per cent of the increased demand for fuel and electric energy was satisfied by an increase in production. In iron and steel production, about 45 per cent of the extra demand was met by increased production. But according to the five-year plan, 67–70 per cent of the extra demand should have been met from decreased material expenses. Things are not so good when one looks at the energy component and metal content in our production: the actual decreases achieved were only 1 per cent and 1.4 per cent, which was even worse than in the previous five-year plan. The input of materials into production in 1986–7 went down by only 0.1 per cent per year on average, as opposed to 0.5 per cent per year in the previous five-year plan. And in 1987 materials consumption did not go down at all; in 1988 it fell by 1.5 per cent.

The fact that our economizing of resources did not go as planned meant that the extracting industries would have to be speedily developed. For every 1 per cent growth in the extraction of raw materials, the processing industry increased production by only 1.3 per cent. This was about half the figure for the 11th Five-year Plan despite a great deal of capital investment in the extraction of raw materials. Because of that, and mainly because of various organizational and other measures, we managed to ensure greater stability in the development of fuel and other raw materials production and to even out some of the imbalances in supplies that had come to the fore during the 11th Five-year Plan.

One of the undoubted achievements of the last two years is the

243

fact that we have managed to halt the decline in the extraction of oil that began during the last five-year plan and have increased annual production from 595 million tons in 1985 to 624 million tons in 1988. We have also managed to overcome stagnation in the extraction of coal, and since 1985 the volume of production has been growing (from 726 million tons in 1985 to 772 million tons in 1988). We have also managed to increase steel production from 108 million tons to 114 million tons while at the same time increasing the production of steel pipes. We have managed to halt the decline in the export of timber; deliveries increased from 281 million cubic metres in 1985 to 297 million cubic metres in 1987.

In 1987 14.2 per cent of capital investments went into the development of fuel and energy, while in the 11th Five-year Plan the average annual figure was 12.9 per cent. However, to provide this money for the extracting industries we have had to cut down on investments in the chemical and building industries and to hold back the growth of capital investment in the engineering industry. In 1986–7 the latter received only 19 per cent of investments, less than intended in the plan. We invest in fuel and energy one and a half times more capital than in the engineering sector and three times more than in the actual production of machinery and equipment for the national economy. As a consequence, re-equipment is not being carried out as intended, and those branches of industry that produce the equipment are increasing production considerably more slowly than intended. The gross imbalance in favour of our raw materials production is a burden to the whole structure of our national economy, retarding it and preventing its development.

The fact that production efficiency could have improved a great deal more than it did is demonstrated in the figures showing increased losses in the development of the national economy. Losses accounted for by growing production costs, together with losses written off on other accounts as non-production costs, have gone up by 30 per cent since 1985, amounting to 22 billion roubles in all. Lost time gives rise to about 30 per cent of this (of which 15–20 per cent is time lost during shifts, 6–7 per cent whole days lost, and 3–5 per cent various after-time wastages). The national economy also loses something like 45 billion roubles' worth of production because of inefficient use of the buildings and other equipment available. Direct and indirect waste also leads to enormous losses of material resources. For instance about 11 million tons of metal are lost every year in the engineering industry, and the co-efficient of use of ferrous metals is 0.72 as opposed to 0.85 in the United States. Cattle losses are also very high, and as a result the state gets 1 million tons of meat less than it should. According to calculations made by the Institute of Economics, 40 per cent of this is lost by the producer, 20 per cent in transportation and storage, and 40 per cent at the retail stage. In the two years of perestroika we have made virtually no progress in cutting back these losses.

Quality of output is an important indicator of efficiency and economic development. Thanks to the work of Gospriyem (the newly established quality control organization) and other measures the quality of our produce has gone up a little. If competitiveness is a sign of better quality, then it should be noted that for the first time in fifteen years the proportion of machinery and equipment in our exports has gone up (this after a period of fairly rapid decline). The co-efficient of renovation in the engineering industry has also gone up: 3.1 per cent of production was withdrawn in favour of new models in 1985, 9.1 per cent in 1987. The production of high-efficiency goods accounts for about 30 per cent of the general growth in the engineering industry.

The figures for the production of new models in the engineering industry bear witness to the acceleration of scientific and technological progress. But these improvements are only the beginning. Our new and more efficient machine tools are not yet in use and have therefore had no chance to increase production efficiency as a whole. It should be noted that the new technologies and systems have still not been fully implemented in the work of factories and enterprises. Nor have we yet managed to set up scientific and technological production consultancies which could help to introduce complete technologies of the highest possible efficiency and thus improve our entire production process. At the moment each enterprise manager selects his own technology and equipment piecemeal, making it impossible to introduce a whole new technology based on the latest equipment.

We have not yet reached the stage where radical improvements in the quality of production will become possible, because at present there are still shortages, the producer still lords it over the consumer, and to great extent distribution is still centralized. Our economic mechanism has not yet started working in such a way as to be able to produce high-quality products.

Our main task is to reorientate our entire production towards the direct satisfaction of social needs. To achieve this, merely moving enterprises formally to a system of cost accounting, self-financing and self-management will not be enough. They must also be allowed choice in the goods they buy, and in order to achieve that we must reduce state purchase orders to an absolute minimum, especially as these seem to have taken the place of the old directional plan. We must also substitute wholesale trading for the centralized distribution of resources and move over to a new sensible price system which will take account not only of costs but also of the usefulness of a product. This will mean that enterprises will find it profitable to produce what is profitable for the whole of the society.

In order to be successful in this transition to wholesale trading and a new price structure, we must achieve a better financial balancing of our economy. The current situation is not very satisfactory. In 1986–7 state income from sales tax and profits tax went down, while expenditure from the state budget went up. This was also particularly true of 1987–8. The deficit in the state budget has increased as a result and is the most important cause of the inflationary trends in our country and of the ever-growing gap between goods turnover and money supply. As a result, still more shortages occurred, because the purchasing power of enterprises was much higher than the possibilities of satisfying their demands with material supplies. This also means that the incentive funds cannot obtain the goods they would want to supply as incentives. All this undermines the possibility of economic reform and requires immediate measures: we must devise and introduce special wide-ranging programmes for the renewal of the national economy. In the event of failure, there will be no transition to the new economic and managerial systems. We must increase the incentives for enterprises and organizations to make themselves far more profitable than they are now, and this must be done first of all by lowering production costs and improving output quality. Every loss-making and non-profitable organization must be dealt with. We must ensure that enterprises have more money of their own to work with, and we must solve the problem of the enormous indebtedness of the collective farms, state farms and many other enterprises.

In 1988, when a sizeable proportion of our enterprises changed over to the new conditions, the overall profits soared by up to 7.8

per cent, while in those enterprises that had made the transition the increase was 10.8 per cent. In 1987 the growth of profits in the national economy was a mere 5 per cent. It would be a good idea to use this improvement in our finances to introduce a whole series of measures to balance the economy.

As we can see, the economic development of the country in the first half of the 12th Five-Year Plan displays some contradictory features. There have been certain positive shifts, but these were connected not so much with any progressive structural changes in the development of the national economy as with an increase in GNP derived from the more traditional sectors of production. The real restructuring of the national economy in order to satisfy social needs more fully is going exceedingly slowly. The nature of our economic growth has not yet radically changed. The improvements in a number of indices have been achieved mostly at the expense of organizational factors and without being backed up by any technical progress or new administrative and economic methods.

In the past, transitions to new economic conditions (as, for example, after the September 1953 Plenum or during the economic reform in agriculture and industry in 1965) had greater and more immediate effects on economic growth rates, and especially on efficiency figures. The slower effects of the present reform are connected with the fact that the most important measures, like the price reform and the transition to wholesale trade, are still ahead of us. We have also made mistakes in our transition to the new economic methods, in that we retained to some extent the administrative 'diktat' in the fixing of state purchase orders and the setting of economic rules and regulations. In most cases this meant that the new economic mechanism was not taken right to the actual producers, the workers, the engineers in the early stages of production, and that very little has changed in the actual provision of incentives. What has actually been done towards the introduction of perestroika has so far been a little half-hearted, and the results have been half-hearted. Only where there have been major changes in the economic mechanism (that is, where there has been a transition to the second form of cost accounting, i.e. at present about 1,000 enterprises) has the effect been considerable: labour productivity rates here doubled or trebled, costs have shot down, and much larger sums have been paid into the incentive and other funds.

The results of the socio-economic development in our country in the first half of this five-year plan demonstrate that we must implement a series of more radical and more extensive measures to restructure our economic system. We have lost some time in our reorganization of the economy, and although we now need to catch up it will still be possible for us to fulfil and to overfulfil the targets of the 12th Five-year Plan, especially in matters concerning the social problems facing our country.